MW01517648

The Xilixana Yanomami of the Amazon

A Xilixana prepares to distribute cooked meat to his guests at the end of a festival (John Peters, 1976).

# THE XILIXANA
# YANOMAMI OF
# THE AMAZON

History, Social Structure,
and Population Dynamics

John D. Early / John F. Peters

University Press of Florida
Gainesville · Tallahassee · Tampa · Boca Raton
Pensacola · Orlando · Miami · Jacksonville

F2520.1.Y3 E29 2000
*0134107935105*
Early, John D.

The Xilixana Yanomami of
  the Amazon : history,
    c2000.

2005 09 26

Copyright 2000 by the Board of Regents of the State of Florida
Printed in the United States of America on acid-free paper

05  04  03  02  01  00  6  5  4  3  2  1

Library of Congress Cataloging-in-Publication Data
Early, John D.
The Xilixana Yanomami of the Amazon: history, social structure, and population dynamics
/ John D. Early, John F. Peters.
p. cm.
Includes bibliographical references and index.
ISBN 0-8130-1762-9 (cloth: alk. paper)
1. Yanomamo Indians—Brazil—Macajaâ River Valley. 2. Yanomamo Indians—Population.
3. Yanomamo Indians—Social conditions. I. Peters, John F.
F2520.1.Y3 E29  2000
306'.089'9808114—dc21  00-024462

The University Press of Florida is the scholarly publishing agency for the State University
System of Florida, comprising Florida A&M University, Florida Atlantic University, Florida
International University, Florida State University, University of Central Florida, University
of Florida, University of North Florida, University of South Florida, and University of West
Florida.

University Press of Florida
15 Northwest 15th Street
Gainesville, FL 32611-2079
http://www.upf.com

# CONTENTS

# TABLES

# FIGURES

# MAPS

# PREFACE

This research began in 1983 with an exchange of letters between the two co-authors. John Peters and his family lived for nine years, 1958 to 1967, among the Yanomami as missionaries. He returned briefly to Canada and then came to the United States for graduate work. In 1972 he was once more among the Yanomami to write his dissertation. After taking a position at Wilfrid Laurier University in Canada, Peters occasionally returned to the Yanomami, but his academic interests drifted away from them as he turned his attention to the topic of the Canadian family. A letter from John (Jake) Early began to pull him back to the Yanomami.

John Early worked extensively both as a Mayan ethnographer and as a community organizer (cooperatives, literacy, and health programs) in Mexico and Guatemala from 1962 to 1970. Then he took a position at Florida Atlantic University and wrote a book about the Guatemalan population, published in 1982. When civil war in Guatemala prevented his return, he switched his attention to other groups. Reading some articles by Peters, he realized that joint work had the potential to produce some needed basic research on the Yanomami. Thus began a sixteen-year collaboration that has required much effort but has been highly rewarding for both.

This book represents the third case history of preindustrial populations researched by Early. These efforts have been an attempt to provide reliable data about preindustrial populations since many existing studies have methodological problems that render the data questionable. We believe these case histories of Yanomami villages present a unique body of data with many theoretical, comparative, and practical implications. In the future, we intend to explore some of these ourselves, but we hope the wider community of researchers, policy makers, community activists, and the general public will find the material of value and will help develop its full potential.

The authors have collected over a thousand slides and pictures of Yanomami in Roraima taken by missionaries over a thirty-five-year period. Early has reduced these to about 250 colored images of ethnographic interest. The authors are producing and will independently distribute a CD-ROM with these images, commentary, and references to be used as a supplement to this and their other books.

We owe debts of gratitude to many people who assisted the research. The Mucajaí people themselves were very cooperative even after they came to realize Peters's change of role from missionary to researcher on his return visits. The missionaries of the Unevangelized Fields Mission cooperated fully as intermediaries between the villagers and the two of us as we sought information by mail, e-mail, or faxes transported by the missionary pilots on their supply flights. This research would have been impossible without the help of Carol James, Carole Swain, Steve and Dawn Anderson, Milton and Márcia Camargo, and Alex and Daura Juniqueira.

Other researchers shared their data with us. Ernest Migliazza was most helpful with the historical background of the Yanomami and gave us full access to his unpublished work. Fr. John Saffirio gave us use of his Catrimani data. Bruce Albert, Gale Goodwin Gomez, and Don Borgman provided information about the Brazilian situation. Hortensia Caballero Arias shared information about the Venezuelan Yanomami area. The Social Science and Humanities Research Council of Canada provided grants and research time. Florida Atlantic University also provided research time.

Several people read earlier versions of the manuscript and made suggestions. Prof. Susan Love Brown of Florida Atlantic University, Prof. Leighton Hazlehurst of Lyndon State College, and Prof. Kenneth Johnson of Thomas College pointed out problems of ambiguity and organization that helped us attain greater clarity. Prof. Dieter Heinen of the Instituto Venezolano de Investigaciones Científicas in Caracas made helpful suggestions. Profs. Raymond Hames of the University of Nebraska and Leslie Sponsel of the University of Hawaii made important recommendations for the University Press of Florida. Adruen Spano of Florida Atlantic University was indispensable in the production of the maps, graphs, and charts. From the University Press of Florida, Gillian Hillis, David Graham, and an anonymous copy editor were diligent editorial guides. While we did not follow all the advice received, the manuscript is much better for having passed through the hands of these readers and viewers. Any shortcomings are our own responsibility. Finally, we would like to thank our wives, Lorraine Peters and Jacky Early, for their patience.

# Introduction

# 1

# The Research

This study is focused on the Xilixana, a group of Yanomami Indians residing in the rain forest of the western part of the state of Roraima in Brazil. Since the 1930s they have lived in three to eight villages located at various times in the vicinity of the middle Mucajaí River (maps 1, 2). (*Mucajaí* is pronounced in phonetic notation as "mu-ka-dza-i" and *Xilixana* as "shi-di-sha-na"). We investigate their history, including their entry into the Brazilian Amazon, an extended period in the Parima Highlands, migration to areas near the Uraricoera and Mucajaí rivers, a period between 1957 and 1960 when they first entered into contact with Brazilians, and the problems created by contact with the national society, especially since 1987 due to the invasion of gold miners into their traditional territory.

In the latter portion of the study we examine the region in which the Xilixana live and compare them with other Yanomami groups found there. The Yanomami are sometimes characterized as "the largest indigenous people in the Americas to retain their traditional way of life" (Ramos 1995:271). As can be seen in the chapters that follow, this statement is quickly losing its aptness to describe the situation of the Yanomami.

We address a number of questions. What was the precontact situation of this group? What were the similarities and differences between the villages? What were the problems posed by contact with the national society? Was there much variation between the villages in their experiences of contact? How can the answers to these questions help clarify the ethnographic literature about the Yanomami? How are the Xilixana and other Yanomami in the Brazilian rain forest affected by the political and economic forces of Brazil and the world system? What is the impact of national development on these tribal communities? What will happen to the Xilixana and other Brazilian Yanomami?

This introduction gives an overview of the Yanomami and outlines the presentation of the research. (We follow in this volume the growing custom of using a terminal *i* for the spelling of *Yanomami,* the generic name for the whole group, instead of *a,* which was used in a previous volume [Early and Peters 1990].)

## I. The Yanomami

The people designated by this generic term live in small settlements scattered over an area lying at approximately 1 to 5 degrees north latitude and 62 to 66 degrees west longitude (map 1). This region falls within the national territories of Brazil and Venezuela. Technically the Yanomami have legal status in the nation in which they live, but until the gold rushes of the 1980s, national penetration was mostly limited to assorted exploratory, missionary, and trading activities. The population of the Yanomami Indians is usually estimated to be between twenty thousand and twenty-two thousand (MacMillan 1995:10; Ramos 1995:19, note 2; and the sources cited in these two references). However, these are rough estimates because of the isolation of a number of groups, and the numbers do not take into consideration the growth or decline of the population during their more recent history. About 60 percent of the population are estimated to live in Venezuela and 40 percent in Brazil. Two 1996 estimates of the Brazilian Yanomami by the Yanomami Health Agency (DSY 1999:23) are 7,882 and 8,768.

In the middle of the Yanomami area rise the Parima Highlands, a north-south spine of uplands and low mountains reaching to 3,000 feet. The division between the eastward- and westward-flowing watersheds from these mountains forms the international boundary between Venezuela and Brazil. In Brazil, the various rivers drain either east into the Rio Branco, which empties into the Rio Negro, or south directly into the Rio Negro, which joins the Amazon River near the city of Manaus. In Venezuela, the rivers drain west and north to the Orinoco River, which flows into the Atlantic Ocean. (The Siapa River with its connection to the Rio Negro is an exception.)

Each Yanomami community is independent with its own headman but with kinship and marriage ties to other communities, usually those in the same region. The people are referred to by a common name because of a similarity of languages and customs indicating a common origin. There is no social structure uniting all Yanomami villages, no union or confederation of all Yanomami. In this study we refer to Yanomami communities as villages although this may be misleading. Yanomami communities are relatively small and usually move every few years. The term *village* as used here does not imply a permanently populated geographical location.

Migliazza (1972:34) has classified the Yanomami into four distinct language groups (map 1), which correspond to different geographical regions within the Yanomami area: the Sanumá (Sanemá) in the northern sector, the Ninam (Yanam) in the eastern sector, the Yanomam in the south-central sector, and the Yanomami (Yanomamo, Yanomamö, Yanomamɨ) in the southwestern sector. Since the latter name is used both for the whole group and for the southwestern group, the context sometimes needs to be examined to clarify the usage. There are some variations of customs among these four groups, with the Sanumá distinctive in several ways.

## II. The Ninam Yanomami

Migliazza (1980:103–4) subdivides the Ninam into three dialectical groups. At the time of his survey the northern Ninam or Xiliana (Shiliana) lived on the upper reaches of the Paragua River in Venezuela and the Uraricaá River and its tributaries in Brazil. The central Ninam or Xilixana (Shilishana) lived on the middle Mucajaí River and are sometimes called the Mucajaí Yanomami. This is the group investigated in the present study. The southern Ninam lived on the tributaries of the Apiaú and Ajarani rivers. Migliazza expresses some reserve about classifying the language of the southern groups as a dialect of Ninam because of intelligibility problems with the other two Ninam dialects. Some (e.g., Chagnon 1972:255) have classified the southern Ninam as a fifth language group. However, based on linguistic structure, Migliazza (pers. comm.) thinks this language should be classified as a dialect of Ninam until further research should indicate differently. Before and since the time of Migliazza's survey in the 1960s, some Ninam villages from all three groups have lived outside the aforementioned river systems. Some of these movements are described in upcoming chapters.

When describing themselves to outsiders, the northern and central Ninam refer to themselves as Xiliana and Xilixana respectively. The people know that this is how they are referred to by outsiders and *Xilixana* has become a designation frequently used in the literature. Its origin is uncertain. Migliazza and Peters believe the term has an origin internal to the group. But it was also a pejorative term used by Carib groups, especially the Yekwana, to refer to Yanomami groups. It is the name of a particular type of monkey that has a prognathic profile. Many Yanomami men frequently place a large wad of chewing tobacco between the lower teeth and lip, which gradually extends the lip. This produces a resemblance to the monkey's profile and hence the name.

## III. The Xilixana (Shilishana, Central Ninam, Mucajaí Yanomami)

This volume is a detailed examination of the villages of the Xilixana. Members of these villages consider themselves a distinct subgroup of Ninam because of dialectical differences from the other Ninam and owing to the marriage and kinship ties uniting the communities. They are here also called the Mucajaí Yanomami because for many of the years between 1930 and 1995, all or the majority of this group lived in villages on or near the middle Mucajaí River in Brazil. This is located at approximately 2 degrees, 45 minutes north latitude and 62 degrees, 25 minutes west longitude (map 2). The Mucajaí River rises in the Parima Highlands and flows in an easterly direction to empty into the Rio Branco at a point approximately 50 kilometers (31 miles) south of Boa Vista, the capital of the Brazilian state of Roraima.

## IV. Research Objectives

We have attempted to gain some insight into the functioning of a tribal group under the very different circumstances during the phases of their history. For the earlier periods, we present in chapters 2 and 3 a synthesis of the history of the Yanomami and the evolution of the Ninam as a distinct subgroup. The history is derived from linguistic evidence, colonial sources, and oral histories from the Ninam themselves. In chapter 4 there is a description of the traditional village, including a model of their kinship classification and its influence on social interaction.

Based on the work of Ribeiro, we develop in chapter 5 a model of past Brazilian experience of contact with indigenous groups. This is a heuristic device to highlight certain points in the later examination of the individual villages. To understand the types of contact and their effects, the model requires an analysis of the population dynamics accounting for changes in the sizes of these communities before and after first contact. The basis for this analysis is a demographic database covering a period of sixty-six years. In chapters 6 and 7 we discuss the methodology for developing this database. There may be skepticism about the validity of data for a sixty-six-year period from a tribal population. The details of the collection and verification of the database are given so that readers may make their own evaluation.

To remove the mystery of mere numbers for those unfamiliar with demography, in chapter 8 we explain the basics of demographic presentation, which provides an understanding of the derivation and significance of the numbers presented later.

The next eight chapters examine the history, social structure, and population dynamics of each of the eight villages that have comprised the Xilixana at various times during the sixty-six-year period covered by the demographic data. To understand tribal populations better, in the following two chapters we compare and summarize the findings from the village case histories.

The final sections of the book place the findings of the research in larger contexts. Chapter 20 indicates the significance of these findings for the clarification of the existing anthropological literature about the Yanomami, and raises some further questions.

Beginning in chapter 21, we examine the history of the contemporary political and economic forces, both national and international, that are shaping the contact situations with indigenous groups in the rain forests of the Amazon. In chapter 22 we show how the pressures described have threatened the survival of other Yanomami groups in Roraima and compare their experiences with those of the Xilixana. Based on these findings, the two subsequent chapters consider the situation of the Brazilian Yanomami at the end of the twentieth century. We develop in chapter 23 an alternative model of the contact experience to the historical one presented in chapter 5. Based on this alternative model, we consider in chapter 24 the key problematic issues of health and land. In the final chapter we speculate on the future of the Yanomami in Roraima, including the Xilixana. Our aim is to contribute to an understanding of the Brazilian Yanomami and to highlight the necessity of knowledge as a basis for confronting their situation at both the policy and action levels.

## V. Previous Work

The demographic aspect of the research extends, and in some places revises, a prior volume entitled *The Population Dynamics of the Mucajai Yanomama* (Early and Peters 1990). It more than doubles the length of the diachronic analysis from a twenty-eight- to a sixty-six-year period by reconstructing the precontact population from 1930 to 1957 and by adding the years 1987 to 1995. The present analysis of the population dynamics is more detailed in employing the individual villages as the units of analysis rather than the aggregate of all the villages used in the previous volume. Each village has its own history and individual characteristics, thereby providing insight into the diversity of tribal population dynamics obscured in the analysis of the aggregate.

## VI. Maps

All the maps have been placed together for convenience as there are multiple references to them throughout the volume.

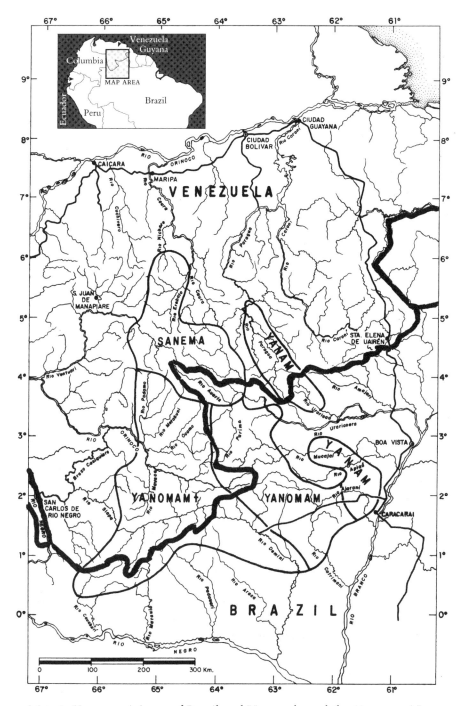

Map 1. Yanomami Areas of Brazil and Venezuela and the Yanomami Language Spoken in Each

Adapted from a map compiled by Roberto Lizarralde in Lizot 1988:490. The language boundaries are based on Migliazza 1972:4c. We thank the publisher, Fundación La Salle in Caracas, for permission to reproduce the map.

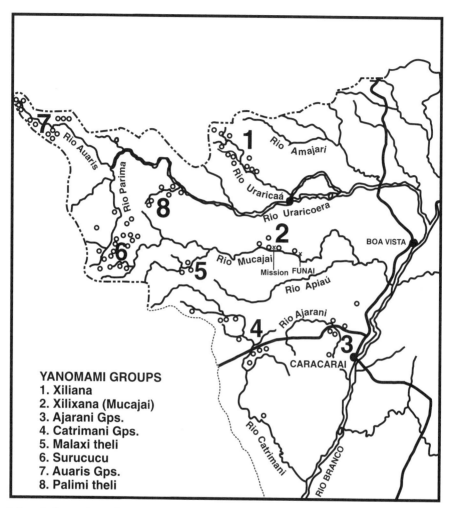

**Map 2. Location of Yanomami Groups in Western Roraima, Brazil**

An enlarged section of the previous map. The numbers indicate the regions occupied by Yanomami population blocs. The small circles represent estimates of locations of Yanomami villages around 1980. Within the Mucajaí bloc (2), reading from left to right, the villages are C, B (off the river), E at the Kloknai stream, and downriver village D. The Mission is located a short distance to the west of village E. The FUNAI post at Comara is located downriver from village D.

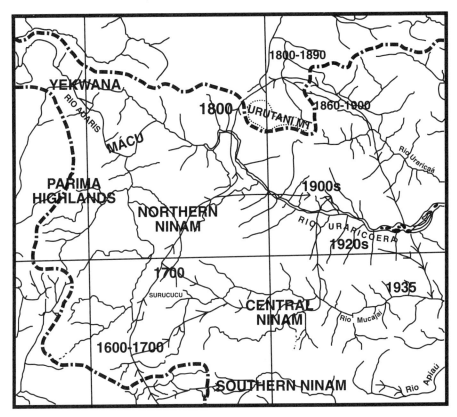

Map 3. Migliazza's Sketch Map Showing Probable Historical Migration Routes of the Ninam

The routes indicated are trails that exist in the twentieth century. Migliazza believes they are quite old and probably used by the Ninam in their migrations.

1. RORAIMA
2. AMAPÁ
3. PARÁ
4. AMAZONAS
5. ACRE
5. RONDÔNIA
7. MATO GROSSO
8. TOCANTINS
9. GOIÁS
10. MATO GROSSO DO SUL
11. RIO GRANDE DO SUL
12. SANTA CATARINA
13. PARANÁ
14. SÃO PAULO
15. RIO DE JANEIRO
16. MINAS GERAIS
17. BAHIA
18. PIAUÍ
19. MARANHÃO
20. CEARÁ
21. RIO GRANDE DO NORTE
22. PARAÍBA
23. PERNAMBUCO
24. ALAGOAS
25. SERGIPE
26. ESPÍRITO SANTO

Map 4. The Regions and States of Brazil

Classification of the regions taking into consideration the main watersheds as well as state boundaries. For a more frequently employed regional classification using only administrative boundaries, see Wood and Carvalho 1988:4–5.

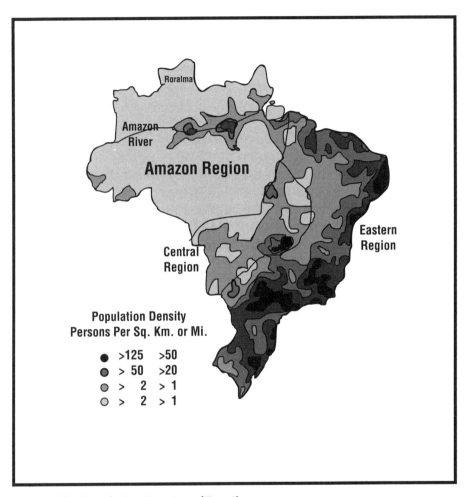

Map 5. The Population Density of Brazil

Adapted from *The World Book Encyclopedia*, copyright 1999 World Book, Inc. By permission of the publisher.

Map 6. Roads and Colonization Projects in Roraima

The source of this map and map 7 is Columbia University Press, 563 W. 113th St., New York, NY 10025. *At the End of the Rainbow* (Diagrams), Gordon MacMillan (1995:19, 37). Reproduced by permission of the publisher via Copyright Clearance Center, Inc.

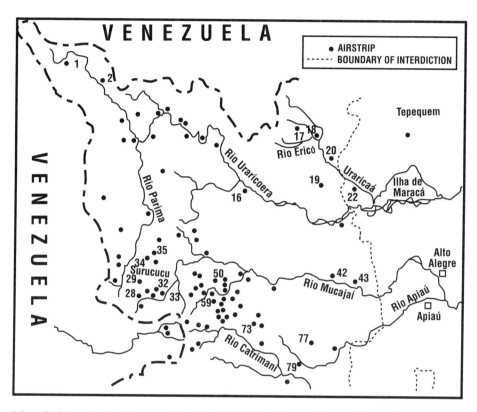

Map 7. Airstrips in Western Roraima Used by Miners during the Gold Rush, 1987–89

Only the airstrips at locations mentioned in the text are numbered. The numbers are retained from MacMillan's map. There has been a slight correction of the location of airstrip 17. The Mission is number 42 and the FUNAI post at Comara is number 43.

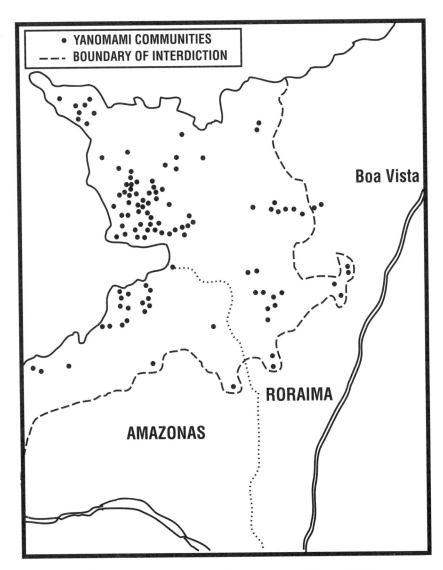

Map 8. Government Interdiction of Yanomami Territory, 1982

Adapted from the 1990 report of Ação pela Cidadania (1990:16). The dots estimate location of Yanomami villages at that time.

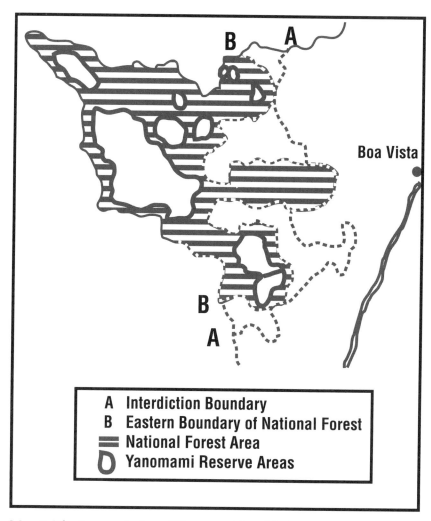

Map 9. The Expropriation of Yanomami Land in Roraima
Adapted from the 1990 report of Ação pela Cidadania (1990:16).

# History and Ethnography

# 2

# A Historical Survey of the Yanomami

The Yanomami have no written history of their own. Some historical perspective can be obtained from patterns of linguistic evolution, from reports of European colonials and explorers, and from oral histories taped between 1957 and 1972 for Migliazza by Ninam elders, Mácu survivors, Yanomam, Yanomami, and members of various Carib tribes. From these sources, Migliazza (Migliazza and Campbell 1988; Migliazza 1972, 1980, 1982, 1998) has reconstructed the movements of the Ninam and Ferguson (1995: 123–48) has synthesized the historical record.

## I. Pre-Columbian Period

Based on approximately 150 probable cognates, Migliazza (Migliazza and Campbell 1988:197–207, 387–402; also Migliazza 1982) hypothesizes that the ancestors of the Yanomami lived on the upper Ucayali River in Peru during the last "Refuge" phase (Meggers 1975, 1976). Then as the reforestation period progressed, proto-Panoan speakers from this group moved to the lower Ucayali River and then eastward into territory currently Brazilian. Speakers of proto-Yanomami separated and slowly moved down the Amazon River to its confluence with the Rio Negro. Years later they moved up the Rio Negro to its juncture with the Rio Branco and spread out, occupying the territory drained by the tributaries of the lower Rio Branco (map 1). In Pre-Columbian times the Branco-Negro-Orinoco region had developed complex societies that were centers of trade networks. Ferguson (1995:69) speculates that the Yanomami participated in this trade. During this period, the Yanomami began moving toward the Parima Highlands.

## II. European Insertion and the Slave Trade

The arrival of Europeans and the subsequent establishment of the New World colonies did not immediately touch the Yanomami region. Portuguese settlements along the coast of Brazil and the Dutch, English and Spanish outposts in the Guiana region were too involved with the founding and administration of coastal plantations and port towns. Their purpose was the production and shipment of raw materials to the mother country.

As time passed, these activities created an increasing demand for unskilled labor, which was usually supplied by slaves. The local supply became insufficient, due mostly to high mortality. To meet the increasing demand, slave traders began to spread out along the waterways toward the interior. They conducted captures themselves as well as inducing indigenous groups, especially the Caribs, to seek out and capture people from other indigenous groups.

Slave raiding reached the Rio Branco in the 1630s if not earlier and continued with various degrees of intensity in and around Yanomami territory to around 1820 (Ferguson 1995:78, 96). Whitehead (1988:30) points out the multiplier effect of slave raiding on mortality. One estimate is that the raiders would kill two people for every slave they captured. More were killed due to the violence between indigenous groups because of the hatred arising from the participation of some in the slave trade. Still more indigenous people were killed by the new infectious diseases transmitted by direct or indirect contact with European slavers and traders.

## III. Results of the Slave Trade

Ferguson (1995:96) describes the results of the period of slavery.

> By the end of the eighteenth century, great stretches of the Branco, Negro, Orinoco and tributary rivers were completely devoid of human life. . . . Genocide is the appropriate term for the effect of the first two centuries of Western contact. Along the waterways that encompass the Yanomami's highlands, a few, small, scattered settlements of "civilized" natives from mixed backgrounds toiled under the uncharitable rule of soldiers, priests or secular directors. In the highlands above the main rivers, behind protecting rapids, there were pockets of survivors—long-term residents or refugees from the lowlands—most numbering a couple hundred or fewer.

## IV. The Withdrawal Period in the Parima Highlands

Probably as a result of the devastation of the slave trade, most Yanomami withdrew to the protection of the Parima Highlands. They engaged in some raiding and trade, but here they were away from the large rivers with their traffic of trade goods and slavers as well as being protected by small rivers and streams choked with rapids. They resisted the few efforts of the Portuguese to entice them out of their highland retreat (Hemming 1987:32, 343).

In the highlands, hunting, collecting, and horticulture provided their subsistence. There is some dispute about the relative importance of each, but they appear to have provided adequate subsistence in spite of periodic shortages. It is generally agreed that the Yanomami population increased during this period. Some ascribe this to the adoption of a type of banana as the staple. Others see the acquisition of steel tools for clearing larger fields as the important factor. In either of these cases, the population increase would be due to a better food supply lowering mortality.

## V. Emergence of the Ninam

It is not known when the Ninam emerged as a distinct Yanomami group. Based on linguistic evidence and the toponymy of the region, Migliazza (1998) thinks the Ninam moved from the tributaries of the lower Rio Branco to the area of the Surucucu plateau in the Parima Highlands by the seventeenth century (see map 3). Migliazza speculates that sometime before 1700 the group to become known as the southern Ninam branched off from the remainder of the Ninam group, left the Parima Highlands, headed east, and settled on the upper Apiaú River, with some later going to the Ajarani River.

## VI. Further Expansion of the Ninam

Because of the increased population and conflict with the Yanomam, the Ninam and other Yanomami groups began to migrate out of the Parima Highlands. This was the push factor. But there was also an important pull factor enticing them out: the desire for metal tools. In 1912 a Ninam group indicated to Koch-Grunberg (1979, 1:209, 210, 213) the importance of hatchets and machetes for making larger horticultural fields than they could make with their traditional nonmetal tools. This particular Ninam group was living in a temporary encampment on the Uraricoera River used for their meetings with Mácu Indians from the Auaris River. During these encounters, the Ninam obtained steel tools and other items.

## VII. The Northern Neighbors of the Ninam

In the movement out of the Parima Highlands, the Ninam were confronted by other Indian groups (see map 3), who fought with them and influenced their moves.

## A. The Yekwana (Yecuana, Maquiritare, Maiongong)

This was a large Carib group who lived in the mountains northwest of the Parima Highlands (see map 3). They also were protected by impassable rapids. The Yekwana social structure was complex enough to coordinate resistance by the various Yekwana communities to European soldiers and slavers. By 1800 they controlled the region of the upper Orinoco, Ventuari, Cunucunuma, and Padamo rivers as well as the country north of the Parima River, including the Auaris River and the upper drainage area of the Uraricoera River. The Yekwana were skilled river people and had a long tradition of trading directly with Brazilians, Venezuelans, and with the British and Dutch in the Guiana region. They also traded with the Europeans through intermediary indigenous groups. Because of their trading activities, they had an ample supply of steel tools. The first Yanomami groups to move north were the Venezuelan Sanumá. They lived interspersed among the Yekwana as clients in a patron-client relationship that gave them access to the steel tools. Tensions leading to armed conflict also arose between the two groups.

## B. The Mácu (Máku)

This group engaged in trading goods from the Orinoco to the Rio Branco using the Uraricoera-Auaris-Padamo rivers. Sanumá invasions pushed them eastward to the lower Auaris and upper Uraricoera rivers. In 1912 Koch-Grunberg (1979, 1:209) found the Mácu to be an important source of manufactured goods for the Ninam, including cloth, ornaments, and especially steel tools. In the 1930s an attack by the Ninam at the Kulekuleima Rapids on the Uraricoera River forced the Mácu to the lower part of the river and into contact with Brazilian peasants, where they were decimated by disease. Migliazza (1980:115) found that by the 1950s there was only one surviving Mácu family living with the Macuxi in the village of Buquerao.

## C. Macuxi

This is a Carib group who lived to the northeast of the Yanomami region on the lower Uraricoera, Surumu, Cotingó, Maú, and Itacutú rivers in eastern

Roraima. They have a long history of contact with Brazilians along the upper Rio Branco and its tributaries.

## VIII. The River System

To set the context for Ninam activity as they moved out of the Parima Highlands, it is helpful to understand the river system of this region (maps 1, 2) and its use as a trade route. The Parima, Uraricoera, and Rio Branco could be considered a single river approximating the shape of an inverted U but with the right downward stroke longer than the left. The portions of the river formed by its changes of main direction have been called by different names. The river rises in the Parima Highlands and flows in a northerly direction for about 80.5 km (50 mi.); here it is called the Parima River. Then it turns in an easterly direction for more than 483 km (300 mi.) and is known as the Uraricoera River. Then it turns toward the south and becomes the Rio Branco, which flows for 563 km (350 mi.) before emptying into the Rio Negro (*Webster's New Geographical Dictionary* 1988:369, 927, 1274). The Rio Negro in turn empties into the Amazon River near the town of Manaus.

Indian traders, especially the Yekwana and Mácu, used the Uraricoera to move goods between the Orinoco and Branco drainage areas. In the Rio Branco area in Brazil, the trade route ascended the Uraricoera and Parima rivers to the confluence with the Auaris River in the Parima Highlands. It continued in a westerly direction up the Auaris River to its headwaters. From this point there was a short portage to the headwaters of the Padamo River, which descends to the Orinoco River in Venezuela. The opposite west-to-east movement followed the same course.

## IX. The Northeastern Expansion of the Ninam

Migliazza's histories (1998) indicate that around 1700 the Ninam began to move in a northeasterly direction into a relatively uninhabited area between the Mucajaí and Uraricoera rivers. The main attraction in the movement toward Uraricoera River was its use as a trade route by the Mácu and Yekwana for carrying steel tools and other manufactured goods. The Ninam could not go in a more northerly direction following the Parima River because this area was occupied by the Yanomam, Mácu, and farther north, the Yekwana.

Sometime between 1750 and 1800, the central Ninam or Xilixana dialect diverged from the northern Ninam or Xiliana dialect (Migliazza 1998).

Some of the Xilixana group probably branched off from the Xiliana and moved east to the upper Mucajaí River and then north to the Uraricoera River (map 3).

The Xiliana reached the Uraricoera River around 1800, with some groups continuing north beyond the Urutani Mountain to the headwaters of the Paragua River in Venezuela, where they remained for some time (Migliazza 1998). In 1839 Robert Schomburgh found Ninam living on the Urawe River near the Urutani Mountain (Migliazza 1972:365). This is a northern tributary of the Uraricoera with headwaters not far from the Paragua-Uraricaá headwaters. Around 1860 some of the Ninam moved to the headwaters of the Uraricaá River in Brazil. Migliazza took up residence among these groups in 1958.

From 1830 on there are reports of Ninam preying on trade canoes along the Uraricoera, especially those of the Yekwana and Mácu. Ferguson (1995:124) notes: "Ultimately, the Ninam come to dominate the Uraricoera and its tributaries from the Auaris down to Maracá Island." The Yekwana continued to travel the Uraricoera in spite of the Ninam raids on their canoes.

The territories north of the Uraricoera were inhabited by other indigenous groups whom the Xiliana absorbed or destroyed. They absorbed the Awake (Urutani), who lived north of the Uraricaá River between the Urutani Mountain and Maracá Island, and the Sape (Kariana), who lived on the upper Paragua. They expelled or destroyed the Carib Porokoto from the Uraricaá (Migliazza 1998).

## X. The Rubber Boom and Increased Trade on the Main Rivers

The Amazonian rubber boom during the latter half of the nineteenth century indirectly affected the Yanomami. While only the upper Orinoco area seems to have been directly involved in rubber tapping, the other areas profited by supplying the needs of tappers and associated workers and from receiving trade goods from missionaries. The cattle industry developed along the Rio Branco area to supply meat, especially for Manaus. The ranches mainly employed Macuxi. Anglican missionaries in British Guiana (later Guyana) were an important source of trade goods poured into the network from the north.

## XI. The Xilixana or Mucajaí Ninam

Migliazza estimates that the central Ninam (Xilixana) broke off from the Xiliana between 1750 and 1800. So far it has been impossible to identify specifically any of the previously mentioned Ninam with the Mucajaí Ninam. Between 1800 and 1900 there may have been other Xilixana groups in addition to those from whom the Mucajaí Ninam descended.

The first known appearance of the specific ancestors of the Mucajaí Ninam in the historical record is the account given to Chagnon by the Yekwana (Chagnon 1972:277–79; Chagnon et al. 1970:342). In the last part of the nineteenth century the Ninam group from which the Mucajaí group descended was living in close contact with a Yekwana group on the upper Auaris River in a patron-client relationship. Chagnon says this was a Ninam village but Migliazza believes it was more likely a temporary encampment while they worked for the Yekwana. In this period the Ninam were highly nomadic. Disputes arose between the Yekwana and the Ninam, who then moved away. Chagnon says they moved downriver to the confluence of the Auaris and Parima rivers. Peters (1998:172) in his research was unable to verify these events. Migliazza (1998) says the Mácu occupied this site at that time, and while the Ninam may have passed through, they probably went on to join other Ninam groups residing in the Paragua or Uraricaá or Uraricoera areas.

Migliazza's interpretation agrees with the accounts given to Peters. The groups who were to become the Mucajaí Ninam were first identified as living in an area north of the Uraricoera River around 1900. They were in contact with other Ninam groups—the Xiliana (the northern Ninam), Wehewe, Koliak, and Gilinai—with whom they intermarried as well as fighting and taking captive women. Later the groups who were the precursors of the Mucajaí Yanomami moved to the region south of the Uraricoera River.

## XII. The Koch-Grunberg Expedition

There are accounts by two explorers, Koch-Grunberg in 1911 and Rice in 1924, of their expeditions along the Uraricoera River in these years. They speak of the Yekwana, Mácu, Macuxi and Xiliana. Holdridge (1933:382) thinks the Xiliana group was Yanomam, although Migliazza (pers. comm.) is not convinced by his argument. Regardless of the particular group, the descriptions by the explorers give some idea of Yanomami life along the Uraricoera at that time.

In 1911 Theodor Koch-Grunberg met two groups of Xiliana and noted that there was a dialectical difference between them. Migliazza believes the first group was the Kasilapai, a Xilixana group who later became one of the Mucajaí villages. They had recently moved to the upper Uraricaá River and were visiting in the area of their former residence near the Uraricoera River, where they met Koch-Grunberg at the Puruname cataract. He describes their previous intense raiding of trading groups along the Uraricoera River but found them at peace in 1911, following the death of their former headman (Koch-Grunberg 1979, 3:242).

The other encounter was on the Uraricoera River near Motomoto at a temporary shelter used by a Xiliana group for their meetings with the Mácu, with whom they traded. Koch-Grunberg (1979, 1:208–14) noted their physical appearance and body ornaments. He found them to be dirty and covered with scabs due to a skin disease. Their infants were thin. Koch-Grunberg was unimpressed and considered them very timid.

## XIII. The Rice Expedition

In 1924–25 A. Hamilton Rice ascended the Rio Branco, the Uraricoera, and a sizable portion of the Parima River. His group met a number of Mácu and Yekwana trading groups on the Uraricoera River. He also had some contact with Ninam groups.

The first encounter took place on the Santa Rosa Channel on the north side of Maracá Island. Rice met four Ninam going upstream in a canoe. They stopped for several hours but there was little communication since the Ninam were not talkative and only one Macuxi in Rice's crew could understand Ninam. Rice remarks that they looked like river people because of their well-developed upper torsos from paddling their canoes.

Late in the afternoon of March 18, 1924, Rice's group noticed a small stream entering the river. It had been cleared of debris for a short distance, providing a landing for small canoes. Rice's party went ashore and was greeted by several men described as dirty, naked, and badly nourished. They gave Rice some bananas. Then they escorted him and his crew to the village house, a circular edifice eighty feet in diameter with a conical roof. The interior was very dark. Rice (1928:216) describes the community in this manner:

> There were some fifty people in all, about one-third of whom were females, short and stocky, all with very young children . . . A disgusting caxiri (beer) of bananas was passed around in gourds, and was apparently what the community lived on, as there were no signs of the usual utensils for preparing mandioca [manioc], either within the house or outside. There were bows, arrows, spears and blow guns, articles of the chase and household utensils, most of them of indifferent workmanship, though one young Indian [believed by Rice to be from another group] with a strong looking consort—I could not make

out whether she was a Shiliana [Xiliana] or not—showed me with much pride an excellent assortment of fish spears, bows, arrows and blow guns.

No steel implements were to be seen. All arrows and spears were tipped with bone or bamboo, but the stumps of the clearing in which stood the house looked as though they had been felled with axes previous to the burning that always follows in the preparation of a clearing, whether for house or plantation.

On his return downstream in early May, Rice (1928:355) found this village abandoned and everything devastated by an invasion of locusts. Farther downriver he found a remnant of the community camped by the river. The majority were in hammocks, so sick with fever that they could not move or speak. Those not in hammocks were weak, emaciated, and starving.

Rice (1928:354) summed up his impressions of the Ninam.

The Shiliana are not the fierce and intractable people that legend ascribes them to be, but for the most part poor, undersized, inoffensive creatures who eke out a miserable existence, barely surviving the privations and diseases of a harsh and exacting environment, a very different nation from the bold and warlike Guaharibos on the west side of the Parima serra.

## XIV. The Xilixana on the Uraricoera River, 1920–1935

In the 1920s the Xilixana or Mucajaí Ninam were living in three villages south of the Uraricoera River. During the 1920s the only known event was a raid by the downstream Macuxi, who stole a Ninam woman. The Mucajaí Ninam in a retaliatory raid killed a Macuxi man.

They told Peters (as earlier groups had indicated to Koch-Grunberg) that during this period they were without steel tools and had only pieces of rock tied to sticks, which they used to chop down the trees of the forest to make room for their gardens. Palm slats were used as knives to cut bush rope. They knew about steel tools and were intent on acquiring some.

In 1932 a Mácu couple and their three young sons were traveling up the Uraricoera River after trading with Brazilians downstream. The Ninam saw their canoe and invited them to come ashore, saying they wished to trade cotton for some knives the Mácu were transporting. Upon landing, the father and one of the sons walked inland with the Ninam toward their dwelling to see the cotton. On the way the Ninam pointed out ripe palm fruit high in a tree. When the father and son looked up, the Ninam grabbed their hair, yanked their heads backward, injuring their backs, and then beat them to death with sticks. Other Ninam were guarding the wife and two younger sons at the riverbank. They told the older boy that his father wanted him. As he went along the path, this son was also killed. This group of Ninam now had some steel tools. The captured woman was taken as wife by one of the Ninam men. The young son was also taken captive but died shortly afterward.

In 1935 an unknown assailant killed a Ninam man. The captured Mácu woman suggested that it might have been a Yekwana group who lived upriver. The Ninam decided to raid this group to seek revenge. Men from all three Ninam villages ascended the river in three sluggish bark canoes. When they approached the Yekwana village, one canoe landed while the other two remained hidden. The Yekwana received the Ninam well and served them food. At a given signal to the concealed Ninam, all attacked the Yekwana. They killed four or five Yekwana men and made off with their steel goods and three Yekwana women and their children. A Yekwana youth escaped and carried news of the attack to Yekwana villages farther upriver.

In fear of retaliation, the Xilixana moved farther inland (south) and east, to the headwaters of the streams flowing into the Mucajaí River. Some months passed. When it appeared that the Yekwana were not going to attack, the Ninam moved back to the vicinity of the Uraricoera where they had previously been. Here all three villages were gathered together preparing for the traditional *yaimo* ceremony. During a rainstorm, they were surprised by Yekwana armed with guns and assisted by allies, some of whom were probably Palimi theli, another Yanomami group. The Yekwana killed the five Mucajaí men they could find. One woman and a young boy also died when caught between the bullets and arrows. At the time of the raid, some of the Ninam men were away from the village hunting or fishing. When they heard the gunshots, these Ninam men circled the path used by the Yekwana and ambushed them on their return, inflicting some casualties.

Once again in fear of retaliation, the three Ninam villages fled. The smallest village moved a short distance while the other two villages went south, out of the Uraricoera watershed to the Kloknai stream, a northern tributary of the Mucajaí River.

## XV. Summary

The early history of the Yanomami led to their occupation of the Parima Highlands, and their eventual movement out of the highlands involved both push and pull factors. Following the emergence of the Ninam Yanomami as a distinct subgroup and the divergence between the Xiliana and Xilixana, both groups moved to an area north of the Uraricoera River. Later the Xilixana communities, who were to become the central Ninam or Mucajaí group, moved to the south side of the Uraricoera. In 1935 they raided the Yekwana for steel tools and women. The Yekwana retaliated in a raid in which they used guns. To avoid further attacks, the Xilixana or Mucajaí Ninam fled south, with all three villages eventually going to the headwaters of the streams flowing into the Mucajaí River and later moving to the river itself.

# 3

# The Xilixana on the Mucajaí River

This chapter continues the history of the Mucajaí Ninam from the time of their arrival in the Mucajaí watershed (map 2) in late 1935 or early 1936 to the invasion by gold miners beginning in 1987.

## I. The Period of Isolation, 1936–1956

Two of the villages remained at the Kloknai stream for some time. No Yekwana or any other group appeared. The three villages were entering a period of isolation in which they would be cut off from all other Yanomami groups for more than twenty years. During this period two of the villages moved a number of times within the hilly forests of the Mucajaí watershed and lived at times along the Mucajaí River itself. Occasionally they would return to the upper part of the Uraricoera watershed, where they were rejoined by the third village. Every two or three years during the dry season, the Yanomami move to a new area for the purpose of hunting in fresh grounds and of clearing trees and vines to make new fields.

A few years after locating near the Mucajaí River, a group of men walked southeast to the vicinity of the Apiaú River searching for a source of steel tools. In a village they found some Aica women, who immediately warned them away as the men were returning. They saw from a distance some Aica men, who shot at them but missed. The Mucajaí men returned disappointed in their search.

The Mucajaí group had a shortage of women and in their isolation had been unable to establish marriage ties with other villages. Sometime between 1936 and 1944, men from the three villages traveled southwest for a considerable distance to raid a village and capture some women. In a mountainous region they came across the Moxatotau, a Yanomami group. The Moxatotau discovered their presence and attacked with arrows. The Mucajaí raiders fled (Peters 1998:175).

In 1944 a young man was passing by a tree located near the confluence of the Mucajaí River and the Kloknai stream. There to his amazement he saw some axes, machetes, and a bolt of red cloth placed in a crotch of a tree.

The cloth was immediately torn into loincloths for the men. Members of the Brazilian Boundary Commission who had passed through the area without seeing the Xilixana had left these gifts. In their exploration of the Demini River a few years previously (Ferreira Reis 1943), the commission had clashed with the Yanomam. The items were a goodwill offering to let the Xilixana know the Boundary Commission party had no hostile intent, in the event that the Xilixana should recognize their presence.

Around 1946 two of the villages were struck by a sickness believed to have been malaria. Several people died. As is the Yanomami custom, the place became identified with the sickness and was abandoned. The sickness was shortly preceded by an event in which connection with the disease is problematical but is taken as certain by the Xilixana. While working in her garden, a woman was grabbed by a man dressed like a Brazilian peasant. She escaped only when another Xilixana woman came to her aid. At the riverbank soon afterward the Xilixana found an abandoned shelter with empty tin cans, a sign of Brazilian presence. They appropriated the tin cans and used these to cut meat. Upset by the presence of the Brazilians, the Xilixana painted themselves black and journeyed downriver to take their revenge on the intruders. They found no one. These Brazilians could have been carriers of malaria, as there had previously been no known malaria in the area.

After these deaths, the three villages moved north, back to the Uraricoera watershed. Two of the villages occupied the area where they had lived prior to the conflict with the Yekwana; the third settled some distance away but remained in contact. The three villages lived at a number of different locations in the Uraricoera watershed during this period. About 1954 the villages returned to the Mucajaí area. One village established their house on the Mucajaí River, a short distance upriver from its confluence with the Kloknai stream. The other two villages were located at a site on the Peiwa stream about 20 km (12.5 miles) or a seven-hour canoe trip upstream from the Mucajaí River.

## II. Breaking the Isolation—Contacts with Other Groups, 1956–1961

In the latter part of the 1950s there was a desperate need for steel tools among the Xilixana. It had been about twenty years since they had obtained these from the Mácu and Yekwana by deception and bloodshed and more than ten years since the Brazilian Boundary Commission's visit. This need led to a series of events that brought the Xilixana group into contact with Brazilians.

In 1956 seven men from two of the villages set out on foot toward the Apiaú River in an attempt to find some Brazilians who would trade steel goods. Near the Apiaú River they came across an Aica village with only women present. The Xilixana continued downriver a short distance. They came across an empty Brazilian rubber camp but could not find the occupants. They returned home empty-handed. Encouraged by this information, another group then set out for the Apiaú, but this time they could find neither Aica nor Brazilians.

The need for obtaining a fresh supply of steel tools persisted. A Yekwana captive, wife of two husbands and mother of some growing young men, suggested a trip down the Mucajaí River to find Brazilians with whom they could trade. She had probably had some experience of this as a young girl on Yekwana trips to the lower Uraricoera. In 1957 a group of men descended the Mucajaí in canoes and contacted some Brazilians. The Ninam traded arrows and canoe paddles for a few axes and knives and then returned upriver. Shortly afterward another group of twenty men and two women made another trip.

In August of 1958 a group consisting of thirty-two men and women from all the villages made a third trip downriver in seven canoes to contact Brazilians and trade for steel goods. They arrived at the ranch Fazenda Itu and traded with the Brazilians (Taylor 1979:76). Tensions arose within the Mucajaí group as they felt they were not receiving sufficient axes and hatchets in the exchange. Some wanted to kill the Brazilians and take their steel goods, but others in the group dissuaded them (Peters 1998:178). They came to realize that the Brazilians wanted them to return at a later date to work in the fields. They would be paid with steel goods.

(In this section and throughout the book, the terms *Brazilian* and *Indian* are used in a cultural sense. In the political sense, all Indians are Brazilians with legal status but some, including the Yanomami, lack the rights of full citizenship.)

While the Xilixana were looking for trade relations with the Brazilians, a group of Americans and Canadians under the auspices of the Unevangelized Fields Mission (UFM), later called Missão Evangélica da Amazônia (MEVA), were making plans to establish missionary stations in the Brazilian Yanomami area. Their initial activity consisted of making aerial surveys over the region. In 1957 they passed over the Mucajaí group and dropped some fishhooks as a goodwill gesture. In October of 1958 there was another overflight, during which they dropped cans tied with red ribbons. The cans contained fishhooks, knives, scissors, and beads. At the same time two missionaries, John Peters and Neill Hawkins, accompanied by two Wai-Wai

Indians began their ascent of the Mucajaí River by canoe to make contact with the Xilixana. On November 20, 1958, they arrived at a village *yano* (house) located close to the river. It was empty as the villagers were having a feast at another location. Two days later the villagers returned to the yano by the river and were delighted with the presence of the outsiders with their steel goods and beads. A small, permanent mission station with an airfield was established near the site at approximately 62 degrees, 14 minutes west and 2 degrees, 46 minutes north.

With the establishment of the mission station and the airstrip, the Xilixana began to receive visits from Brazilians and others connected with the national society. In 1959 four prospectors visited the villages on their way by boat to the Parima Highlands. In 1961 a Brazilian Air Force major visited the mission. He urged the missionaries to find a new location for a longer airstrip to accommodate larger air force aircraft. June 17 of the same year saw the arrival of representatives of the air force, army, and ministry of justice. The airstrip, with its role in Brazilian control of its borders, was their concern. Although the missionaries constructed airstrips for their mission posts, all the strips remained the property of the Brazilian government, with open access to all unless restricted by the government.

Based on the information they had obtained from the visiting prospectors, toward the end of 1960 the Xilixana traveled for several days upriver and visited another Yanomami group, the Malaxi theli. This was the beginning of trade and marital relationships between these two groups that still continued in 1999.

The missionaries accompanied by Xilixana made several survey trips to neighboring Yanomami groups. These trips became important for the future of the Mucajaí group because the introductions led to marital exchanges and affinal kinship ties with these groups.

In February 1959, three missionaries with two Wai-Wai Indians visited the Aica on the Apiaú River. In January 1960 Mucajaí men made the same trip to invite the Apiaú group to visit the Mucajaí villages and establish intergroup relations. Shortly afterward, ten Aica arrived at Mucajaí for a feast. In August, Peters and four Mucajaí men traveled to the Aica on the Ajarani River. In May 1961 Peters and some Mucajaí men traveled to the Malaxi theli; a repeat visit took place in December. In October of the same year Peters with six Mucajaí men visited for five days a Yanomami village on a tributary of the Ajarani River. And that December ten Mucajaí men visited the Palimi theli on the Parima River. While there they met some visiting northern Ninam, the Xiliana.

Thus in the five years between 1957 and 1961, the Mucajaí group broke out of their isolation. They had established contact with the Brazilian farmers and ranchers on the lower Mucajaí, the missionaries, and the military. Other Yanomami groups contacted were the Malaxi theli on the upper Mucajaí, the Aica of the Apiaú and Ajarani Rivers, and the Palimi theli on the upper Uraricoera. Many of these contacts resulted in long-standing relationships with important demographic consequences for the Xilixana population; these consequences are examined later in the histories of the individual villages.

### III. Interacting with Rural Brazilians

After the arrival of the missionaries, the villagers continued to travel downriver and spend a few days each trip with Brazilian farmers and ranchers. These trips were motivated as much by the desire to learn about the ways of the Brazilians as by the wish to trade. Yanomami subsistence had much in common with the subsistence of the Brazilian frontiersmen. Both groups hunted, fished, and felled trees to grow gardens with their staples of bananas and manioc. Like the Xilixana, the Brazilians possessed few consumer goods. For travel, the Brazilians walked and canoed, just as the Yanomami did.

During the 1960s and the early 1970s, the contact increased. The Xilixana received requests from the farmers and ranchers to come and work for them at harvest time and to help clear new fields. These work periods lasted for several weeks, during which time the Xilixana were absent from their villages. Peters (1973:150) estimates that the Mucajaí villages received about a total of two hundred dollars a year in either cash or trade goods from their work for the Brazilians at that time. During these work periods on the Brazilian farms and ranches on the lower Mucajaí, the Xilixana would accompany the Brazilians on trips to Boa Vista, where they began to learn more about the ways of rural Brazil.

In the 1970s some villagers were stricken with tuberculosis. All of the sick families were connected with individuals who had worked for Brazilians. The Xilixana were already aware of the danger of disease from outside contact because of their experiences from 1957 to 1960. The missionaries continually warned them of the danger. As a consequence, while not avoiding all outside contact, they diminished the frequency of their outside trips and became cautious about interaction with Brazilians.

Up to this point we have been considering the history from the viewpoint of events unfolding in the Xilixana villages. To understand further aspects of the history, other events taking place in Roraima need to be considered.

## IV. The Gold Rush in Roraima

Brazilian gold miners visited the Xilixana villages beginning in 1987. Events on the Mucajaí River should be seen against the broader background of events to the east in Boa Vista and to the west in the Surucucu region of the Parima Highlands and in neighboring Paapiú in the Couto de Magalhães riversed, a tributary of the upper Mucajaí.

Boa Vista is the political and economic center of the state of Roraima. Its location on the Rio Branco gives it water access to all the rivers of the area. But more important for the miners is the aviation center. A small plane from the airfield in Boa Vista can reach any location in western Roraima where an airstrip can be cleared. Monbiot (1991:65) reports that the Boa Vista airport was the second busiest in Brazil, with daily traffic of three hundred small planes taking off and landing. With the comings and goings of the miners, pilots, mechanics, construction workers, ranchers, and settlers, Boa Vista has taken on many of the characteristics of a roaring frontier settlement.

Surucucu is located in the Parima Highlands about 200 km (125 mi.) west of Boa Vista, with the Mucajaí villages in the middle of the flight path between them. Paapiú lies to the east on lower ground. The Paapiú airfield was first built on the initiative of the Malaxi theli to woo the missionaries downriver to visit them with medicine and trade goods. In 1986 the military enlarged it into a wide, mile-long airstrip. The following year an estimated forty thousand gold miners poured into the highlands and fanned out over a wide area.

Armed clashes between the miners and the Yanomami inevitably developed as the miners ran roughshod over the surrounding areas. Part of this region was the home of the Malaxi theli, with whom some of the Xilixana had kin relationships. By 1989 the Yanomami area was in the grip of a malaria epidemic spread by the conditions created by the miners. Because of the epidemic and the resulting pressures brought by national and international groups, the government finally expelled the miners from the Yanomami area. The miners retreated to Boa Vista to wait out the period of protest. By 1992 an estimated eleven thousand had resumed their mining activities, only to be expelled again.

Some miners ascended the Mucajaí River on their way to the highlands. Boatloads of miners and their equipment passed by the Mucajaí villages located near the river. While the traffic was irregular, the missionaries estimate that about twenty miners and their equipment passed each day during the height of the gold rush from 1987 to 1989. The miners stopped at the villages in the vicinity of the river and wanted the villagers to provide food, labor, sex, and so on. The miners needed extra help to move their boats upriver through the rapids or to portage around them. At first the Mucajaí people welcomed the miners, as they were a source of many kinds of manufactured goods as well as cash. Sunglasses, stereo radios, and watches became important items in the Mucajaí inventory of manufactured goods. From 1987 to 1990 the government expelled the Mucajaí missionaries for reasons which have remained obscure. Miners and personnel of the Fundação Nacional do Índio occupied the mission post at Mucajaí. There were armed clashes between miners and some Xilixana with casualties on both sides; the demographic impact of all this activity is examined in later chapters. In the 1990s after action by the government to deter the miners, the traffic of miners on the river diminished substantially. There was little mining in the middle Mucajaí area itself. The river became polluted with mercury coming down from the highlands, but the people began drawing their water from creeks that did not have their sources in the areas of intense mining.

## V. Classification: The Historical Periods

As we have seen from this outline of Xilixana history since their arrival in the Mucajaí watershed in 1935, during this period they passed from being a group of three small villages isolated from all other Yanomami groups as well as rural Brazilians to being a group of six larger villages interacting with other Yanomami groups and with Brazilians.

Part IV of the present work examines the population dynamics of the Xilixana from 1930 to 1995. Demographic data for each of the sixty-six years show the levels of fertility, mortality, migration, and consequent population increase or decrease of each village as they experienced these events, and historical factors influencing these rates are assessed. But annual data are too discriminate and subject to volatility owing to the small numbers. The data need to be classified by the differing historical conditions that influenced their magnitudes over the sixty-six-year period. Based on the history presented in this and the previous chapter, a fourfold classification of historical phases is used in the chapters to come.

The twenty-seven-year period from 1930 to 1956 was the Precontact period. Although there were raids on other indigenous groups between 1930 and 1935, for most of this period the Mucajaí people were cut off from contact with other Yanomami groups and the nation.

From 1957 to 1960 the Mucajaí Yanomami broke out of their isolation and quickly came into contact with rural Brazilians, missionaries, and other Yanomami groups. This is here called the Contact period, shorthand for first contact, as the contact continued in the subsequent periods.

From 1961 to 1981 the Mucajaí Yanomami and the missionaries formed a distinct community that gradually established kinship links with other Yanomami groups. To a much lesser extent they also established economic links with some Brazilians. This is called the Linkage period.

The phase from 1982 to January 1, 1996, is called the Brazilian period. During this time, the Xilixana gradually learned about Brazilian rural life, interacted with the miners, and became aware of political events in Roraima with implications for the Yanomami. They also realized the threat of disease in their contacts with Brazilians, which led to restraint in these contacts. The beginning of this period was around 1982 when Xilixana mortality began an upward trend owing to infectious diseases related to interaction and linkages with the national society.

# 4

# The Xilixana Village

This chapter describes some typical physical and social characteristics of Xilixana villages, the only communal unit of Yanomami society. It emphasizes the importance of the faction in the social structure and role of kinship classification in determining social behavior.

## I. The Village and Its Environs

All the individuals who are members of a village live within the confines of a single dwelling. It is located near a water source, near land that is suitable for making gardens, and where the surrounding forest can provide a sufficient supply of game, fruits, nuts, berries, and firewood.

For the Xilixana the village house (*yano*) is a circular dwelling that may be anywhere from 15 to 23 meters (16 to 25 yards) in diameter, depending on individual preferences and the size of the population. The circular walls are made of palm leaves hung on a frame of poles. The roof is cone shaped, again made of leaves attached to a frame of wooden poles. It covers the entire area within the walls. The houses have no openings except for the entry door. Consequently the interiors are without outside light except for some reflection through the leaves on a bright day or when the leaves are pulled aside to admit light.

Smoke lingers in the darkened dwelling from the numerous fires, which are the focal points of activity for each family. These fires are placed toward the outer circle within the dwelling. The hammocks of each family, hung from the support poles for the walls and roof, are grouped triangularly around the family fire. The wife's hammock is hung about 30 centimeters (about one foot) off the ground with her husband's hammock directly above. She keeps the fire going throughout the night to ward off the chill of the darkness. Infants sleep in the hammock with the mother until they are about three years of age. The older children have their hammocks on the other sides of the triangle or, if more room is needed, from a pole added for this purpose.

Each dwelling has a large vacant inner circle. This is used as a passageway from the door to the various family hearths. It is also the play area for

4.1. A traditional Xilixana village dwelling, the *yano* (Andersons, 1976).

4.2. A family section with hearth and hammocks within the *yano* (Andersons, 1970).

the children. Its most important use is for dancing and ritual activities. In other Yanomami regions the roof may not cover this inner circle, and this allows these houses to be much larger. While these larger dwellings have more light, they are more easily penetrated by rain and are colder at night.

During the Linkage period, there were some changes in the materials used for the construction of houses. The walls of the village yano were made of mud instead of palm leaves. Many of the yanos began to feature multiple doors as well as one or two vents or windows in the roof to allow more light into the interior and to evacuate the smoke. These changes emulated features of the houses of the Yekwana and rural Brazilians.

In the Linkage period some families abandoned the village yano and built their own individual rectangular dwellings of mud, following the rural Brazilian custom. Families needed more space as they began to accumulate manufactured goods. In addition, security of these goods became a problem in the communal yano. The mud walls provided better insulation against the heat as well as being less of a fire hazard than the traditional palm leaves.

Several arrangements of village houses emerged in the Linkage and Brazilian periods. One village retained the traditional yano where all the villagers resided. Other villages built rectangular mud houses for individual families or factions (discussed later) but retained a village yano where the headman and his faction resided. The rectangular houses formed a circle around the yano. Still other villages did away with the traditional yano and had only rectangular mud houses, which could have varying arrangements relative to each other.

Traditionally each village has a main yano as described. However, some villages may have a secondary yano. This occurs when a village plants additional gardens that are at least a three-hour trip from the main yano. While working these gardens or hunting and gathering in the forest in this area, the villagers temporarily occupy the secondary yano. Some headmen have also constructed secondary yanos at the mission post for use by their family and villagers when they visit the mission to receive medical treatment.

An area of trees and underbrush close to the village house is cleared or thinned for planting gardens. Each family cultivates its own section. Approximately half of the garden is planted with both bitter and sweet manioc. Numerous varieties of plantains and bananas are the other staple. Additional foods grown are yams, sweet potatoes, and sugarcane. The gardens also produce plants used for purposes other than food, including cotton, tobacco, and seeds of the bixa tree for producing red body paint. Additional gardens may be planted in another area some distance from the village house because of good soil or hunting conditions.

The surrounding forest provides various kinds of palm fruit, berries, nuts, and honey as well as the third staple, game meat. Tapir and peccary (sometimes called wild pig) followed by the spider and howler monkeys are the preferred game foods. Several times a year, especially when preparing for ceremonies during which gifts of game meat are distributed, the Xilixana will go on trekking expeditions to hunt game. These treks last between three and fifteen days.

There have been eight villages comprising the Xilixana population bloc at various times between 1930 and 1996. Not all of the villages have been in existence for this entire period. In 1930 when the Xilixana were living south of the Uraricoera River, there were only three villages, and they continued during the Precontact period. In this study they are designated villages A, B, and C. At the beginning of the Contact period in 1957, village A fused with village B; thus villages B and C comprised the group when the Xilixana were contacted by Peters in November 1958. During the Linkage phase the group expanded to four villages: in 1960 village D fissioned from village C, and village E fissioned from village D in 1962. At one time in the Brazilian phase the group expanded to seven villages, but it contracted to six in 1988 and remained at this number in 1998. In 1984 village F fissioned from village D and village G from village C. Village H fissioned from village B in 1986 while in 1988 village F disintegrated. These fissions and fusions are discussed in detail later.

## II. Kinship: The Logic of Yanomami Social Interaction

The logic behind much of the social structure of Yanomami villages is provided by the kinship system. In the minds of the people it is a logical construct that defines the kin relationships between people and, in so doing, automatically defines the expected social interactions among them. Complex societies would call these interactions political, economic, religious, and social as well as familial activities. Once kin are defined, non-kin are automatically defined. In other words, the kinship system defines an individual's social position relative to all members of the village, both kin and non-kin. Various elements make up the logic of Yanomami kinship.

Biological descent is the primary principle of classification in Yanomami kinship. However, in considering an anthropological society, we must ask whose biology of reproduction is being used as the basis of reckoning descent. Historically, various cultures have explained the reproductive process according to the principles of their own worldviews and ethnophysiology. In the Yanomami view of reproduction, the fetus is derived exclusively from male semen and requires multiple acts of insemination, which contribute to its development. The female womb is necessary for the nourishment of the fetus received from the male(s). In the Yanomami view, there is the possibility of multiple biological fathers.

Each individual is classified by a patrilineal descent category derived from the father. Therefore all villagers who are descended from a common male ancestor have the same descent category. If multiple paternity is involved, the primary father, usually the primary husband of the mother, is used in tracing the line of descent. In addition to biological descent through the male line, marriage, adoption, and occasional redefinition of a kinship relation are also sources of kinship in the Yanomami system.

## III. Categories of Kinship Classification

Figure 4.3 shows in symbolic form some of the kinship terms used by the Yanomami. This is a model that has been found useful in explaining the essentials of Yanomami kinship. For clarity, the model makes the simplifying assumptions of a single village in which inhabitants have one of two possible descent categories and marry within the village. (In reality, there may be more than two descent categories present in a community and marriages may take place with people from other villages.) The referent point of the diagram is ego (E), who may be of either sex. In the diagram, each type of symbol refers to a specific kinship term. The repetition of a symbol means that the same kin term (and therefore type of social interaction) is applied to all those relatives for whom it is used.

Within the nuclear family ego calls his/her male genitor by the Yanomami term for father, which is symbolized by the horizontally divided triangle. Ego calls his/her female genetrix by a kin term meaning mother and symbolized by a striped circle. Ego calls his/her male siblings by a term meaning brother and symbolized here by a blank triangle. Ego calls his/her female siblings by a kin term meaning sister, symbolized by a blank circle. Moving beyond the nuclear family to ego's other kin, the system's logic begins to reveal itself. In the generation prior to ego's and within the patrilineal line, the brothers of ego's father are also called father. This is because the father and his brothers have the same descent category. The children of father's brothers are called by the same kin terms as ego's siblings, brothers and sisters, because they also have the same patrilineal descent category as ego and his/her biological siblings.

Within the matrilineal line mother's sisters are called by the kin term of mother. They have the same descent category as ego's mother. Ego's mother has a different descent category than ego because if this were not so, she would not have been allowed to marry ego's father as the marriage would

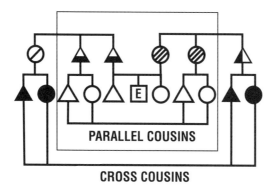

4.3. Some Yanomami kinship terms.

have been incestuous. In this model, the husband of mother's sister (not shown in the diagram) also must have the same descent category as ego and his father; that is, he is a brother (not necessarily biological) to ego's father. He must have a different descent category than his wife to avoid an incestuous marriage, and by simplifying assumption, there are only two descent categories in the community. Therefore ego also calls the children of mother's sister and her husband by the kin terms of brother and sister since they have the same descent category. This is not always the case as the simplifying assumption is not always present.

Father's sister (cross sex) is called by a distinctive kin term symbolized by a circle with a stripe through it. She has married a man (not shown in the diagram) with a different descent category than her own (otherwise incestuous) and with the same descent category as ego's mother because, by assumption, there are only two descent categories present. In other words, he is a brother to ego's mother. By the patrilineal rule, children of father's sister have the descent category of their father, which in this model must be different from ego's. Ego calls them by the kin terms symbolized by a blackened triangle for the male and a blackened circle for the female. These terms could be translated as "potential husband" or "potential wife," meaning someone whom ego is eligible to marry according to the kinship logic. The anthropological term for this relationship is *cross cousin*.

Mother's brother (cross sex) is symbolized by a vertically divided triangle. He has a different descent category than ego because it is the same as mother's descent category (which must be different from ego's for her to have married ego's father). His children (his wife is not shown in the diagram) have his descent category because of the patrilineal rule. The kin term for the male is symbolized by the blackened triangle and for the female by the blackened circle. These are the same symbols as for the children of father's sister because by the logic of the model they are cross cousins to ego.

Two families whose children have different descent categories frequently enter into agreements to exchange women as wives—that is, sisters marry brothers. This is the preferred form of marriage but frequently is not possible.

As described, the logic of this kinship system classifies members of the same descent category in the same generation by similar kin terms distinguished only by sex. These, in turn, are distinguished from individuals with different descent categories by different terms of kinship. These analytical terms are shown on the lower part of figure 4.3. The cross cousins are the members of the same generation as ego but with different descent categories. Since they do not have the same descent category, they are not kin even though the semantic of "kin terminology" is used to describe the system. In contrast to the cross cousins, the parallel cousins are members of the same generation with the same descent category as ego. Therefore all are called brothers and sisters even though it is known that they are not from the same biological parents. It should be noted that these descent classifications are logical categories in the minds of the people and do not comprise actual social groups.

This type of kinship system emphasizes the distinction between people with the same descent category as ego and those with a different descent category. In figure 4.3, the distinction is between those within the rectangle and those outside it. Within and without the descent category, it distinguishes only by sex and generation.

The simplified model illustrated here is seldom adequate to explain real situations. Many complications arise whereby the core logic of the model becomes highly complicated. Some of these complications are polygyny, polyandry, serial monogamy, age imbalance of generations, adoption, women captured in raids, redefinitions of relationships, and incestuous marriages that are not prevented. In spite of these complications, all the villagers know their descent category and relationship to every other individual in the village and many in other villages. They also know the relationships of all the villagers to one another.

## IV. Significance of Kinship Logics

While the classification of kin is a logical exercise producing a cognitive map in the minds of the villagers, it is not simply a logical exercise. It determines various types of intravillage as well as intervillage behavior. When two Yanomami meet for the first time, they immediately begin discussing kinship so that they can establish the proper manner in which they should act toward one another. If strangers—including anthropologists—should reside for a period of time in a village, they must be adopted as a specific type of kin by someone in the village. This is not an honorific but a practical necessity so that the logic of the system can be applied to the stranger by all the other villagers. In this way they will know how to interact socially with the stranger. Here are some examples of how the kinship logic determines social behavior.

The functioning of this kinship logic can be seen in the occupancy of the interior space of the yano. A reproductive family is marked by the descent category of the primary husband. The wife cannot have the same descent category as her husband since the marriage would have been incestuous. She does not change her descent category with marriage. But the family group is frequently identified by the descent category of the primary husband. All the families identified by the same descent category make their fires and hang their hammocks next to each other in the outer sector of the circular yano. This means that the children of these families are brought up in close proximity to each other. Father and his brothers perform many economic and ritual activities together, with the children in attendance as a group. If ego's primary father should be occupied with other matters, then the father's brother may temporarily take parental responsibility in place of the father. This physical closeness and interaction illustrates why *father* is also an appropriate kin term for children to use for father's brother.

Perhaps the most striking example of the kinship logic defining social interaction is the selection of marriage partners. In tribal societies marriage is not primarily viewed as the union of two individuals, as its legal definition makes it in industrial societies, but as the union of two kin groups, however these may be defined. In Yanomami culture, the negative rule is that it is incestuous to marry someone with the same descent category; that is, a sibling or parallel cousin whose term of address is brother or sister. The positive rule is that one marries someone with a different descent category, frequently a cross cousin from the same logical generation (although those of the same logical generation may not be close in age). There are some exceptions to the positive rule, such as captives.

Within a village these rules can exclude ego's marriage to a sizable portion of the marriageable group. It depends on the number and size of the factions (discussed later) as well as the number of descent categories among the villagers. In addition, the preferred form of marriage involves the exchange of women between two families identified by different descent categories. Therefore ego's chances may be further diminished if ego's family is unable to enter into such agreement. Early and Peters (1990:103–14) have discussed these problems in greater detail and some of the means taken to cope with them. Marriage itself creates a whole new set of affinal relationships. Of special importance is the relationship of a son-in-law to his father-in-law and mother-in-law.

The model does not mean to imply that marriage is restricted to a mate from the same village. This is usually the preferred form, although at times impossible. It is preferred on the boy's part because it means he can spend the period of bride service for his new in-laws within the village where his own family resides. If the marriage is between villages, the boy would have to spend up to several years of bride service in her village with her family and only at the end of this period is he free to return with his family to his original village. On the girl's part it allows her to remain in the village of her family after the period of bride service. Here she is more at home and her family of origin can provide quick protection if there should be trouble in the marriage.

Kin relationships also define how goods and services are exchanged among Yanomami. These are called reciprocity exchanges. The meat brought by the hunter is not the property of the hunter. It must be distributed among other members of the village. The necessity to share and the amount shared depend on the closeness or distance of the kin relationship between the hunter and the other members of the community. His relationship to his immediate in-laws is of special importance. By the basic law of reciprocity, kinship dictates sharing by those who have with those who are in need. The strength of the obligation and what must be shared is defined by the kin relationships. Assistance in the preparation of food for feasts is a service rendered according to kinship obligations to the one responsible for the feast. For societies that are organized by kinship principles, kinship with reciprocity rights and obligations are all the same thing. It could be said that they are the two sides of the same coin. This use of kinship logic to define exchange is totally different from a market system employing the logic of supply and demand and from various systems of redistribution.

Yanomami frequently visit other Yanomami villages. These visits create the need for hospitality, which includes food and drink to refresh themselves and a place near a fire where visitors can hang their hammocks. Kinship determines such obligations. In time of conflict, these obligations are extended to support and assistance in raiding enemies.

## V. Xilixana Descent Categories

Genealogical work has identified eleven men born around 1875 who were the individuals providing Xilixana the descent categories used in the Pre-contact period. These men became fathers in the decade before the turn of the twentieth century and some continued to father children to around the time of the Yekwana conflict. Since that time, some descent lines (categories) have flourished while others have gone out of existence. The principal descent lines were carried by six of these eleven male ancestors and are designated A through F in upcoming discussions.

Descent category A was carried by a famous Xilixana shaman who had six wives and fathered at least twenty-three children. His first wife was killed by the Xiliana. With this shaman monopolizing the women, his descent line has flourished and in the Brazilian period remained the most common descent category among the Xilixana.

Descent categories B and C were carried by Xiliana in-migrants. Descent category D was carried by a man about whom we know nothing. Descent category E was carried by another Xiliana who in-migrated in his late teens for marriage. A Xilixana who stole his second wife from the Xiliana carried descent category F.

The O-U classification means other or unknown descent categories. There were five additional descent categories in the Precontact period, but these lines had died out by the beginning of the Contact period. Most of the discontinued lines involved secondary husbands in polyandrous unions, men who never became primary husbands. There are several individuals whose fathers are unknown.

The final category refers to additional external in-migrating males joining the Xilixana after 1930. They have a descent category from their original village. The in-migrants become fathers and thereby introduce new descent categories into the Xilixana population. Since some of the male in-migrants were Yanomami brothers, they have the same descent category. Consequently the new categories are fewer than the number of external in-migrating males.

## VI. The Social Structure of a Yanomami Village

The categories of kinship classification exist in the minds of the villagers and are one of the logics behind the formation of social groups, but these categories themselves are not social groups. The social groups comprising Yanomami social structure are the family, the factions, the village group, and the regional blocs of villages.

Husband, wife, and children form the basic family unit, which is symbolized by having their own hearth in the communal house. Males and females have distinct roles and depend on each other for subsistence and social definition. There are no adult males or females who have not been married. A male is defined as provider of the main support for the family, especially by hunting. The female's primary function is to bear children but she also provides food for the family by preparing meals, gathering firewood, and tending the garden. A barren female is looked down upon. Others without a family of their own may attach themselves to such a family, especially elderly parents. These arrangements can be modified due to polyandry, polygyny, and other marital arrangements. The family is identified by the descent category of the primary husband, as already explained, but no one changes descent category upon joining a family group. The family unit is seldom an autonomous unit within the village but is meshed into the next level of organization.

Family units form social groups that can be called factions (Lizot 1988:554–58). The core of a faction usually consists of mature males with the same patrilineal descent category, often a father and his sons or a group of biological or Yanomami brothers, the latter being parallel cousins. Their wives and children are also part of the core of a faction. Additional members may be sons-in-law, elderly parents especially if widowed, and other individuals or families not in a position to form an independent faction. One of the core males is looked upon as the headman of the faction. A group of individuals or nuclear families lacking kin connections in a village may form a quasi-faction with a headman. Occasionally a single family of procreation may comprise a quasi-faction.

Most factions are identified by a descent category derived from the dominant males of the faction. It usually applies to a majority of the faction's members, including the children. But not all members of a faction have that descent category; for example, the descent category is different for wives, and may be so for some grandparents, in-laws, isolated individuals, or non-kin nuclear families. By becoming members of a faction, people do not change their descent status.

Factions usually attempt to build up their numbers and thereby increase their influence in village affairs. An important function of the faction is to arrange the marriages of its female members. These arrangements are frequently made for the purpose of creating alliances with other factions.

Factions are not necessarily long-term, permanent groups. They can go through cycles of growth and decline depending on the ability of the headman of the faction, a faction's sex ratio of fertility, the pattern of mortality of its members, the ability to attract new adherents, and the ability of a sufficient number of its members to remain in the village or faction when marriage considerations may pressure them otherwise.

Traditionally the entire population of a village lived in the single communal house. A village may contain only one or two factions, which may or may not be identified by the same patrilineal descent category. Within the communal house, there are distinct areas formed by the adjoining hearths of members of the same faction. Individuals in the yano are identified with a hearth family and a faction. The villages move after a period of years when the soil of their gardens becomes fatigued and the game of the adjoining forest diminishes, although they tend to remain in the same general area. As already noted, as the term *village* is used in this study, it does not imply a permanently occupied geographical site.

Although each Yanomami village is an autonomous community, villages enter into social relationships with other villages, usually those within the same region. The basis for these relationships is usually affinal kinship arising from marriage and/or kinship because of a common origin. The kin bonds between two villages include political alliance and periodic exchanges of goods. But the solidarity of such bonds can sour, so that fights erupt and raiding takes place. Groups of villages descended from a single village of origin have been called population blocs (Chagnon 1992:80) or agglomerations (Lizot 1994:216), following Riviére. The Mucajaí groups, because of their historical and marriage ties, are a population bloc although it is impossible to designate the single village of origin.

Among the Ninam, the solidarity between related villages is expressed by the *yaimo* ceremony. This is a ritual in which the host village invites members of the other villages to a gathering. The ceremony includes dancing, shamanic contact with the spirits, distribution of food, and a long ceremonial dialogue followed by exchange of various items. Among its many functions, the ceremony serves as an expression of solidarity by the population bloc descended from the same ancestors. Since the 1970s there have been other social gatherings that serve a solidarity function, such as work projects and political meetings.

## VII. Leadership and Decision Making

At times decisions must be made affecting the entire village, such as about construction of a new yano or renovation of the existing one, starting a new garden, the organization of a feast, or the preparations for an attack on an enemy village. A village discussion may take place, usually dominated by the leaders of the factions and by any other persons respected because of experience or special abilities. A woman may speak, especially if she is the mother of several adult males. The headman of the village is the leader of one of the factions, frequently the largest. His role is mainly that of a *primus inter pares,* and he can act only by example and persuasion. Village decisions involve an extended discussion by the headmen of the various factions and other important people, in which a gradual consensus is reached about a course of action.

Members of each faction in a village recognize as their leader one of the core males. The role is ill-defined as to both function and selection. It functions by persuasion and example, not by command. It usually falls to an older man who wants the role, has the ability to lead people in this way, and has a family unit of sufficient size, especially in number of grown sons, to carry out communal tasks. The father usually has dominance over the sons, but this can vary depending on the age, health, and ability of the father. Since the strength of a faction and its influence within the village is partly dependent on numbers, a father may attempt to attract additional families to his faction. A common way of doing this is to encourage a son-in-law to remain after he finishes his period of bride service and not to return to his original village. Some inducement is usually given, frequently the promise of a second wife who is a younger sister of his first wife. Any male without kin ties in a village (usually an in-migrant) will be recruited to join a faction to increase its influence.

## VIII. Village Fission and Fusion

Fissioning takes place when a group of considerable size—usually a faction or factions influenced by their headman or headmen—moves out of a village and establishes a new village. Demographically this is out-migration from the original village without any in-migration, since there is no receiving population but a new village is founded. Fusion is the opposite demographic process to fission. It takes place when a village dissolves and its members join (in-migrate to) an already existing village. Fusion frequently takes place when village populations become too small to carry out ordinary village activities.

## IX. Size of Populations of Yanomami Villages

As background for the demographic part of this study, it is helpful to know what previous studies have found about the size of the populations of Yanomami villages. Table 4.1 presents a survey compiled from several

Table 4.1. Population Size of Yanomami Villages

| Population | Brazil | | Venezuela | | | |
| | | | Atabapo | | Rio Negro | |
| | N | % | N | % | N | % |
| --- | --- | --- | --- | --- | --- | --- |
| <20 | 3 | 14.3 | 19 | 12.0 | 1 | 1.8 |
| 20–49 | 16 | 76.2 | 53 | 40.4 | 14 | 25.3 |
| 50–99 | 2 | 9.5 | 31 | 31.3 | 21 | 38.2 |
| 100–149 | - | - | 7 | 15.1 | 18 | 32.8 |
| 150–249 | - | - | - | - | 1 | 1.1 |
| 250+ | - | - | 1 | 0.6 | - | - |
| Total | 21 | 100 | 111 | 100 | 55 | 100 |

Sources: Saffirio and Hames 1983:8; Ramos 1979a:14, 1995:34; Oficina Central de Estadística e Informática 1985:195–246.

sources. The Brazilian studies are by individual anthropologists. The Venezuelan data are from the government's Indigenous Census of 1982 (Oficina Central de Estadística e Informática 1985), which in many areas was supervised by anthropologists.

All the Yanomami in Venezuela live in the departments of Atabapo and Rio Negro of the state of Amazonas (Oficina Central de Estadística e Informática 1985:71). The department of Rio Negro contains the villages with a higher incidence of conflict, which Chagnon studied. As Chagnon noted, the conflict leads to higher concentrations of village populations than in areas with a lower incidence of conflict, such as Atabapo. This is verified in table 4.1, which shows that in the department of Rio Negro, there are more villages with populations between 50 and 99 (average 82.5) than in any of the other ranges of population size. The population range with the highest percentage in Atabapo is for villages with populations between 20 and 49 (average 47.8). The Atabapo average of 47.8 is slightly lower than averages of two population blocs within Atabapo: 59 for thirty-five villages of the central Yanomami (Lizot 1977:501) and 52 for eight Haiyamo villages (Hames 1983:408). It is higher than an average of 44 found for seven villages of the Shitari (Hames 1983:424 citing Fredlund).

Village populations from 20 to 49 were also found to be the range for the majority of twenty-one Brazilian villages: the Sanumá in the Auaris watershed, the southern Ninam in the Ajarani watershed, and the Yanomam in the Catrimani watershed. The smaller size of the Brazilian villages compared with Atabapo villages in Venezuela is probably due to the overall lower density of the Yanomami population in these areas. The table indicates that village populations below 20 people are rarely found.

# 5

# Contact with the National Society

The Xilixana villages entered into contact with Brazilians in 1957 on their first trip downriver to obtain steel tools, as we have seen. They have maintained this contact in some fashion for over forty years since that time. We turn now to the ensuing motivation of the Xilixana to maintain contact and to the history of the Brazilian experience of contact with its indigenous groups. This serves as background for examining the results of the contact experiences of the Xilixana villages.

## I. Motives for Initial Xilixana Contacts

As noted in chapter 3, during the Precontact period the Xilixana were eager to make contact with Brazilians and to obtain manufactured goods from them. The trips to the Apiaú River and down the Mucajaí River beginning in 1957 were undertaken for this purpose. The Xilixana welcomed missionaries for the same reason. Table 5.1 reflects a pattern in these desires for manufactured goods, as shown by the sequence in which they were requested and acquired by the Mucajaí people during the Contact and Linkage periods. The table distinguishes tools, household items, and clothing, although some items overlap these categories.

The first column of the table lists the western goods possessed by the Xilixana at the time of the arrival of the missionaries in 1958. These were the remains of the tools and a few items of clothing acquired from the Yekwana, the Boundary Commission, or the downriver farmers and ranchers. All the tools were instruments for cutting many kinds of objects, a "general" type of tool. Only the men occasionally wore the western clothing. (The man wearing the long woman's slip was an anomaly to the western eyes of the missionaries, but this culturally conditioned way of viewing clothing was nonexistent for the owner of the slip.)

The missionaries kept a stock of various tools for the maintenance of the mission post. These western goods immediately aroused great interest and elicited requests from the Xilixana, being the very items for which they had been seeking a source. These goods are marked by an $x$ in the second column and indicate the priorities of the Xilixana at that time. Again the em-

Table 5.1. Western Goods Possessed or Requested by the Xiliana

| Type | Item | Possessed 1958 | Requested 1958 | Requested 1960s | Possessed 1972* |
|---|---|---|---|---|---|
| Tools | Machete | 5 | X | - | 28 |
| | Ax | 3 | X | - | 16 |
| | Knife | 3 | X | - | 20 |
| | Hoe | 1 | - | - | |
| | Adze | - | - | X | 2 |
| | Dirt digger | - | - | - | 6 |
| | Fish line | - | X | - | 7 |
| | Fish hooks | - | X | - | |
| | Gun & shot | - | - | X | 7 |
| Household Goods | Matches | - | X | - | |
| | Metal pots | - | X | - | 17 |
| | Grater board | - | - | - | |
| | Salt | - | - | X | |
| | Kerosene lamps | - | - | X | |
| | Flashlights | - | - | X | |
| | Braz. hammocks | - | - | X | |
| | Scissors | - | X | | |
| | Needles | - | - | X | |
| | Beads | - | - | X | |
| | Mirrors | - | X | - | |
| | Soap | - | - | X | |
| | Radio | - | - | - | |
| Clothing | Shirts | 2 | - | - | 18 |
| | Caps | 1 | - | - | |
| | Slip | 1 | - | - | |
| | Shorts/pants | - | - | X | 9 |
| | Skirts/blouses | - | - | X | |

\* by 50% of adult male population
- none or not pertinent
blank = not enumerated

*Source:* Peters 1973:136, 113, 115, 117 revised

phasis was on cutting tools. The Mucajaí people integrated the manufactured tools into their already existing cultural patterns in place of their traditional, less efficient tools.

The third column indicates the additional goods requested during the 1960s. The emphasis now shifted to household goods and clothing. Among the tools, the emphasis moved to tools for specialized purposes. The adze was employed in the construction of canoes and the gun for hunting. Some items, such as salt, soap, and Brazilian hammocks, may be considered as the beginnings of a desire for consumer goods.

The fourth column is a list of how many items of some specific tools that twenty-six Mucajaí men, or approximately half of the adult male population, possessed in 1972. The increase since 1958 indicates the strength of their desire for manufactured goods and why they persistently sought to contact Brazilians. By the middle of the Linkage period, most families had at least one machete, ax, knife, grater board, and metal pot. Many had a number of these items. Saffirio (Saffirio and Hames 1983:15, 20–21) found similar patterns among the Catrimani Yanomam.

Clothing became an item of major importance. At first the use was utilitarian, as protection against insects, which became more prevalent in the periods after the Precontact phase. Clothing served for warmth as well as prestige. Later, the importance of clothing became social as contacts with Brazilians increased. Negatively, the Xilixana did not wish to be gawked at or made a spectacle of by Brazilians either on the lower Mucajaí or in Boa Vista. The Fundação Nacional do Índio had encouraged a return to the traditional loincloth for the men and apron for the women, but the Xilixana would hear none of it. In the Brazilian period, they guffawed when shown pictures of their kin in such dress from the early 1960s.

The missionaries had introduced Brazilian currency, the *dinheiro,* to the Ninam in 1962 as they began to substitute it for the trade goods they had been giving in exchange for work at the mission post and for objects made by the Yanomami for the tourist trade. Women as well as men became recipients of cash. The women cut grass at the mission post and sold garden produce and bead work they had crafted. The estimated income from these sources for the whole group was about thirteen hundred dollars per year. The Brazilian farmers and ranchers also began to pay for labor by cash rather than barter.

As the desire for more manufactured goods increased, there was a need to obtain more cash. In the early 1970s the work downriver on Brazilian farms and ranches began to take on greater importance, especially during harvest periods. While the Yanomami had always been aware of the danger of disease through contact with Brazilians, their desire to obtain manufactured goods had overcome this fear up to this point. But around 1975 several Mucajaí people became sick with tuberculosis, and as mentioned, it struck in families in which a member or relative had been working for Brazilians. A reaction began to set in so that the Mucajaí people lessened the frequency of their trips downriver and became cautious about contacts with Brazilians. The withdrawal was not complete, but it led to diminished contact. As a consequence, it reduced the flow of cash and slowed the acquisition of manufactured goods. This, in turn, lessened the pressures for changes of the reciprocity and kinship systems as had been experienced by the Catrimani groups (Saffirio and Hames 1983:22–27).

## II. Motives of the Missionaries for Contact

While the motives of the missionaries are often seen as religious in the sense of conversion, the religious motivation of the MEVA missionaries included providing human services to the Xilixana community.

The religious goal of the missionaries was to found a self-sustaining Xilixana church with a lifestyle based on an evangelical interpretation of the Bible. The missionaries translated portions of it into Ninam. Being baptized was the symbol of commitment to this way of life. Elements of traditional Yanomami culture explicitly rejected by the missionaries were the practice of shamanistic rituals, the use of hallucinogenic drugs, and infanticide. About 10 percent of the population were baptized, although not all continued the baptismal commitment. The traditional worldview remained the definer of the situation for the vast majority of the Mucajaí villagers. Among converts, many elements of the traditional worldview remained (Peters 1998:200–6).

For most Xilixana, the major importance of the missionaries lay in their

5.1. A missionary provides medical assistance (Andersons,1970).

5.2. A missionary teaches about the encounter with the nation (Andersons, 1972).

roles as healers and traders. The necessity of medical assistance was always an explicit goal of the missionaries. With the increase of health problems in the Brazilian phase, the medical work absorbed much of the missionaries' time, on some occasions to the point of exhaustion requiring withdrawal and recuperation.

Personnel at the mission post had anticipated a minimal trading role. They exchanged items for services as well as game and garden products received. Salt, fishhooks, axes, and knives were the most desired items. But this trade expanded, and soon a half day, then two half days a week were designated as "trade days." Eventually a room adjacent to the maintenance shop was built to store trade items. Trade days became occasions of social gatherings. The villagers showed keen interest in the expanding stock of the store and the acquisitions of their kin and friends. These activities introduced the Xilixana to the use of money and gave them some understanding of the logic of market exchange. The store was an educational as well as an economic effort. The medical and economic assistance of the missionaries profited all the Xilixana without any discrimination or requirements connected with the missionaries' religious activity.

All the roles mentioned involved education of the indigenous population about aspects of the national society. In addition, the missionaries had a more focused educational role in the form of a literacy program. While reading of the Bible was an important goal, other kinds of instructional materials were used.

In the Xilixana case, the one, two, or three missionaries present at any one time were Canadian or American or, later, Brazilian. In working with indigenous groups, a missionary is never simply a bearer of a religious message but also brings his or her own cultural ways, since these become an unconscious part of the missionary's psychological being. For this reason, missionaries were as much transmitters of ideas and of a limited range of artifacts based on western technology as they were conduits of a religious message. While the missionaries had only simple, practical manufactured items for their work or personal care, these were objects of intense interest to the Yanomami.

The Xilixana and the missionaries formed their own community in semi-isolation from the national society. The main link was the occasional airplane bringing in supplies and mail. The everyday life of the missionaries consisted of associating with the Yanomami in one of their four roles. They came to know one another as individuals with varying types of interaction depending on individual personalities. As in any community, these interactions involved a range from deep friendship to antipathy. The stereotype of an acculturated, submissive, and permanently sedentary Indian group dominated by missionaries does not fit the Mucajaí situation.

## III. A Model of the Brazilian Experience of Contact with Indigenous Tribes

The contact of the Xilixana, as of all of the Yanomami, has taken place relatively late in the history of contact between national societies and indigenous groups. Brazil has had a long history of contact and at the beginning of the twentieth century, initial contacts were still taking place in the eastern regions of Brazil. These contacts were bloody and brutal as Indian lands were forcibly taken over; many Indians were killed and the survivors were banished. Large-scale massacres of Indians were reported in many of the eastern states.

Hemming (1978, 1987) has detailed this aspect of Brazilian history. Darcy Ribeiro (1967) has summarized the main strands of it by analyzing the intensity of contact between the known Brazilian indigenous groups and the national society in 1900 and by showing what subsequently had happened to these groups by 1957 (table 5.2). In 1900, 46 percent (105) of the known tribes were not yet in contact with the national society or had had an encounter and had then withdrawn into isolation from it. By 1957 about a third of this group (33) remained isolated, and about two thirds (72) had entered into contact with the national society. As a result of these contacts,

Table 5.2. Number and Percentage of Known Brazilian Indigenous Groups by Intensity of Contact in 1900 and 1957

| Intensity of Contact | 1900 | (%) | 1957 | | | | |
|---|---|---|---|---|---|---|---|
| | | | Isolated | Intermittent | Permanent | Integrated | Extinct |
| Isolated | 105 | (45.7) | 33 | 23 | 13 | 3 | 33 |
| Intermittent | 57 | (24.8) | - | 4 | 29 | 10 | 14 |
| Permanent | 39 | (17.0) | - | - | 3 | 8 | 28 |
| Integrated | 29 | (12.6) | - | - | - | 17 | 12 |
| Total | 230 | (100) | 33 | 27 | 45 | 38 | 87 |
| | | | Percentages | | | | |
| Isolated | | 100 | 31.4 | 21.9 | 12.4 | 2.9 | 31.4 |
| Intermittent | | 100 | - | 7.0 | 50.9 | 17.5 | 24.6 |
| Permanent | | 100 | - | - | 7.7 | 20.5 | 71.8 |
| Integrated | | 100 | - | - | - | 58.6 | 41.4 |
| Total | | 100 | 14.3 | 11.7 | 19.6 | 16.5 | 37.8 |

*Source:* Ribeiro 1967:92.

almost half (33) of the tribes had become extinct. Of the 125 tribes that were already in some degree of contact in 1900, 43 percent had become extinct by 1957. Altogether of the 230 known tribes in 1900, 38 percent (87) were extinct by 1957. In brief, contact for an indigenous group poses a serious problem of survival or extinction. If survival, how many and under what conditions?

From the Brazilian historical experience, Ribeiro formulated a model to explain what happens to indigenous groups subsequent to their contact with the national society. The model is not restricted to Brazil but describes the historical experience of many nations, including the United States and Canada. Ribeiro distinguished four degrees of intensity of contact, depending on the degree of penetration by the national society into areas traditionally occupied by indigenous groups. He shows what usually happens to the indigenous group at each stage. Table 5.3 presents the stages of contact and their characteristics. In the last two stages the tribal group becomes part of the national group, so that at this point *contact* is no longer an apt word.

A. Initial and Intermittent Contact

In this stage indigenous areas are penetrated by extractors of forest raw materials. Ribeiro is thinking primarily of rubber tappers, timber cutters, and hunters of animal hides. These people are usually in small, mobile bands encroaching on areas traditionally used by indigenous groups for their subsistence. In encounters with extractors, the indigenous groups are

Table 5.3. Model of Brazilian Experience of Contact with Indigenous Tribes

| Stages of Contact | National Groups in Contact | Results of Contact for Tribal Groups | | |
|---|---|---|---|---|
| | | Land | Population | Culture |
| Isolation | - | Intact | Increase | Intact |
| Intermittent | Extractors | Intact | 50% decrease | Intact |
| Permanent or Extinction | Agriculturists and ranchers | Decrease | Continued decrease | Modified |
| Integrated or Extinction | Rural-National | None | Increase | Lost |
| Assimilated National | - | - | - | - |
| Alternative Second Stage | | | | |
| Drawn-out Intermittent Service Agency | | Intact | Decrease but <50% | Intact |

*Source:* Ribeiro 1967

attracted to their steel tools. The results of this contact can be examined by the impact on land, population, and culture of the indigenous group.

While in some cases friendly relationships between extractors and indigenous groups have been developed, the more common outcome is an attempt by the extractors to expel the Indians from their lands, with ensuing armed conflict. Because the extractors are small mobile bands, these conflicts can last for long periods without any decisive outcome but can allow the indigenous groups retain their land.

In the 1980s a new kind of extractor arrived in the western rain forest of Roraima: Brazilian gold miners. This confrontation is not with the Brazilian mining industry as defined by large national and transnational corporations with their permanent mines, large capitalization, and organized, wage-earning miners. Most of the Yanomami contacts in Roraima have been with Brazilian *garimpeiros*—small-scale, independent miners who are not interested in establishing a long-term presence in any one place. This characteristic, combined with their clashes with the Yanomami and periodic expulsions by the federal police, has resulted in intermittent contact.

In areas where the miners conduct operations, relationships tend to deteriorate, leading to violence, which also contributes to the contact remaining intermittent. Albert (1994:47–48) has provided an excellent description of how such conflict typically develops.

When gold miners first entered the Yanomami area, they arrived in small groups. Since they were few in number, they felt endangered by the more numerous Indians and tried to buy goodwill through the liberal distribution of food and goods. For their part, the Indians had little or no experience with Whites and considered this attitude to be a demonstration of generosity that they would expect from any group that wished to establish bonds of neighborly alliance. At this early stage of cultural misunderstanding, the Indians did not yet feel the health effects and ecological impact of the mining activities. . . . As the number of gold miners increases, it was no longer necessary to maintain the initial generosity. The Indian turned from being a threat to being an annoyance with their incessant demands for the goods that they are accustomed to receiving. The gold miners got irritated and tried to shoo them away with false promises of future presents and with impatient or aggressive behavior.

At this stage of contact, the Indians began to feel the rapid deterioration of their health and means of subsistence caused by the gold mining. The rivers were polluted, the game was scared away by the noisy machinery, and many Indians died in constant epidemics of malaria, flu, and so on, all of which factors tended to destroy the economic and social fabric of their communities. Due to this situation, the Indians came to see the food and goods given by the miners as a vital and indisputable compensation for the destruction they had caused. When this was refused, a feeling of explicit hostility welled up within them.

Thus they arrived at a deadlock: the Indians became dependent on the prospectors just when the latter no longer needed to buy the former's goodwill. This contradiction is at the root of all the conflicts between the Yanomami and gold miners. From there, the possibility of minor incidents degenerating into open violence increases. And since the disparity in force between the prospectors and the Indians is enormous, the scales always tip against the Yanomami.

This type of situation clearly shows the extent to which the logic of the gold mining repels the participation of the Indians and even their mere presence. Because they use mechanized techniques to extract the gold, the miners have no interest in the Indians as a labor force or anything else. From the miner's point of view, they are, at best, a nuisance, and, at worst, a threat to their safety. If gifts and promises do not get rid of them, then the solution is to intimidate or even exterminate them.

There is an inevitable and invisible biological problem in the early meeting of indigenous tribes and members of the national population. The human body carries within it various microscopic entities, a number of which cause sickness without death to the person carrying them. People in large populations have been continually exposed to these organisms and have developed defenses against them. But when such a carrier first comes into contact with people from isolated, small-group societies who lack these microscopic entities and the defenses against them, infectious diseases such as measles, whooping cough, and the common cold erupt. They can lead to epidemics, death, and tribal extinction.

Ribeiro sees indigenous populations as having decreased by at least 50 percent as a result of diseases contracted in their intermittent meetings with members of the national population. All contacts between relatively isolated indigenous peoples and national populations pose this problem. It has been known and documented for centuries. Once the initial shock has passed, it takes time for indigenous groups to evolve their own defenses and to develop some immunity to these diseases. Members of national societies, either those who enter into contact situations and deliberately refuse to take preventative measures, or those who understand the danger but deliberately induce others to enter into such contact, are engaged in a type of biological warfare.

If an indigenous group survives biologically and retains its land, the initial and intermittent contacts do not alter the traditional culture. However a new element is usually added: the desire for manufactured goods and the necessity of acquiring cash or producing goods to trade for manufactured goods. Ribeiro (1967:85) notes some of the implications of these felt needs: "They found themselves obliged to carry on their normal subsistence tasks and also either to devote an increasing amount of time to the production of surplus articles for exchange with Whites, or to hire themselves out as a labor force. Their culture and their language were beginning to reflect these new experiences."

## B. Permanent Contact

In the next stage, agriculturists following behind the extractors move into Indian areas. In certain ecological areas, ranchers also invade Indian regions. These are large waves of people, hungry for land and determined to remove Indians from it. The conflict is usually brutal and bloody. The impact on the indigenous group is all embracing.

The national groups continue to desire land and/or labor from the tribal group. Acquiring them poses a problem for national groups. With regard to labor, why should indigenous people desert their traditional subsistence and submit themselves to the rigors of the labor market to earn a wage? While the indigenous desire for manufactured goods is strong, it usually is not strong enough to drive such people into full-time employment as wage laborers. If land is the main concern of the national group, the question becomes: What means can be taken to acquire Indian land in a situation where people do not perceive land as a commodity that can be transferred by sale but depend on it for their subsistence and security?

The solution to these problems is to force the indigenous population into the market economy. The way to accomplish this is by driving a wedge between the indigenous population and their independence—an independence afforded by their traditional factors of production—so as to leave them with no options except to become wage laborers. This is the classic imposition of the capitalist mode of production (see Wolf 1982, especially 77–79). Land seizure is the means, either for itself or as a way to force the indigenous group into the labor market. Land expropriation can take many forms: armed invasion, swindle, legal trickery, abuse of governmental powers. Historically, permanent contact has involved large reductions or loss of lands traditionally used by indigenous groups.

Due to disease and the loss of life in attempting to defend their land, the indigenous population usually continues its decrease so that the surviving group, if there is one, is a small remnant compared with the group that made the initial contact.

Because of the land shortage, Indians are forced into the labor market, usually in agriculture, to work for wages. In addition, cash has become a necessity because of the felt need for manufactured goods. The introduction of the market greatly modifies traditional patterns of social structure, especially kinship and reciprocity. Ribeiro (1967:86) described the conditions of permanent contact from the Brazilian historical experience: "A great part of the cultural autonomy of these groups had been lost as they became completely dependent upon a supply of metal, salt, medicine, cloth, and other such industrial products. Those traditional customs compatible with their new situation were preserved, although at the same time profoundly modified by the cumulative effects of the ecological, economic, and cultural constraints of this stage of their integration. The number of individuals able to express themselves in Portuguese had soared, amplifying their channels of communication with the national society."

C. Integration

As noted, *contact* is not an apt word for this stage. By now the indigenous group is part of the national population, distinguished from it only by retention of those cultural characteristics not in opposition to those of the market, technology, and law of the national culture. Indians have become members of the rural sector of the nation—peasants, by anthropological classification. The group retains its identity as an ethnic minority, usually discriminated against by other members of the national population.

At this stage practically all the original indigenous territory has been lost due to settler invasion, forcible expulsion, or legal trickery. Indians are usually landless peasants in the national culture. Ribeiro (1967:86) describes these groups as "islands in the midst of the national populace," their economic role "that of a reserve labor force or of specialized producers of certain marketable commodities. They were an unwanted minority, restricted to segments of the lands they had formerly held or cast out of territory rightfully theirs and forced to roam from place to place . . . [and] were enduring the most precarious conditions of life in the greatest dependence and misery."

With regard to population, Ribeiro finds evidence that after the devastating losses of the previous stage, the surviving remnant begins to stabilize and slowly increase its population. At this stage the Indians are part of the rural peasantry retaining a few cultural characteristics as symbols of ethnic identity. Ribeiro (1967:87) describes the changing Indians as having "forgotten their own language. . . . [They] could have passed unperceived had they themselves not been certain of their identity as a people and loyal to their ethnic background."

## D. Assimilation

The next logical step in the model is assimilation. At this point ethnic identity is lost and the Indian is completely absorbed into the national population. Frequently this involves marriage with non-Indians. Ribeiro does not describe this stage because the Indian groups are no longer identifiable.

## IV. Violence: The Dominant Characteristic

Ribeiro sees the Brazilian historical experience of contact as being a situation of violent conflict in which the Indian population is decimated by disease and warfare. The remnant Indian groups that survive are driven from their land and lose their traditional culture as they are forced into the agricultural labor market. The violence, disease, and resulting mortality stemming from contact situations triggered a national debate. As a result, in the first decade of the 1900s, a small military group revolving around Marshal Candido Rondon proposed that a government agency be established to protect Indians against the destructive effects of frontier expansion.

## A. Indian Protection Service (SPI), 1910–1967

This led to the establishment in 1910 of the Indian Protection Service under the leadership of Rondon. The SPI developed a strategy for the pacification of uncontacted Indian groups. Gifts of steel tools, beads, and mirrors were left at strategic places. There was a period of waiting for the Indians to come forth and accept the gifts. Then SPI agents would enter the Indian villages and try to convince the people that the government would be their protectors against the greed of extractors and settlers expanding the frontier. The pacification program was initially successful and allowed peaceful entry by Brazilians into parts of São Paulo, Paraná, Santa Catarina, Minas Gerais, Espírito Santo, and Maranhão. But restraint by the settlers and protection of the Indians turned out to be a temporary situation. In case after case, collectors of forest products and settlers ignored SPI agents, overran Indian lands, and frequently influenced state governments to legalize their land seizures.

## B. Xingu National Park, 1961

Three brothers, Orlando, Claudio, and Leonardo Villas Bôas, were members of the Rondon group within the SPI. The experiences of the SPI had convinced them that a more aggressive strategy beyond pacification was needed for the protection of Indian rights. There was a need to provide Indians with the security of a landed area where they could continue their traditional way of life; where infectious disease could be partially controlled by restricted access, allowing the buildup of immunity; and where medical programs focused on Indian needs could be established. Only with their land protected could indigenous people gradually learn about and work out the problems of cultural contact. The brothers believed that based on the Indian desire for manufactured goods and given time for a gradual and protected transition, the Indians would eventually seek integration into Brazilian society on their own terms.

In the 1950s the Villas Bôas brothers worked in the area of the upper Xingu River. They attempted to implement the new strategy as best they could as SPI agents but eventually proposed their model for legal implementation because of the needed tools provided by the law. In 1961 the government established the Xingu National Park (a reservation) in northern Mato Grosso with the brothers as the directors. It was an attempt to protect Indian groups and their lands from a society bent on expansion and industrialization and from a national underclass seeking to escape poverty. The fight against disease and land seizures by ranchers from the latifundia tradition continued. In recent years, there have been invasions of the park, epidemics, and the forced departure of some groups. Those remaining face the precarious situation of all indigenous groups in the Amazon.

## C. Fundação Nacional do Índio (FUNAI), 1967–1997

By the late 1950s many of the personnel of SPI had lost the Rondon spirit and degenerated into a group of criminally abusive Indian agents. An investigation was launched and the activities of the SPI became a national scandal publicized by the Figueiredo Report. In 1967 the SPI was abolished and a new government agency, the Fundação Nacional do Índio or Brazilian National Indian Foundation (FUNAI), was created. Its charter stated that it was to respect Indian traditions, to guarantee possession of their lands including exclusive use of natural resources, to preserve the physical and cultural integrity of Indian communities in contact with the national society, and to defend spontaneous (gradual) rather than forced (rapid) acculturation. These objectives were to be carried out by establishing in Indian areas FUNAI posts, which would provide access to medical care and would be agents of communication and interpretation between the Indians and the national society.

With the announcement in 1970 of the Program of National Integration (PIN) and its provision for the construction of the Transamazon Highway, FUNAI was assigned the task of pacifying the thirty Indian tribes who lived along the projected route. PIN defined pacification as ensuring, by protecting highway workers against Indian attacks, that the Indians did not become an obstacle to the rapid occupation of the Amazon. This was an obvious rejection of the Rondon–Villas Boas legacy on which FUNAI had originally been founded and meant the subordination of FUNAI to the goals of the PIN project.

## D. The Model: An Alternative Intermittent Stage

As a result of the experiences of the SPI, Ribeiro added to his model an alternative description of the intermittent stage. This could be termed the conditions of peaceful contact, as distinguished from the conflictive ones of the main model. Based on the programs of the SPI and the Villas Bôas brothers, the initial contact is with a national group concerned with "protective intervention." The SPI defended the Indians against invasion by settlers and provided them with necessary human services. Where successful, this resulted in a protracted intermittent stage that allowed Indians to adjust to the new situation. Unfortunately most cases of SPI intervention were eventually thwarted by invasions of Indian lands and a reversion to the conditions of permanent and integrated contact as summarized in the conflictive model. Ribeiro sees the indigenous population as declining in the protracted intermittent stage but not to the degree that it does in the more frequent conflictive situation.

## E. The Model and the Xilixana

The Ribeiro model poses the problems to be investigated in the chapters about the Xilixana villages. In the Precontact phase, what were the population dynamics of these tribal villages in the Brazilian rain forest? In this period of isolation from the national society without the advantages of modern medicine but with their own methods of curing, did these groups barely grow, grow very slowly, or grow moderately or rapidly? What were the important demographic factors in their degree of growth? How does the Precontact period contrast with the period following initial contact? What were the important demographic factors in the Contact, Linkage, and Brazilian phases? Did the Xilixana villages follow the demographic pattern laid out by Ribeiro's model? How has contact impacted the land and culture of the Xilixana?

The experience of how Brazil has attempted to wrestle with the problems posed by the contact of its people with indigenous groups shows the problematic nature of the contact experience. Ramos (1998) has detailed the political aspects of these efforts. Historically, increasing intensity of contact between tribal groups and elements of the national society has brought cultural change and decline or extinction for tribal groups. Has this been the Xilixana experience? These questions are be examined later as part of the history of each village. While many theoretical questions concerning population dynamics can be asked about tribal groups, understanding the growth or decline of their populations is the most fundamental of all.

## V. Summary

This description of changes that have taken place in Ninam villages as a result of contact with Brazilians, the history of Brazilian experience with its indigenous populations, and the ethnographic and historical accounts in the preceding two chapters, provide background for the analysis in part IV of the population dynamics of the eight villages that have comprised the Mucajaí Yanomami from 1930 to 1995. But before beginning that analysis, we describe in part III the methodology for the collection and presentation of the demographic data and for the critical process of evaluating its quality. Any analysis of data simply accepted without a critical process risks being a house built on shifting sand.

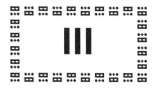

# Methodology

# 6

# Sources and Critical Appraisal of Data for the Years 1959 to 1995

The Ribeiro model of the previous chapter has indicated the importance of understanding the size and changes in the size of the indigenous population before and after the initial contact as well as reasons for the changes. The model suggests that mortality was the main cause. But a change in the size of a population is always a four-variable problem: births minus deaths plus in-migration minus out-migration. Therefore the model requires a demographic analysis of the village populations as the basis for explaining their population dynamics. Prior to this analysis, Part III is a methodological section identifying how the field data about these demographic variables were gathered, how the demographic database was formulated, and how it was critically evaluated to ensure its validity for the analysis in part IV. For those unfamiliar with demographic discourse, we discuss in chapter 8 the meaning of the demographic expressions and their calculation and presentation in the tables.

## I. Defining the Study Populations

Peters first encountered the Xilixana in November 1958 when they lived in two villages near the middle Mucajaí River. Readily identifiable since they had been isolated from other groups for a number of years, they became the study population. Their past, back to the time when they lived near the Uraricoera River before retreating to the Mucajaí watershed, was investigated in ethnohistorical and genealogical work. People are considered members of the study population as long as they have been residents of a village that either preceded or traced its origin to the two villages encountered by Peters in 1958. Missionaries have been in continual contact with the Mucajaí group since 1958 except for the period 1987 to 1990, when the Brazilian government forced them to leave.

As noted, in this research village populations are defined as distinct communal units regardless of geographical location. Under traditional conditions, the communality arose from the fact that people lived in a single yano with a recognized headman. Usually the village yanos were at some distance

6.1. Aerial view of the mission (Andersons, 1976).

from each other. In the Linkage and Brazilian periods, a village was defined by a common headman who presided over the group's concern with a set of tasks and interests. Although the arrangement of the individual houses of a village could vary, they formed a cluster that was easily recognizable.

Physical continuity of the structure does not enter into the definition of a village population. Village yanos are not enduring structures and new ones are built every few years in new locations, sometimes at a considerable distance. The Brazilian-style mud houses periodically undergo extensive renovation and reconstruction. For the purposes of this study, these changes do not constitute a demographic migration. The population in the new location is considered the same population as in the previous location.

In this study internal migration takes place when an individual moves from one village to another within the Mucajaí group. This is an out-migration from the viewpoint of the village left and an in-migration from the viewpoint of the receiving village. External migration takes place when an individual moves either into a village from outside the population bloc or from one of the villages to a community outside the Mucajaí group.

When does a fission begin? Xilixana villages traditionally consisted of a single dwelling for all members of the village. Frequently the fissioning process was incremental. One faction or several would build a new dwelling adjacent to or a short distance from the dwelling where they previously lived with other factions. The construction of a second dwelling at the same site was usually the prelude to moving farther away at a later date. The question posed by this situation is: At what point in time does fission occur whereby the population of one village becomes two distinct village populations? Is it with the construction of another yano, no matter how close or far that is from the original dwelling? Or does fissioning require the second house to be some distance from the first? If so, what distance is required? A demographer needs to pinpoint methodologically the time of beginning of new villages. This cultural requirement of the demographer does not exist for the Yanomami, and so they provide no answer. Here we have taken fission to begin when a faction or combination of factions separates and occupies a distinct dwelling with its own headman, regardless of its location with respect to the former dwelling.

Peters and the missionaries gradually accumulated ethnographic information about the Mucajaí Yanomami. Peters's first encounter and some of the details of the field situation have been described elsewhere (Early and Peters 1990:7–12, Peters 1998:45–58). This research project began in 1983. It triggered further ethnographic enquiry to help interpret the demographic data. The ethnographic information became a qualitative database.

## II. The Methodological Problems of Population Data from Anthropological Societies

Six methodological criteria for building and evaluating demographic databases employed in the analysis of the population dynamics of anthropological societies are explained in a previous work (Early and Headland 1998:170–71). These criteria are:

1. Is the database composed of valid data? Due to cultural differences, the difficulty of acquiring quantified data from anthropological populations makes this the most problematical aspect of this type of research.
2. Was obtaining demographic and population data the main objective of the research? Owing to the difficulties of obtaining such data, unless it is the main focus of the research, the results are often incomplete and of little analytical value.
3. Were data obtained on a sufficient number of demographic variables so that the analytical power of the demographic equations can be employed?
4. Were the data longitudinal? Analysis involving a short period of time, especially a single year, is unsatisfactory for understanding of population dynamics.

5. Were the data subjected to a critical process to check on the aforementioned difficulties? Without such a process, there can only be skepticism about the analysis based on them.

6. Were the demographic data integrated with historical-ethnographic and/or biological data so that there is some understanding of population dynamics and not mere numbers? In this chapter and the next, we explain how this research attempted to comply with these criteria.

## III. The Quantitative Database

This database was built using as its basic unit the demographic history of individual people for each year of their lives from birth to their death or the ethnographic present. The advantage of using individual people and annual data is that in later analytical work, the data can be combined in many ways without being limited by larger aggregations of the original data.

A. Database Variables

To build a database about the demographic history of each individual, information was needed about the following variables:

1. Name
2. Sex
3. Date and village of birth with names of parents
4. Descent category of father
5. Date and village of death with information on its cause
6. Date, reason, and village of in-migration and out-migration
7. Source and quality codes to keep track of the source of the data and the methodological quality of the source
8. As much information as possible about fetal deaths, which include deliberate abortions, late miscarriages, and stillbirths

For purposes of calculation, computers require complete dates with the three elements of year, month, and day. Due to estimation, late recording, or incomplete knowledge on the part of the missionaries, a few dates were incomplete and could not be recaptured. In these cases simplifying assumptions using midpoints were employed. If the day of the month was missing, it was assumed to be the fifteenth. If the month was missing, it was assumed to be the first of July. All dates were coded for quality according to the number of elements known exactly or requiring estimation.

All the above information was coded and entered into a Paradox 4.0 database program. The complete demographic record of an individual may fall within one of the historical periods discussed in chapter 3 or that record may embrace several or all four historical periods. The methodologies to acquire and verify data about demographic events varied by historical period. The main division was between demographic events before or after January 1, 1959, which marks the absence or presence of the missionaries. This is equivalent to the Precontact and early Contact period versus the later Contact, Linkage, and Brazilian periods.

B. Sources of Data for Demographic Events after 1958

The missionaries kept records of the births and deaths from 1959 to 1995. The single exception was their absence from 1987 to 1990, when vital records were kept by the government agency FUNAI. When this research project began in 1983, migration was reconstructed from the historical memory of both the missionaries and individual Yanomami. This was not difficult since external out-migration was almost nonexistent and most in-migrants were still present.

Censuses were enumerated in 1972 and 1979. This added to the database individuals who were born before 1959 and were still alive. It also gave the population totals by sex and age for these two years. This was used as a check on the same figures derived by simply summing the individual records of the database showing those alive in these two years.

Genealogies were constructed for every mother in the database and included paternity. At first the information was drawn from the sources mentioned. Then interviews were conducted with the mothers themselves or with knowledgeable Yanomami to check the information and make additions for time periods not covered by the other sources. While the vital registration gave information on the later Contact, Linkage, and Brazilian periods, the censuses and genealogies began the process of reconstructing the Precontact period, discussed more fully in the next chapter.

Residential histories detail the years in which an individual lived in a specific village. They were constructed by reading an individual's demographic record. A person was born in a village in a determined year, lived in that village all subsequent years to the year of death or to the year of out-migration to another Mucajaí village or outside the group. A computer program turned this information into age-sex distributions for each year of the research period for each village.

There may be some question about the validity of the death records derived from death registration, censuses, and genealogies because of discussions in the literature about the Yanomami prohibition against speaking of the dead. Among the Xilixana, there is no absolute prohibition. There is reluctance to refer to the dead by their personal names, but other reference terms can be substituted to specify individuals. Since the missionaries knew individuals by personal name while they were still alive, there was no problem in identifying them when they died for the death register. Reference terms were used when talking about individuals who died before the arrival of the missionaries. Because of the long-term residency of the missionaries and Peters's familiarity with the population, the Xilixana were less guarded in observing name taboos. Names were also mentioned when Yanomami assistants began to understand the focus of the research. These observations are also true of infanticides, which are discussed in detail in our previous volume (Early and Peters 1990:59–60).

## IV. The Need: A Critical Evaluation

Collecting the field data and entering it into the database program was only the beginning of the construction of the database. Before using it for demographic analysis, there was the long, critical process of verifying the completeness of the enumeration of the population and the accuracy of the information about its characteristics. Because of human error and cross-cultural differences, the first compilation of such a database is seldom, if ever, satisfactory. There were different kinds of database problems depending on the sources of the data.

In collecting data there is always confusion about the details of some demographic events, resulting in incorrect and missing data. Even when the field data are correct, there are always some clerical errors made in assigning code numbers and/or typing them into the computer. Occasionally data were missing. This was due to such factors as confusion, oversight, late recording of an event leading to uncertainty about elements of dates, and under-enumeration during the FUNAI period.

The database needed a critical evaluation to detect and correct any such problems. Some errors were detected simply by the logical discipline required for entry into the database. Internal comparisons of database variables turned up some coding and typing errors. Such errors usually introduce some kind of logical or known inconsistency in the record of an individual person. Some examples would be a male becoming a mother, a person dying before his or her date of birth, improbable ages at various points of the life cycle, or conflict with the known history of an individual. Problems were also detected by the construction of fertility histories, addressed in the next chapter. Peters was able to rectify most problems by mail inquiry and/or return visits to the Mucajaí mission in 1973, 1979, 1987, 1992, 1994, 1995, and 1996.

# 7

# Reconstruction of the Precontact Population and Critical Evaluation of the Database

The main method for the reconstruction of the Precontact period was compiling fertility histories for every mother in the population. Every person who lived at any time in the study population should appear in a fertility history except external in-migrants or children of mothers who externally out-migrated to other groups. External in-migrants were either still alive after 1958 or listed as a parent in the genealogies. There were no cases of female external out-migrants until 1968. Therefore the fertility histories became the basis for reconstructing the Precontact population and the first two years of the Contact period.

## I. Initial Sources of the Fertility Histories

Genealogies for births prior to 1959 and the registration of births after 1958 provided the initial information to construct fertility histories. For each mother this gives a preliminary list of her children in sibling order. To this were added all known dates of birth and the age of the mother at each birth after 1958.

These data were the starting points of additional information deduced by the logical patterns contained in the biological and cultural clocks regulating the beginning, spacing, and termination of childbearing. The basic strategy was to develop criteria from the portions of the fertility histories known to be accurate and use them to reconstruct the Precontact population. The use of fertility histories for this purpose assumes that the fertility structure has remained relatively constant over the time periods used for derivation and application of the criteria. This was verified by ethnographic enquiry and by finding a close approximation of the fertility indices generated by analyses of both synchronic and actual female cohorts (Early and Peters 1990:51).

To complete the fertility histories, information was needed about missing birth dates, age of the mother at the birth of each child, and missing dates of death. A previous volume (Early and Headland 1998:70) shows some examples of typical fertility histories.

## II. Estimation of Birth Dates

Depending on the known dates in a fertility history, three variations of the same method were used to determine birth dates in the Precontact period.

### A. Fertility Histories Containing at Least One Sibling with a Known Date

In most cases, missing birth dates were estimated by taking the last known birth date in a fertility history and subtracting from it the average length of a birth interval to estimate the missing birth date of the previous sibling. This procedure was then repeated for next prior sibling and so on in chainlike fashion back to the first sibling. We have previously (Early and Peters 1990:37–51) described the biological and cultural patterns of Yanomami reproduction, which create a rhythm in childbearing. The average length of a birth interval expresses this rhythm.

To obtain as accurate an estimate as possible, only birth intervals with exact data were used to calculate the average. From the quality codes regarding the number of known elements of the two birth dates defining each interval, an additional code was made for the quality of the interval itself. This quality code indicated whether the two birth dates defining the interval were both exact or partially estimated as to year, month, and day. Only birth intervals defined by two exact dates at least as to year and month after 1957 were used for calculating the average. This average was then applied in the chainlike fashion already described to the last known birth date in a fertility history.

To gain greater precision, several averages for the length of the birth intervals were calculated, depending on the type of birth interval. The length of a birth interval can vary due to the presence or absence of fetal, infant, or child mortality within it. An interval that contains no fetal, infant, or child mortality between the time of the two defining live births of the interval is called a regular interval.

Fetal deaths (deliberate abortions, stillbirths) can prolong the length of an interval between two live births because of the time required for carrying the fetus. Within this type of interval, there can be further systematic variation depending on the type of fetal death. Deliberate abortions usually take place in the second month of pregnancy (Early and Peters 1990:76–77), while stillbirths (including recorded miscarriages) are usually later and may be full term.

Deaths of infants, including infanticides and deaths of young children to about 2.5 years, can have the opposite effect. They shorten the length of a birth interval because such deaths end the necessity of breast-feeding with its contraceptive effect. This allows the possibility of subsequent pregnancy and birth sooner than when the mother continues to nurse the infant for two to three years. The result is a shorter birth interval than the regular interval.

For these reasons, the birth intervals defined by birth dates exact as to year and month are classified in order of expected decreasing length as: (1) an interval containing a stillbirth; (2) an interval containing a deliberate abortion; (3) a regular interval which contains no fetal, infant, or early child mortality; (4) an interval in which the preceding sibling died between the second month and up to 2.5 years of age; and (5) an interval in which the preceding sibling died within the first month of life.

All the intervals in each of these five classifications were listed along with the names of the children and of the mothers. Instances of unusual lengths were examined to see if they could be explained. Extremely short intervals usually indicated an error in the data and were removed from the distribution until they could be corrected or verified. Unusually long intervals could indicate missing births and needed field verification. The reasons for some unusually long intervals may be known, such as widowhood, extended absence of a husband, and so forth. These were also removed from the distributions and placed in a separate category called extended intervals.

The average length of the birth interval for each classification was then calculated from the cases remaining in the distributions. The average for an interval in which an infant died within the first month was 1.9 years; for an interval in which an infant died between the second and twenty-seventh month, it was 2.1 years; for a regular interval, the average was 3.2 years; for an interval containing an abortion, 3.8 years; for an interval containing a stillbirth, 4.1 years (Early and Peters 1990:46). The appropriate average was then applied to the last known birth date in a fertility history in the chainlike procedure noted to estimate missing birth dates in the Precontact period.

## B. Fertility Histories with No Known Birth Dates

There were some fertility histories in which all the births occurred prior to 1959 and dates were therefore unknown. But a number of these histories contained a female child who later became a mother with her own children in a more recent fertility history. If the date of birth of her first child was known, the mother's age at the date of this birth could be estimated from the average age at first birth (see later discussion). Then the birth date of the mother herself could be estimated in the earlier fertility history where she appears with her siblings. This gave one fixed date in the list of siblings. By adding or subtracting the appropriate average lengths of birth intervals in chainlike fashion to the siblings before and after this mother, all the remaining birth dates were estimated.

## C. Fertility Histories with No Females Who Later Became Mothers

There were a few histories without any birth dates for the children and in which none of the females lived to become mothers. In these histories the date of birth of one of the children was estimated by his or her age relative to that of a person in another history whose date of birth either was known or had been estimated. The sibling with the best quality of data for the compared person was selected as the starting point. Again using the chainlike calculation for siblings before or after the sibling now with an estimated birth date, the remaining birth dates of the history were calculated.

All the estimated birth dates were confirmed by listing these dates in chronological order and checking the sequence with several Yanomami assistants. This resulted in some small adjustments.

## III. Estimation of Death and Migration Dates Prior to 1959

These were estimated by finding out who was born shortly before or after the death or migration of the person under consideration. With the birth dates previously determined, this method gave estimates of dates of death and migration (method of relative age).

A concentrated effort was made to enumerate infanticides during the Precontact period. Some may have been missed. But the investigators believe the enumeration is of high quality. The information was obtained from several Yanomami women and verified with other Yanomami as much as possible. One of the Yanomami assistants in the research was an older woman who began her own childbearing in 1939 when the female population of reproductive age was relatively small (to be discussed later), and their pregnancies and births were well known and discussed among the women. Also, from the data on birth spacings during this period, there was little room for omitted infanticides, and the few possible intervals were carefully investigated.

## IV. The Critical Process

The fertility histories were used not only for the initial reconstruction of the period prior to 1959 but also for the critical evaluation and correction of the initial reconstruction and for some of the evaluation and correction of data in the period after 1959. In addition to the spacing averages, the fertility histories were used to calculate other averages to be used as criteria of reasonableness.

## A. Criteria of Reasonableness

The first criterion is the average age of the mother at the birth of her first child. The pattern behind this criterion is the result of the biological clock of sexual maturation and the cultural clock regulating diet and the age of initial sexual union. An average was calculated from cases where the birth dates of both mother and first child were known to be exact as to year and month. The average of 16.8 years from the previous volume (Early and Peters 1990:42) was used. Peters thinks this average is a little high for the period before 1959, when there was a substantial shortage of young females in the population. In the 1990s the average was 19.9. This was the first decade in which some women did not have their first birth until in their twenties. It reflects a trend toward a later age of first marriage. For the period before 1959 it was more appropriate to use most of the criteria from the previous volume (Early and Peters 1990) rather than updating them. Another criterion is the average age of the mother at the birth of her last child. This was taken from the previous study, where the average was forty years of age (Early and Peters 1990:41).

## B. Detection and Correction of Problems

The construction of the database, the fertility histories, and the use of the estimation methods described yielded initial dates of births, deaths, and migration for the periods prior to and after 1959. But the results were not simply accepted. The information was subjected to careful scrutiny to ensure further the quality of the data before they were used for analysis of population dynamics.

The basic strategy was to use the better parts of the database and ethnographic information to check the remainder. Intervals shorter than expected could indicate a problem with the defining dates of the interval or confusion about the identity of individuals or their mothers. Some individuals were double-entered because of name confusion. Intervals longer than expected could indicate possible omission of some births, especially from 1987 to 1990 when the missionaries were absent. Unexplainable problems were entered into a log for field verification and explanation.

The village of birth was checked by the mother's residential history compared with the village in which the birth of the children took place. De jure place was always used—that is, village of customary residence of parents. The father's residential history was also listed and checked for coherence, although there were marital and other situations in which coherence was not expected.

Given the total fertility rate of seven to eight live births from 1959 to

1986 (Early and Peters 1990:48), did a fertility history appear to be lacking some births? Did the estimated dates for other children cohere with known temporal relationships to individuals in other histories and/or with ethnohistorical indications? The reasonableness of the age of the mother at the birth of each child, especially the first and last children, was evaluated. Also checked was the reasonableness of the age of the same female in two different fertility histories. In the first, she appears with her mother and siblings. In the second and later history, she is a mother with her own children. Her date of birth must cohere with that of her siblings in the first history and with the date of birth of her first child in the second history. A problem in any one date in a history raised questions about all the other dates in the same history since they were interconnected.

Logical coherence was achieved only by everything falling into place. In a few cases small adjustments were made to achieve this coherence. The interpretation of any history used any relevant information about the individuals in the history. Many logical clues were available depending on the depth of the information about the individuals involved. A list was made of all suspected problems and questions that needed to be asked.

The problem at this point was to correct the erroneous data, find missing values, or verify unusual data. If checking the trail from the original recording of the data to its being entered into the computer did not solve the problem, a direct or indirect return to the field was required. An indirect return was made through exchanges of letters with the missionaries who succeeded Peters at the mission after his departure in 1967. In spite of their busy schedules, they were cooperative in every way possible. Peters himself made seven return visits from 1973 and 1996 to collect or verify information. The primary purpose of the later visits was the reconstruction of the pre-1959 population. The list of problems and questions helped frame explicit questions about possible births, deaths, and dates. This work brought to light missing individuals, some of whom had died young and had been omitted from the genealogies compiled in the original fieldwork; others were older people who had died early in the Precontact period.

This description of the critical methodology is a linear presentation for the sake of clarity and brevity. But in reality, it was a constant dialectical process of entering data into the database, checking, detecting problems, correction, return to the field, and starting the cycle all over again.

Although the dates derived by estimation are not exact, they are valid for analytical use as long as the estimation procedure is shown to be reasonable. Exact dates are not necessary for many types of demographic analysis. In this study, the individual years of the research period are collapsed into four main historical periods of five or more years. The age-specific demographic rates collapse the individual ages at which the demographic events took place into age classifications of five, ten, or fifteen years. These are robust procedures that can tolerate some error in the estimation of dates. The demographic rates result from the frequency of a demographic event being divided by the size of the appropriate population. This means that the estimation error often shows up somewhere beyond the first decimal place, a realm of insignificance for demographic purposes.

## V. Dates of Historical Events

Dates of historical events prior to Contact, described in chapters 2 and 3, were estimated in much the same way as the demographic events. All ultimately depended on the dates of births. However there were several events of special importance for which additional information was available.

The conflict with the Yekwana was a major event in the history of the Mucajaí group. One of the captured Yekwana women had two children after 1958, which means the chain calculation of the birth dates of the older children began with an exact date. Her fertility history was known to be complete. She was one of the main sources of genealogical information about many people and completely understood genealogical questions. She was not married prior to her capture and her first menses took place shortly after her capture. By the chain calculation her first child was born in 1939. This indicates that the conflict took place around 1935.

The fertility history of the captured Mácu woman was used to estimate the date of this event. At the time of her capture she was immediately taken as a wife by one of the Mucajaí men. By the chain calculation her first child among the Mucajaí was born in 1933. Therefore the capture of the Mácu woman and the killing of her first husband and two children is estimated to have taken place in 1932.

Information about the Boundary Commission helps estimate the dates of their gifts. Brazil and Venezuela had agreed that the boundary between their nations was a line in the Parima Highlands marking the division between the eastward-flowing streams feeding the Rio Branco in Brazil and the westward-flowing streams flowing into the Orinoco River in Venezuela. But no one knew exactly where this line fell because the sources of the rivers in the Parima Highlands were not well understood. Between 1939 and 1943 the commission conducted four surveys to help determine this line. In 1939–40 there was an aerial survey of the region. In 1941 a ground expedition ascended the Rio Demini to the highlands (Ferreira Reis 1943). In 1942 another expedition ascended the Catrimani River. There are two published accounts of the fourth survey, conducted in 1943 (Ferreira Reis 1944; Dias de Aguiar 1944). The primary emphasis was an aerial survey of the Mucajaí, Parime, Majari, Uraricaá, Parima, and Auaris rivers. In 1943 members of the expedition were also on the ground in the highlands. Observations about the Mucajaí River were made as a result of overflights; no explicit description of a land expedition on the Mucajaí is given, though Dias de Aguiar (1944:20/238) notes in passing that it took four to five months to traverse the Mucajaí. The gifts were left during this phase of the commission's work, but it is not known whether they were left on an ascent up the river or a descent downriver. The intense aerial activity was toward the end of 1943. A period of time passed between when the gifts were left in the tree and when the Mucajaí people found them, but it was not a long period because the red cloth was still in good condition. Given these clues, we estimate the find to have taken place in early 1944. This date became an important item in a memory calendar Peters used to verify the estimated birth dates. The dates for the remainder of the events discussed in chapters 2 and 3 were estimated by reference to the Yekwana, Mácu, and cloth episodes or by reference to the dates of births or deaths of specific individuals.

## VI. Starting and Ending Points of the Research Period

When the database had been finally formulated, the first question was the starting point of the analysis. In what years were the data first of sufficient quality to be used for analytical purposes? The quality of the database becomes more problematical as the years recede from 1958. There are individuals in the database going back to the nineteenth century, with the earliest estimated birth date being 1840. When the critical evaluation showed that the estimation methods were yielding consistent data back to 1930, this was selected as the starting point of the study. The older people in the population after 1958 remembered genealogical and historical information back to this period. The completeness of the demographic information before 1930 became questionable and the history was extremely vague. The end point of the demographic study is December 31, 1995, which for demographic purposes is considered the same as January 1, 1996. With the methodological work discussed here and in chapter 6, the database was now ready to be used in the analysis of the population dynamics of each village.

# 8

# The Demographic Presentation

In an effort to make the story of the Xilixana intelligible to as broad a readership as possible, we here explain the conventions used to express the magnitudes of the demographic variables and the quantitative relationships between them. Demography is the quantitative language used to describe population dynamics. The use of a quantitative language permits better evaluation of the importance or nonimportance of various factors in the increase or decrease of the size of a population. Without its use, such analysis can become merely logical speculation. As with any language, it has its own vocabulary. For this reason, this chapter is a primer in demography for those who may find it helpful for understanding what follows. We attempt to answer the basic questions: How are the numbers formulated, what terms are used for them, and what do they mean? Those familiar with demography may choose to skip the chapter.

## I. Demography and Population Analysis

*Demography* is used in several senses, which can be confusing. Demographers usually distinguish two basic senses: formal demography (narrow sense, demographic analysis) and social demography (broad sense, population analysis). Formal demography (Shryock and Siegel 1973:2) is "concerned with the size, distribution, structure and change of populations. Size is simply the number of units (persons) in the population. Distribution refers to the arrangement of the population in space at a given time, that is, geographically or among various types of residential areas [here, the villages]. Structure, in its narrowest sense, is the distribution of the population among its sex and age groupings. Change is the growth or decline of the total population or of one of its structural units. The components of change in total populations are births, deaths and migrations."

Social demography (Hauser and Duncan 1959:2–3) is "concerned not only with population variables [formal demography], but also with relationships between population changes and other variables—social, economic, political, biological, genetic, geographical, and the like. The field . . . is at least as broad as interest in the determinants and consequences of population trends."

There is a third and very loose sense in which the word is used. Social demography starts with formal demography and frequently comes back to it. Formal demography is the cornerstone on which the rest of the analysis is built. However some usages skip the requirements of formal demography and use the word *demography* in the sense of almost any quantified variables that are perceived to have some relationship to population size but are not explained in terms of formal demography. This usage is found in some specialized areas of anthropology, such as anthropological genetics. It is also found in "seat-of-the-pants" demography, the attempt to make a formal demographic argument without the data required by formal demography.

Part of this research is a study in anthropological demography. It begins with and usually returns to formal demography in the analyses. The explanation of the components of change beyond the variables of formal demography is usually done by ethnography, history, and occasionally biology. These are usually qualitative explanations, although quantitative forms are used wherever possible.

## II. The Basic Demographic Equation

A single equation is at the heart of formal demography. It says that during a determined time period, the change of the size of a population, either increase or decrease, is the result of the births (B) minus the deaths (D) plus the in-migration (I) minus the out-migration (O) of that period. The equation can be written:

$$P2 - P1 = + B - D + I - O$$

P2 is the population at a later point in time while P1 is the population at an earlier point in time. Population change is always a four-variable problem. Even if the magnitude of a variable is negligible, the analysis must establish this. The four variables are frequently referred to as the components of change.

The equation can also be written in a shorter form, which combines the six variables into three compound variables.

$$TI = NI + NM$$

TI is the total increase or decrease of a population (P2 – P1); NI is the natural increase or decrease (B – D); and NM is the net migration (I – O). All three compound variables may have negative values. The equation can be rearranged algebraically into various other forms. While this equation is utter simplicity from a mathematical viewpoint, its analytical power is great. All the factors responsible for population change, whether biological, social, or ideational, must act through one or a combination of these four variables.

The absolute values of the four components of change can be compared between populations only if the sizes of their populations (P) are the same, which is rarely the case. Analytical methodology constantly compares phenomena. Therefore these values are expressed in a comparable form by dividing them by the size of their populations (P). By convention, the value of a population at midyear or midpoint is used as the denominator of annual rates or any other time segment. Demographic rates of this form are called "crude" rates (C...R) for a reason to be explained later. The basic equation links these rates in the same way as it links the absolute numbers of the same variables and reads:

$$CTIR = CBR - CDR + CIR - COR$$

The compound form of the equation can also be used for the crude rates.

### III. The Age-Sex Structure of a Population

While knowing the size of a population and the magnitudes of its components of change is important, many analyses of formal demography need more information. For this reason, the demographic profile of a population usually includes its composition by age and sex expressed in a cross tabulation. The ages may be grouped in various ways. Demographic convention, influenced by the structure and availability of data in industrial systems, has established five-year age categories to age eighty-five as the standard, with the exception of the first year of life. As is the case with many anthropological populations, the Yanomami village populations are small and estimation techniques have been used to determine ages in some cases. For these reasons, ten- and fifteen-year age categories to age seventy have been used here except for the early years of the life cycle. Again for comparative purposes, the absolute numbers of the age-sex cross tabulation are divided by the size of the population to obtain a percentage distribution.

We can now return to the question of why the crude rates are called "crude." The probabilities of the ages at which births, deaths, and migration take place are not spread evenly over the human life cycle. These probabilities tend to cluster within certain ranges of age. For example, women have children only within a specific age range. The probability of dying is greater at certain ages than others. Therefore the age-sex distribution of a population should be taken into consideration when examining the components of change. The crude rates are "rough" because they ignore the age structure. Their denominators are simply the size of the total population. Strictly speaking, the crude rates of the components of change for two populations can be compared only when the populations have like age-sex structures. However, because age-sex structures may not change quickly, crude rates are frequently compared, although this problem should always be kept in mind. This is especially the case with anthropological populations because of small-number volatility (discussed later) and when comparing populations with distinctly different social structures.

## IV. The Population Graph and the Tables

Each chapter in part IV opens with a graph showing the annual sizes of the village's population. Four standardized tables follow—depicting the demographic profile, fertility, mortality, and migration—which explain the changes of the population seen in the graph. The four historical periods described in chapters 2 and 3 provide the horizontal headings for the tables. Villages not in existence during all four historical periods employ a table with only the pertinent periods.

   In the construction and use of the tables, we have attempted to take into consideration the varying needs of different readers. For the nonspecialist, the more pertinent information for the analysis is taken from the tables and repeated in the text. Nonspecialists could simply follow the analysis in the text and only occasionally refer to the tables to see the wider context. To probe the information at a deeper level, specialists may wish to turn to the details in the tables as questions arise. Data of such detail and quality are seldom found; for this reason, the tables present the data in detail and serve as an archive to which readers may later wish to refer for information about tribal population dynamics.

   In the tables all rates and percentages have been rounded so that the results of additions or subtraction are not always exact. These tables are somewhat compressed and may be confusing to those not familiar with demographic conventions and relationships. The following sections examine the formats of the tables to facilitate reading them. We use the tables for village A (chapter 9) as examples.

## V. The Demographic Profile or Overview (Table 9.1 as an Example)

### A. Absolute Numbers (9.1.a)

The table opens with the size of the village population at the beginning and end of each historical period along with the increase or decrease of the population during these periods. Within each phase, the basic equation in its simple and compound forms provides the format for presenting the absolute numbers (N) of the components of change labeled in the extreme left-hand column of the table. The absolute numbers indicate possible volatility in the data arising from small numbers. They also provide the figures for those who may wish to "play with the numbers" and to test relationships they may see in the data and that are not discussed in the text.

### B. Crude Rates (9.1.b)

The second section of the table expresses the variables of the basic equation as crude rates. By demographic convention, these crude rates are per 1,000 population. This is in preference to using the decimal form, which would result from simply dividing each variable by the size of the population. Frequently anthropological populations, including the Xilixana, amount to less than a thousand people and therefore this conventional form could be misleading. However, since most of the literature uses this form of expression, it has been retained to facilitate comparison. This part of the table enables the reader to understand the contribution of the crude rate of each of the components to the rate of total increase.

### C. The Age-Sex Distribution (9.1.c)

The third section of the table further examines the population (P) by decomposing it into its age-sex structure. The first three lines give the absolute values of the population by sex. Below this is the percentage of the total population that is female. We use this as the sex ratio of the population in place of the more conventional expression, which is really a male ratio and at times not quickly intelligible. Also, in this research the percentage of females in the total population has proven to be an important variable. For the convenience of those accustomed to the conventional form, the male and female percentages of a population are converted in table 8.1 into the conventional expression for the sex ratio of a population.

The final portion of table 9.1 is a cross tabulation of age classified in fifteen-year categories by sex. It is expressed in percentage form for comparative purposes. These percentages are rounded so that their sum is not always an exact 100 percent. The format for ages in the left-hand column is

Table 8.1. Conversion of Male and Female Percentages of Population to the
Conventional Expressions for the Sex Ratio of the Population

| % M | % F | Ratio | % M | % F | Ratio | % M | % F | Ratio |
|---|---|---|---|---|---|---|---|---|
| 99 | 1  | 9900 | 66 | 34 | 194 | 33 | 67 | 49 |
| 98 | 2  | 4900 | 65 | 35 | 185 | 32 | 68 | 47 |
| 97 | 3  | 3233 | 64 | 36 | 177 | 31 | 69 | 44 |
| 96 | 4  | 2400 | 63 | 37 | 170 | 30 | 70 | 42 |
| 95 | 5  | 1900 | 62 | 38 | 163 | 29 | 71 | 40 |
| 94 | 6  | 1566 | 61 | 39 | 156 | 28 | 72 | 38 |
| 93 | 7  | 1328 | 60 | 40 | 150 | 27 | 73 | 36 |
| 92 | 8  | 1150 | 59 | 41 | 143 | 26 | 74 | 35 |
| 91 | 9  | 1011 | 58 | 42 | 138 | 25 | 75 | 33 |
| 90 | 10 | 900  | 57 | 43 | 132 | 24 | 76 | 31 |
| 89 | 11 | 809  | 56 | 44 | 127 | 23 | 77 | 29 |
| 88 | 12 | 733  | 55 | 45 | 122 | 22 | 78 | 28 |
| 87 | 13 | 669  | 54 | 46 | 117 | 21 | 79 | 26 |
| 86 | 14 | 614  | 53 | 47 | 112 | 20 | 80 | 25 |
| 85 | 15 | 566  | 52 | 48 | 108 | 19 | 81 | 23 |
| 84 | 16 | 525  | 51 | 49 | 104 | 18 | 82 | 21 |
| 83 | 17 | 488  | 50 | 50 | 100 | 17 | 83 | 20 |
| 82 | 18 | 455  | 49 | 51 | 96  | 16 | 84 | 19 |
| 81 | 19 | 426  | 48 | 52 | 92  | 15 | 85 | 17 |
| 80 | 20 | 400  | 47 | 53 | 88  | 14 | 86 | 16 |
| 79 | 21 | 376  | 46 | 54 | 85  | 13 | 87 | 14 |
| 78 | 22 | 354  | 45 | 55 | 81  | 12 | 88 | 13 |
| 77 | 23 | 334  | 44 | 56 | 78  | 11 | 89 | 12 |
| 76 | 24 | 316  | 43 | 57 | 75  | 10 | 90 | 11 |
| 75 | 25 | 300  | 42 | 58 | 72  | 9  | 91 | 9  |
| 74 | 26 | 284  | 41 | 58 | 69  | 8  | 92 | 8  |
| 73 | 27 | 270  | 40 | 60 | 66  | 7  | 93 | 7  |
| 72 | 28 | 257  | 39 | 61 | 63  | 6  | 94 | 6  |
| 71 | 29 | 244  | 38 | 62 | 61  | 5  | 95 | 5  |
| 70 | 30 | 233  | 37 | 63 | 58  | 4  | 96 | 4  |
| 69 | 31 | 222  | 36 | 64 | 56  | 3  | 97 | 3  |
| 68 | 32 | 212  | 35 | 65 | 53  | 2  | 98 | 2  |
| 67 | 33 | 203  | 34 | 66 | 51  | 1  | 99 | 1  |

used throughout the book for both tables and graphs. This format is coming
into increased usage in age tables, being more economical and mathemati-
cally exact. For each age classification, only the age at the beginning of the
classification is listed, in this case the age years 0, 15, 30, 45. The end of the
classification is understood to be the last possible age before the beginning
of the next age category. Therefore in this case, the first category means 0,
standing for at birth, up to less than 15 years of age, the beginning of the

next age classification. This format is used in tables and graphs regardless of the number of years included in each age classification.

## D. The Additional Tables

The demographic information contained in the overview table is absolutely essential for understanding changes in the size of a population. But for many types of demographic questions, it is insufficient. The age structure of a population can change over time. This change can be brought about by a change in any one or a combination of the four components of change. In turn, the change of the age structure can bring about changes in the magnitudes of these components. For example, if there is an increase in the relative number of reproductive females in a population, this will probably bring about an increase of the crude birth rate. This, in turn, changes the age structure by increasing the relative number of young people in the population. Therefore for a more comprehensive understanding of the population dynamics, the age structure of the four components of change, fertility, mortality, and two migrations, needs to be examined.

## VI. Fertility (Table 9.2)

This table is an example of the format used for the further examination of fertility. The fertility tables are based on the female population (abbreviated as Pf). The "indicator" column lists the name of the demographic expression. The first line repeats the crude birth rate from the overview table (9.1), thereby linking it to the information of that table.

## A. The Reproductive Population

The next line gives the reproductive female population age 15–44 (abbreviated as Pf 15–44) as a percentage of the total population. When there is a change in the crude birth rate, there are two possible demographic sources of this change: a change in the average number of children that women in the reproductive population are bearing, and/or a change in the percentage the female reproductive population is of the total population. In any comparison of crude birth rates, the percentage in this line of the table gives an indication of the importance or nonimportance of a change in size of this age-sex group relative to the total population. It is derived from the age-sex distribution in the overview table (9.1.c) and is called the reproductive ratio.

In this study the reproductive ratio is used as an additional sex ratio of the population because it is a better index of the impact on fertility of the female age structure of the population. Based on the years when there was sexual balance in the Xilixana population and data from a Yanomami group in the Parima Highlands (Schkolnik 1983:114), the female population age 15–44 should constitute about 20 percent of the total population when the population is sexually balanced.

## B. Fertility by Female Age Groups

Indicators in the next set, the age-specific fertility rates, give the birth rates per 1,000 population by five-year age segments of the mothers' ages at the time of the birth of their children. If a birth should take place to a mother under age fifteen or over forty-five, it is included in the first or last classification. To calculate these rates, the number of births to a certain age group of mothers is the numerator and the number of females of the same age group is the denominator.

In some investigations, data are not available about the age of the mothers at the births of their children. Yet the analytical question may require information more precise than that given by the crude birth rate. In this situation, some control for the female age structure is obtained by using the general fertility rate, which employs the total number of births divided by the number of women of reproductive age in the population. It is not used in the analysis here but is included in the tables for possible use by other researchers.

The total fertility rate is the average number of live births a woman will have if she survives her entire reproductive period. It is calculated by summing the preceding age-specific rates in their decimal form (not per 1,000 population) and multiplying the sum by the number of years included in the age classifications, in this case five. The age-specific rates represent a single period in time, while the definition of the total fertility rate implies passage of the mothers through time. Therefore it assumes that the level of the age-specific rates will remain constant through the lifetime of the average woman. This assumption needs to be kept in mind when employing these rates.

## C. Levels of Analysis

The first column of the fertility table is headed "Level of Analysis." The fertility rates just described operate on three levels of demographic abstraction. The first level looks at the total village population. The crude rates describe this level. The next level is a portion of the population within the village. For fertility it is a particular age-sex segment, the reproductive women, which is the female population age 15–44. The five-year age classifications decompose the reproductive women into six subgroups. The third level is an average individual. For fertility it is the average woman over her reproductive span that is expressed by the total fertility rate. It is important to keep these three levels of abstraction in mind because their magnitudes do not necessarily move in tandem. An increase or decrease at one level does not automatically mean an increase or decrease of the indices for the other levels.

## D. The Absolute Values

This section of the table gives the absolute numbers on which the above crude rates are based. These are complete enumerations of the variables for each village, so there is no sampling error.

## E. Descent Categories

The last part of the fertility table lists the percentage of the village population that belongs to the various descent categories (A–F, other/unknown, or external in-migrant) discussed in chapter four. These are listed in this table because of the Yanomami brother-sister relationships. If a village has a high percentage of its population with the same descent category, many people are siblings or parallel cousins to each other and prohibited to marry. This may depress fertility by delaying age at first marriage and first birth.

## VII. Mortality (Table 9.3)

Table 9.3 is a sample of the format used for the further examination of mortality. The first indicator is a repetition of the crude death rate, thereby linking this table to the overview table (9.1).

## A. Deaths by Age Groups

The next group of indicators are age-specific mortality rates calculated in the same manner as age-specific fertility rates. The classification of deaths by age yields some of the smallest numbers in the study and therefore is especially subject to volatility. Ten-year age classifications have been used to mitigate error due to estimation of age and to diminish the number of age classifications with few or no cases.

Because of this problem, life table values including life expectancy have not been used for the demographic profiles of the villages. Chapter 19, concerning the aggregate of all the villages, has larger numbers and therefore transforms the age-specific mortality rates into "q" rates, the life table expression for the probability of dying within the various age intervals.

For some purposes, a more convenient way of expressing the same level of mortality is the use of survival rates (l) from the same life table. They show the percentage of a group born in the same time period who can expect still to be alive at various ages as the group becomes older and experiences death.

A third way of expressing the same mortality is the life expectancy of an average individual, derived from the same life table as the two previous indices. Life expectancy varies with the age of an individual. By convention, the life expectancy at birth ($e_0$) is frequently used as a single indicator of the mortality level of a population. For example, in 1990 in the United States the average life expectancy for a person born in that year was 75.4 years. The value of the life expectancy at birth depends on the mortality values for all the other age classifications. Therefore the accuracy of the life table projection of life expectancy at birth is diminished when there are no cases in one or more of the age classifications due to the small size of the population.

## B. The Absolute Values and the Reasons

The next section of the mortality table gives the absolute values by sex of the deaths. The last section of the table gives the distribution of the absolute numbers of deaths by their cause and sex. A very broad system of classification has been used. "Infanticide" has been made a specific category because the Yanomami do not consider it a homicide. There are only two disease categories because of the difficulties of specific diagnosis. "Infectious Diseases" mainly include pulmonary and gastrointestinal infections contracted by human or insect contact. The category includes pneumonia, measles, whooping cough, tuberculosis, malaria, venereal disease, dysentery, and diarrhea. Frequently an individual's history of morbidity will include more than one of these categories leading to the death. In the upcoming village histories when there are no known cases of a particular cause, that cause has been omitted from the table.

## VIII. Migration (Table 9.4)

The migration table includes in-migration (abbreviated as I), out-migration (abbreviated as O), and their resultant, net migration (abbreviated as NM). It opens with the crude migration rates repeated from the overview table.

## A. External and Internal Immigration

The crude rates are immediately subdivided into their external and internal components. External migration means that the village the migrant came from or went to was outside the Mucajaí bloc of villages as defined in this study. Internal migration means that the migrant came from or went to another Xilixana village.

## B. Migration by Age Groups

The age-specific rates use fifteen-year age classifications, which roughly divide the population into the young, the reproductive, and the old. These rates include both external and internal migrations.

## C. Absolute Values and Reasons

Absolute numbers and their distribution by reasons and sex are given in the last part of the table. "Marriage" includes not only those who actually married but also family members who changed their village of residence to be with one of the married persons. A number of these are children who remained with mothers widowed or divorced. "Captives" refer to those taken in raids, again including children taken with their mothers. "Fission-Fusion" refers to those who migrate when a village subdivides. "Avoid Conflict" refers to an individual or a family group migrating as a means of escaping a conflict situation. Fission can also occur for this reason. Fission usually involves a larger group and the founding of a new village, while the avoidance of conflict as used here refers to an individual or family moving to another village. "Family" is a broad category meaning a migration to be with specific kin people. Important here are widows and widowers or divorced people returning to their families of origin and children who have lost one parent or both. In the upcoming village histories when there are no known cases of a particular reason, that reason has been omitted from the table.

## IX. The Volatility of Small Numbers

As seen in table 4.1, Yanomami villages have populations usually ranging from about 20 to 100 inhabitants, which is typical of many tribal populations. For small populations such as these, the annual number of births, deaths, or migrations can be a single digit number or nothing. This is one of the reasons that the village data will be grouped into larger time and age classifications, but the resulting sums are still what statisticians call small numbers. For example, in a population of 50 people at midyear, the small difference between 3 or 4 deaths in that year is the difference between crude death rates of 60 and 80. This would be a huge difference if large numbers were involved and may indicate a change in the mortality structure. The difference in this example is probably due to the chance difference between 3 or 4 deaths during the year than to any change in the mortality structure. A similar problem arises when comparing the same demographic index for two different populations or for the same population in different time periods.

In these situations, a statistician may ask whether the difference between the two indices can be conceived as solely due to the small magnitudes involved (small number volatility) or whether the difference can be conceived as due to other factors. Based on probability theory, various statistical tests have been developed to determine whether the magnitudes of these differences could arise solely by chance or whether something more than chance may be involved. If the test shows the difference may be due to something more than chance, the test is said to show a "significant difference." If the test shows the difference could arise by chance alone, sometimes it is said that the difference is a statistical artifact without analytical significance. In publishing the results of quantitative research in social science, the use of such tests has at times become ritualistic.

These tests may introduce certain assumptions and consequent biases into any discussion in which they are employed. It is important to examine these assumptions with their problematic application to small number anthropological populations. The first assumption may be that these are large number populations of which the villages are small number representatives or samples. But tribal village populations are not large number populations. Therefore, the use of these tests insinuates this contrary-to-fact assumption into the discussion and throws it out of focus. The second assumption follows from the first. It assumes that the demographic indices for the villages represent samples. This is incorrect for two reasons. As just stated, they are not samples of large number populations. In addition, they are not samples of small number populations since the tables represent complete enumerations of the demographic indices. The use of significance tests muddies this important point. A third assumption that sometimes creeps into discussions results from a misunderstanding of the word "significant." It has a restricted technical meaning. A significance test indicates the probability that the difference between two indices is due to chance. Depending on the limits of probability set by the researcher (sometimes an arbitrary decision) and the test result, a difference is said to be significant or not. If the test indicates the probability that the difference could arise by chance, such a difference is sometimes dismissed as a statistical aberration. Tests showing a significant difference say that it is improbable (but not impossible) that the difference arose by chance. This implies that other factors are involved. But the test does not say what the specific factors are or how important they may be in determining the difference. In brief, "significant" in this context does not mean "important." Therefore, by themselves, the use of such tests does not convey as much information as may appear if "significant" is not understood in its correct sense.

For these reasons, we have not employed these tests in the following chapters. They would add little to the analysis and possibly confuse it, distract from the points at issue, and result in unnecessary clutter. This study takes for granted small number volatility as influencing the varying levels of the demographic indices of the villages and asks about their impact on the growth or decline of these populations as well as the historical and ethnographic factors giving rise to the small numbers. If other researchers wish to make use of the contrary-to-fact assumption that these villages represent samples of some large or small number construct, the tables provide the data with which to calculate various tests of significance. Such an assumption may be useful for certain scientific purposes. But it remains a contrary-to-fact assumption.

## X. What Do All These Numbers Mean?

We have explained demographic concepts, conventions, and quantitative relationships to help those unfamiliar with demography. There is an additional problem for such readers, however. It is a familiar social science problem: What have you got when you have got it? What do all these numbers mean? We attempt to throw some light on these questions in the analyses in the upcoming chapters. But as background, it is helpful to have some acquaintance with the significance of the quantitative levels of the components of change, especially fertility and mortality.

### A. Fertility and Mortality

Both of these variables have a biological as well as a social structure. The biology imposes certain limits of possibility that create a range of expectations for these rates. Within this range enter other biological, social, or ideational factors, so that particular rates may be characterized by qualitative adjectives as high, moderate, or low. However, there is no consensus about the specific quantitative values of any of the components to which these qualitative modifiers apply. Much depends on the demographic unit taken as the standard of reference and the type of problem under discussion.

Modern demography grew out of the need for population data as a basis

Table 8.2. Qualitative Descriptions for Quantitative Ranges of Crude Birth and Death Rates

| Qualitative | Crude Rates | | Examples | | |
| Descriptions | Birth | Death | Continent | Birth | Death |
|---|---|---|---|---|---|
| Low | <20 | <10 | N. America | 14 | 9 |
| Moderate | 20–<40 | 10–<20 | S. America | 24 | 7* |
| High | 40–<60 | 20–<40 | Africa | 40 | 14* |
| Extremely High | 60+ | 40+ | | | |

* under-enumerated

for policy in public health and public administration. National governments with their censuses and collections of local vital registrations became
the primary users of and support for demographic data. As a result, the
national state has become a frequent unit of reference. The United Nations
in their annual Demographic Yearbooks present these data and a useful
summary is published annually by the Population Reference Bureau. These
values are frequently used as comparative referents for demographic data.
Perusing these data, we made an editorial and somewhat arbitrary decision
to apply the qualitative terms *high, moderate,* and *low* to certain quantitative levels of fertility and mortality as shown in table 8.2. Crude rates of
fertility (Haub and Cornelius 1997) for the continents of North America,
South America, and Africa have been used as examples. The crude death
rates for South America and Africa should be higher as death registration is
probably the most under-enumerated of the components, especially in these
areas. The accuracy of national registration systems as well as the levels of
fertility and mortality are highly correlated with the level of economic development and industrialization of a region.

The demographic history of the United States may also be helpful for
giving some perspective on the meaning of the quantitative levels of the
crude birth rate. In 1800 the crude birth rate for the United States was 55.0
(high). About 1860 it declined to 44.3 (still high). About 1880 it declined
further to 39.8 (beginning moderate). Around 1911 it declined still further
to 29.9 (still moderate). In 1932 during the Depression years, it declined
again to 19.5 (beginning low). In 1947 with the economic recovery due to
WWII and the ensuing baby boom, it rose to 26.6 (moderate) and continued
in the 20s until 1965 when it declined to 19.4 (beginning low). In the late
1990s it was around 15.0 (low) (United States Bureau of the Census
1975:49; 1996:75).

Table 8.3. Years Required for a Population to Double in Size at Various Annual Percentage Rates of Increase

| Annual % Increase | Years for Population to Double |
|---|---|
| 0.1 | 693.5 |
| 0.5 | 139.0 |
| 1.0 | 69.7 |
| 1.5 | 46.6 |
| 2.0 | 35.0 |
| 2.5 | 28.1 |
| 3.0 | 23.4 |
| 3.5 | 20.1 |
| 4.0 | 17.7 |
| 4.5 | 15.7 |
| 5.0 | 14.2 |
| 5.5 | 12.9 |
| 6.0 | 11.9 |

The historical data about the United States crude death rates are not as complete, nor do they have the same quality. The best early data are from Massachusetts in 1860 with a rate of 18.7 (moderate). United States rates begin in 1900 with 17.2 (moderate). In 1982 these rates dipped below 10.0 (low) and in the late 1990s were about 8.8 (United States Bureau of the Census 1975:63, 59; 1975:90; 1996:90). The demographic record for the United States begins after the widespread epidemics of infectious diseases that elevate the crude death rates of other areas of the world.

B. Migration

With regard to in-migration and out-migration, it is more difficult to make any such determination of ranges because the biological factor is of less immediate importance. Usually the levels of migration are lower than those of fertility and mortality.

C. Rates of Population Increase

The rates of total increase and natural increase are additional demographic values that may need interpretation. A convenient way to think about their significance is to ask oneself this hypothetical question: If an annual rate of increase should remain constant over a number of years, how many years would it take for the population to double in size? Table 8.3 answers this question. Decimal values not included in the table can be approximated by interpolation.

This is not a table of predictions but merely a hypothetical projection of quantitative relationships to give some idea of the implications of the various magnitudes of population increase. For example, it informs a society of the time frame in which it must increase its production to take care of the doubling of the population.

It should be noted that table 8.3 is a compressed distribution; that is, small quantitative differences can have important implications. Even though population increase is frequently expressed as a percentage (which is per 100 population) instead of as per 1,000 population, the percentage distribution does not run from a possible 0 to 100 percent as it may for other distributions. The biological limits on fertility and mortality usually restrict the distribution of natural increase to the range shown in table 8.3. If one thinks of the distribution as ranging from 0 to 100 percent, a change from 1 to 2 percent can appear insignificant. But a change of this magnitude in this distribution is the difference between a population doubling in thirty-five years and in seventy years. The apparently small 1 percent difference is, in reality, a considerable difference in the time required to muster additional resources. (Table 8.3 was calculated by the mathematical equation for incremental growth, more commonly known as the formula for compound interest. The equation for continuous growth could also have been used. It would have yielded slightly different answers.)

## XI. Summary

The fundamental concepts of demography and their quantitative relationships as expressed in the basic demographic equation have been described. The concepts are expressed by the use of absolute numbers, crude rates, and age-specific rates. In chapters to follow, the four standardized tables present these demographic values and their interrelationships for each of the eight villages and for the aggregate of the group. The basic equation is the logic of the overview table. It shows the role of each component of change in the overall change of the size of the population. The other three tables investigate each component in greater depth by examining age-sex structures as well as giving the reasons for mortality and migration.

# The Villages

# 9

# Village A

In 1930 while living to the south of the Uraricoera River, the Xilixana were composed of three villages designated here as villages A, B, and C. In 1935 all were involved in the conflict with the Yekwana. Following this conflict, village A moved farther inland away from the Uraricoera River, while villages B and C moved south to the Mucajaí watershed and eventually to the banks of the river itself. Later villages B and C returned to the streams that flowed north to the Uraricoera River. Some time after this all three villages moved south to the Mucajaí watershed. The history of village A, the smallest of the three villages, is the focus of this chapter.

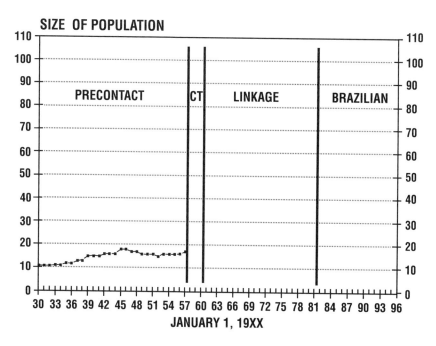

9.1. Village A population.

## I. The Village in 1930

At the beginning of 1930, village A consisted of only 11 people, as shown in figure 9.1 and table 9.1. The village was composed of a single faction, which was a polyandrous family with members from three generations. Two members of the family were external in-migrants from Xiliana groups. The demographic problem for this type of village was whether it could maintain itself with such a small population in the face of the tasks of providing food, attracting marriage partners, and maintaining natural increase by its fertility outstripping its mortality.

## II. Precontact Phase, 1930–1956

Village A was able to manage these problems and maintain itself during the Precontact phase. It increased its population from 11 to 17 due to the interaction of the four demographic components of change.

Group fertility was barely in the moderate range with a crude rate of 22.6. The average mother in the population had high fertility as seen in the 7.1 total fertility rate. Group fertility was moderate because there were so few women of childbearing ages in the village population. Only 33.9 percent of the population was female (table 9.1.c). Women of childbearing ages comprised only 10.7 percent of the village population instead of the expected 20 percent with a balanced sex structure. The problem of sexual balance was further complicated because almost 50 percent of the village had the same descent category, with those in the younger ages being brothers and sisters to each other.

There were six deaths in this phase, one newborn and the rest adults. In 1946 there were three deaths, apparently from malaria related to the temporary presence of Brazilian peasants in the area as discussed in chapter 2. (Table 9.3 lists these as unknown because of the uncertainty.) The crude death rate was a moderate 15.1. The moderate rates of group fertility and mortality resulted in a natural increase of 15.1 (1.5 percent) for the Precontact phase.

The small population was also increased by the in-migration of three young men for marriage, although not all their partners had reached sexual maturity. All the marriageable males and females were related as brother-sister since there was only a single polyandrous family in the village and all the children took their descent category from the primary husband. Therefore any marriage between them would be incestuous and prohibited. Marriage partners had to come from outside the village. Their in-migration was

Table 9.1. Village A: Demographic Profile, 1930–57

| 9.1.a | 1930 | Precontact | 1957 | Contact | 1957 |
|---|---|---|---|---|---|
| Population | 11 | | 17 | | 0 |
| Total Incr. | | | 6 | | −17 |
| Nat. Incr. | | | 3 | | −4 |
| Births | | 9 | | 0 | |
| Deaths | | 6 | | 4 | |
| Net Migration | | | 3 | | −13 |
| In-mig. | | 3 | | 0 | |
| Out-mig. | | 0 | | −13 | |

| 9.1.b | | Crude Rates | | | |
|---|---|---|---|---|---|
| Total Incr. | | | 15.1 | | −1,000 |
| Nat. Incr. | | | 7.5 | | −266.6 |
| Births | | 22.6 | | 0.0 | |
| Deaths | | 15.1 | | 266.6 | |
| Net Migration | | | 7.5 | | −733.4 |
| In-mig. | | 7.5 | | 0.0 | |
| Out-mig. | | 0.0 | | 733.4 | |

| 9.1.c | | Population: Age by Sex | | | |
|---|---|---|---|---|---|
| Population | 11 | | 17 | | 0 |
| Male | 7 | | 11 | | 0 |
| Female | 4 | | 6 | | 0 |
| % Female | 36.4 | | 35.3 | | 0 |
| % Age-Sex | % M | % F | | % M | % F |
| 0 | 18.2 | 12.9 | | 11.0 | 11.4 |
| 15 | 16.6 | 5.4 | | 19.8 | 7.6 |
| 30 | 11.9 | 5.2 | | 27.0 | 3.0 |
| 45 | 19.3 | 10.3 | | 11.8 | 8.4 |
| Total | 66.1 | 33.9 | | 64.7 | 25.3 |

an important factor for the continued independent existence of this faction and village during this phase.

The village maintained itself during this phase with a 15.1 (1.5 percent) rate of total increase. The moderate fertility was higher than the moderate mortality. The three in-migrants for marriage with no out-migration gave a positive net migration. Although the population increased from 11 to 17 at the end of the phase, the village remained with the disadvantages of being a small population.

Table 9.2. Village A: Fertility Rates and Descent Categories

| Level of Analysis | Indicator | Age/ Sex | Phase Precontact |
|---|---|---|---|
| Village | Crude Birth | - | 22.6 |
| | Pf % Pop. | 15–44 | 10.7 |
| Female Reproductive Population | Age-Specific Rates | 15 | 222 |
| | | 20 | 400 |
| | | 25 | 133 |
| | | 30 | - |
| | | 35 | 400 |
| | | 40 | 267 |
| | General | 15–44 | 212 |
| Avg. Female | Total Fert. | 15–44 | 7.1 |
| N Births | Total | | 9 |
| | | M | 4 |
| | | F | 5 |
| Village | % Descent Categories | | |
| | A | | 21.7 |
| | B | | - |
| | C | | - |
| | D | | 6.6 |
| | E | | 46.5 |
| | F | | - |
| | Other/Unknown | | 15.6 |
| | External In-mig. | | 9.5 |
| | Total | | 100 |

## III. Contact Phase, 1957

The village ceased to exist in the first year of the Contact phase. We have noted the need of the Xilixana for steel tools. In 1957 a group of men from villages A and B traveled downstream and found some Brazilians with whom they bartered canoes and arrows for axes, knives, and machetes. But this first contact proved deadly. Upon their return, two men aged 72 and 59 along with the latter's son of 13 became ill with colds, which turned into pneumonia. A 55-year-old woman in the village also died. These Yanomami had not been exposed to the respiratory infections common among Brazilians. The man of 59 years was the headman of the village. The other older

Table 9.3. Village A: Mortality Rates

| Level of Analysis | Indicator | Age/ Sex | Phases | |
|---|---|---|---|---|
| | | | Precontact | Contact |
| Village | Crude Death | | 15.1 | 266.6 |
| Age Groups | Age-specific Rates | 0 | 111 | - |
| | | 1 | - | - |
| | | 5 | - | - |
| | | 10 | - | 333 |
| | | 20 | - | - |
| | | 30 | - | - |
| | | 40 | 24 | - |
| | | 50 | - | 1,000 |
| | | 60 | 62 | - |
| | | 70 | - | - |
| N Deaths | Total | | 6 | 4 |
| | | M | 3 | 3 |
| | | F | 3 | 1 |
| N Reasons | Infectious Disease | M | - | 3 |
| | | F | - | 1 |
| | Unknown | M | 3 | - |
| | | F | 3 | - |

man had been important in the village's identity. Leadership in the village fell to a son-in-law in his thirties, himself an in-migrant from village B. The loss of key members of the community, the small size of the surviving population, and the ties with village B resulted in the fusion of all 13 survivors into village B in 1957.

## IV. Summary

Village A is an example of a Yanomami village coping with the problems of maintaining itself with such a small population. The village consisted of a faction who preferred to live by themselves in a small group while maintaining ties with a larger village. Although village A had a modest natural increase during the Precontact phase, this increase would have been greater if group fertility had not been restrained by a shortage of reproductive females

**Table 9.4. Village A: Migration Rates**

| Level of Analysis | Indicator | Age/Sex | Precontact I | Precontact O | Precontact NM | Contact I | Contact O | Contact NM |
|---|---|---|---|---|---|---|---|---|
| Village | Crude Rate | - | 7.5 | - | −7.5 | - | −733.4 | −733.4 |
| | External | | - | - | - | - | - | - |
| | Internal | | 7.5 | - | 7.5 | - | −733.4 | −733.4 |
| Age Groups | Age- | 0 | 8 | - | 8 | - | 800 | 800 |
| | specific | 15 | 23 | - | 23 | - | 1,000 | 1,000 |
| | Rates | 30 | - | - | - | - | 1,000 | 1,000 |
| | | 45 | - | - | - | - | 333 | 333 |
| N Migration Total | | | 3 | 0 | 3 | 0 | 13 | −13 |
| | | M | 3 | 0 | 3 | 0 | 8 | −8 |
| | | F | 0 | 0 | 9 | 0 | 5 | −5 |
| Reasons: Internal Mig. | | | | | | | | |
| | Marriage | M | 3 | - | | - | - | |
| | Fission- | M | - | - | | - | 8 | |
| | Fusion | F | - | - | | - | 5 | |
| | Family | M | - | - | | - | - | |

in the village population. With the population remaining small upon entering the Contact phase, the death of four members within one year, including the headman, resulted in the extinction of the village. Here *extinction* means dissolution of the village, but there were more out-migrating survivors than dead. In qualitative discussions of indigenous extinction, frequently no distinction is made about the level of analysis—faction, village, or population bloc. Extinction is often interpreted as primarily mortality. As a case history, village A is an example of extinction in which the amount of dispersion (out-migration) is greater than the number of dead.

# 10

## Village B

This village existed in 1930 in the region to the south of the Uraricoera River and entered the Mucajaí watershed after the conflict with the Yekwana in 1935. After wandering between the two watersheds, in 1954 village B settled on the Peiwa stream at a site about an hour's walk north of the Mucajaí River.

The people of village B were called the Kasilapai. In Ninam, this means "long lipped." The Ninam men, like many Yanomami, have the custom of chewing large wads of tobacco. They keep the tobacco between their lower teeth and lip, which gradually thickens and extends the lip. According to Cocco (1987:29–30), *Kasilapai* is a Mácu term that the Mácu originally applied to all Ninam. The Mácu passed on the term to their allies, the Yekwana. The Yekwana in turn were the early sources of information about this region. In this way *Kasilapai* became one of the terms by which the

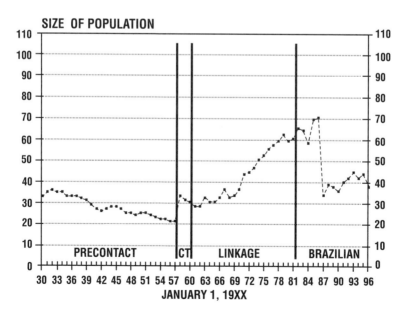

10.1. Village B population.

Ninam became known by outsiders. Among the Mucajaí group, it is used only for the members of village B and later village H. Since contact, the village B community has preferred to be known as Amnas bèk or Oliak bèk, names associated with areas where they have resided.

Village B still existed in 1999. It is one of only two villages to have been in existence the entire sixty-six years of the demographic part of the research. Figure 10.1 shows the variation in the size of the population during this period; from 33 in 1930 to 37 in 1996, but with a high of 70 in 1986 and a low of 21 in 1956 and 1957. The table outlines the population dynamics of the four historical periods.

## I. Precontact Phase, 1930–1956

During this phase the population declined from 33 in 1930 to a low of 21 at the beginning of 1956, the last year of the Precontact phase. This decline was due to both natural decrease (–1.1 percent) and a negative net migration (–0.5 percent). The downward trend of the population and its small size raised questions about the village's ability to survive. The components of change explain the downward trend.

Group fertility was low with a crude rate of 18.5 instead of the expected 40s or 50s for this type of population. However, the average female had 7.9 live births during her reproductive span. As with village A, the low group fertility was due to a shortage of females. Women comprised only 21 percent and women of reproductive age only 9.4 percent of the village population (table 10.1.c) instead of the expected approximations of 50 percent and 20 percent. In addition, one of the these females was sterile until her death in 1959 at the age of 29. There were only four females of reproductive age in the village during most of this phase, all in polyandrous unions. Although there was an extreme shortage of females, the last part of table 10.2 shows a variety of descent categories, so that the kinship structure did not pose a marriage problem.

Group mortality was high with a crude death rate of 29. There was a death as the result of a snakebite, one accidental homicide, one from pneumonia, and one premature infant death, and there were three infanticides. Two infants were rejected because they were female. The reason for the third infanticide is unknown. The remaining causes of death are also unknown (13/22). The mortality in this phase was greater than the low fertility, resulting in a –10.6 crude rate of natural decrease (–1.1 percent).

There was only one death in the village as a result of the Yekwana conflict. At the time of the retaliatory raid by the Yekwana, the men from

**Table 10.1. Village B: Demographic Profile, 1930–96**

| 10.1.a | 1930 | Precontact | 1957 | Contact | 1961 | Linkage | 1982 | Brazilian | 1996 |
|---|---|---|---|---|---|---|---|---|---|
| Population | 33 | | 21 | | 28 | | 65 | | 37 |
| Total Incr. | | −12 | | 7 | | 37 | | −28 | |
| Nat. Incr. | | −8 | | −8 | | 41 | | 11 | |
| Births | | 14 | | 2 | | 55 | | 36 | |
| Deaths | | 22 | | 10 | | 14 | | 25 | |
| Net Migration | | −4 | | 15 | | −4 | | −39 | |
| In-mig. | | 2 | | 17 | | 7 | | 21 | |
| Out-mig. | | 6 | | 2 | | 11 | | 60 | |

**10.1.b** Crude Rates

| 10.1.b | 1930 | Precontact | 1957 | Contact | 1961 | Linkage | 1982 | Brazilian | 1996 |
|---|---|---|---|---|---|---|---|---|---|
| Total Inc. | | −15.8 | | 59.1 | | 40.1 | | −42.2 | |
| Nat. Incr. | | −10.6 | | −67.5 | | 44.4 | | 16.6 | |
| Births | | 18.5 | | 16.9 | | 59.6 | | 54.3 | |
| Deaths | | 29.0 | | 84.4 | | 15.2 | | 37.7 | |
| Net Migration | | −5.3 | | 126.6 | | −4.3 | | 58.8 | |
| In-mig. | | 2.6 | | 143.5 | | 7.6 | | 31.7 | |
| Out-mig. | | 7.9 | | 16.9 | | 11.9 | | 90.5 | |

**10.1.c** Population: Age by Sex

| 10.1.c | 1930 | Precontact | | 1957 | Contact | | 1961 | Linkage | | 1982 | Brazilian | | 1996 |
|---|---|---|---|---|---|---|---|---|---|---|---|---|---|
| Population | 33 | | | 21 | | | 28 | | | 65 | | | 37 |
| Male | 26 | | | 16 | | | 17 | | | 33 | | | 19 |
| Female | 7 | | | 5 | | | 11 | | | 32 | | | 18 |
| % Female | 21.2 | | | 23.8 | | | 29.3 | | | 49.2 | | | 48.6 |
| % Age-Sex | | % M | % F | | % M | % F | | % M | % F | | % M | % F | |
| 0 | | 26.0 | 3.7 | | 11.0 | 11.4 | | 26.1 | 24.5 | | 27.4 | 23.5 | |
| 15 | | 25.9 | 2.0 | | 19.8 | 7.6 | | 7.9 | 13.4 | | 14.0 | 14.3 | |
| 30 | | 13.9 | 7.4 | | 27.0 | 3.0 | | 10.2 | 5.0 | | 3.4 | 8.0 | |
| 45 | | 13.0 | 8.2 | | 11.8 | 8.4 | | 9.6 | 3.1 | | 7.4 | 2.0 | |
| Total | | 78.8 | 21.2 | | 69.6 | 30.4 | | 53.9 | 46.1 | | 52.2 | 47.8 | |

Table 10.2. Village B: Fertility Rates and Descent Categories

| Level of Analysis | Indicator | Age/ Sex | Phases | | | |
|---|---|---|---|---|---|---|
| | | | Precontact | Contact | Linkage | Brazilian |
| Village | Crude Birth | - | 18.5 | 16.9 | 59.6 | 54.3 |
| | Pf as % Pop. | 15–44 | 9.4 | 10.5 | 18.5 | 22.3 |
| Female Reproductive Population | Age-Specific Rates | 15 | 571 | 125 | 371 | 228 |
| | | 20 | 200 | 400 | 286 | 333 |
| | | 25 | 308 | - | 358 | 235 |
| | | 30 | 294 | - | 305 | 270 |
| | | 35 | 150 | - | 250 | 235 |
| | | 40 | 53 | - | 200 | - |
| | General | 15–44 | 197 | 138 | 322 | 243 |
| Avg. Female | Total Fert. | 15–44 | 7.9 | 2.8 | 8.9 | 6.5 |
| N Births | Total | | 14 | 2 | 55 | 36 |
| | | M | 8 | 2 | 30 | 19 |
| | | F | 6 | 0 | 25 | 17 |
| Village | % Descent Categories | | | | | |
| | A | | 16.3 | 20.9 | 27.5 | 24.7 |
| | B | | - | - | - | - |
| | C | | 10.7 | 7.8 | 13.1 | 7.7 |
| | D | | 28.7 | 33.0 | 33.6 | 55.4 |
| | E | | - | 13.9 | 2.2 | - |
| | F | | 23.1 | 15.7 | 11.3 | 1.9 |
| | Other/Unknown | | 19.5 | 8.7 | - | .3 |
| | External In-mig. | | 1.7 | - | 12.3 | 10.0 |
| | Total | | 100 | 100 | 100 | 100 |

villages A and B were hunting and fishing away from the village. Only the women of villages A and B and the visitors from village C were at the yano, where the yaimo ceremony was being held. The lone mortality from village B was a Yekwana woman who had been previously captured by the Xiliana. The men from villages A and B did not return to the yano until the Yekwana were leaving and attacked them as they retreated.

Owing to the small number of females of marriageable age, three men out-migrated to village A and two to village C for marriage. There was one external in-migration, the previously mentioned Yekwana woman captured in the raid in 1935 who was accidentally killed in the retaliatory raid. The resulting crude rate of net migration was –5.3.

Table 10.3. Village B: Mortality Rates

| Level of Analysis | Indicator | Age/ Sex | Precontact | Contact | Linkage | Brazilian |
|---|---|---|---|---|---|---|
| | | | | Phases | | |
| Village | Crude Death | | 29.0 | 84.4 | 15.2 | 37.7 |
| Age Groups | Age-specific | 0 | 214 | - | 109 | 111 |
| | Rates | 1 | 19 | - | - | 61 |
| | | 5 | 12 | - | - | 9 |
| | | 10 | 24 | 39 | 11 | 29 |
| | | 20 | 24 | - | 26 | 27 |
| | | 30 | 27 | 143 | 10 | - |
| | | 40 | 22 | 154 | - | 36 |
| | | 50 | 14 | 316 | - | 34 |
| | | 60 | 24 | - | 57 | 150 |
| | | 70+ | - | - | 167 | 1,000 |
| N Deaths | Total | | 22 | 10 | 14 | 25 |
| | | M | 13 | 7 | 8 | 12 |
| | | F | 9 | 3 | 6 | 13 |
| N Reasons | Infectious | M | - | 5 | 3 | 5 |
| | Disease | F | 1 | 3 | 2 | 3 |
| | Non-infect. | M | 2 | 2 | - | 1 |
| | Disease | F | - | - | - | 2 |
| | Infanticide | M | - | - | 1 | - |
| | | F | 3 | - | 2 | 2 |
| | Homicide | M | 1 | - | 2 | 1 |
| | | F | 1 | - | - | - |
| | Accidents | M | 1 | - | 1 | 1 |
| | | F | - | - | 1 | - |
| | Unknown | M | 9 | - | 1 | 4 |
| | | F | 4 | - | 1 | 6 |

At the end of this phase the village faced a demographic crisis that threatened its existence. Mortality was high. Higher fertility was needed for the village to survive and grow. But there was a large sexual imbalance that threatened its fertility and forced males to out-migrate to other villages to find wives. The village population had declined to 21 people with one reproductive female in her forties toward the end of the period. Had these conditions continued, the population of the village probably would have declined further and the village would have become extinct.

**Table 10.4. Village B: Migration Rates**

| Level of Analysis | Indicator | Age/Sex | Precontact I | Precontact O | Precontact NM | Contact I | Contact O | Contact NM | Linkage I | Linkage O | Linkage NM | Brazilian I | Brazilian O | Brazilian NM |
|---|---|---|---|---|---|---|---|---|---|---|---|---|---|---|
| Village | Crude Rate | | 2.6 | 7.9 | −5.3 | 143.5 | 16.9 | 126.6 | 7.6 | 11.9 | −4.3 | 31.7 | 90.5 | −58.8 |
| | External | | 1.3 | - | 1.3 | 33.8 | - | 33.8 | 5.4 | 1.1 | 4.3 | 1.5 | - | 1.5 |
| | Internal | | 1.3 | 7.9 | −6.6 | 109.7 | 16.9 | 92.8 | 2.2 | 10.8 | −8.6 | 30.2 | 90.5 | 60.3 |
| Age Groups | Age-specific Rates | 0 | - | 5 | −5 | 204 | - | 204 | 6 | 9 | −3 | 27 | 89 | −62 |
| | | 15 | 5 | 24 | −19 | 174 | - | 174 | 10 | 20 | −10 | 48 | 80 | −32 |
| | | 30 | 6 | - | 6 | 141 | 28 | 113 | 14 | 7 | 7 | 13 | 93 | −80 |
| | | 45 | - | - | - | 42 | 42 | - | - | 17 | −17 | 32 | 128 | −96 |
| N Migration Total | | M | 2 | 6 | −4 | 17 | 2 | 15 | 7 | 11 | −4 | 21 | 60 | −39 |
| | | F | 1 | 6 | −5 | 8 | 2 | 6 | 3 | 9 | −6 | 11 | 32 | −21 |
| | | F | 1 | - | 1 | 9 | - | 9 | 4 | 2 | 2 | 10 | 28 | −18 |
| Reasons: External Mig. | Marriage | M | - | - | | - | - | | 1 | 1 | | - | - | |
| | | F | - | - | | 1 | - | | 3 | - | | 1 | - | |
| | Captive | F | 1 | - | | 3 | - | | 1 | - | | - | - | |
| Reasons: Internal Mig. | Marriage | M | - | 5 | | - | - | | 2 | - | | 1 | 2 | |
| | | F | - | - | | - | - | | - | 1 | | - | 6 | |
| | Fission-Fusion | M | - | - | | 8 | - | | - | - | | 1 | 22 | |
| | | F | - | - | | 5 | - | | - | - | | 1 | 16 | |
| | Avoid Conflict | M | - | - | | - | - | | - | - | | 2 | - | |
| | | F | - | - | | - | - | | - | - | | 3 | 1 | |
| | Family | M | 1 | 1 | | - | - | | - | - | | 1 | - | |
| | | M | - | - | | - | 2 | | - | 9 | | 7 | 8 | |
| | Unknown | F | - | - | | - | - | | - | - | | 4 | 5 | |

## II. Contact Phase, 1957–1960

At the beginning of this phase, village B along with village A lived a day's journey upriver and inland from where the Kloknai stream empties into the Mucajaí River. There were several medium-sized rapids and one large one between these two points. In 1960 the village moved to the mission post to be closer to the supply of metal goods and medical services.

In spite of the expected high mortality and the loss of population usually connected with first contact experiences as predicted by Ribeiro's model, this village increased 5.9 percent (59.1) to 28 people during the Contact phase. This population increase resulted from considerable volatility in the components of change during this period.

The low fertility of the previous phase continued into this phase with a crude rate of 16.9. The reason was the same as in the previous phase. Owing to the out-migration of males for marriage, there was a decrease in the sexual imbalance, but females still constituted only 30.4 percent of the total population and, more important, reproductive females only 10.5 percent, about half of the expectation for a sexually balanced population of this type.

The crude death rate was an extremely high 84.4. Most of the deaths were due to pneumonia, the result of infections acquired from contact with people outside the Mucajaí group. Contrary to the experience of village A, mortality from contact with the Brazilians was not high. The first trip downriver with village A was in 1957. However, village B with almost three times the population suffered only one fatality as a result of the trip. The reason for this differential is unknown. The second and third trips took place in 1958 after the fusion of village A into this village. In early 1959 a man died from a respiratory infection and sometime later a woman who had come from village A died.

The high mortality occurred in 1960, probably from contact with Yanomami on the upper tributaries of the Mucajaí. In February 1959 four prospectors passed through village B on their way to the upper Mucajaí. A year later two of the prospectors returned and sought the help of the Mucajaí people to go downriver to Boa Vista. The prospectors told village B about the Malaxi theli, the Yanomami who lived in the area of the Couto de Magalhães River, an upper tributary of the Mucajaí River. The prospectors informed village B that the Malaxi theli wished to meet the Xilixana.

Acting on this information, three canoes of men from village B ascended the Mucajaí River. After a journey of about five days, they met the Malaxi theli and visited them for several days. Upon their return downstream, the men from village B were accompanied by three Malaxi theli men. The Malaxi theli also visited village C and the mission post. Later two men from village B accompanied the Malaxi theli back to their village and then returned to their own village. This was the first sustained contact the Xilixana had had with any other Yanomami group since 1935.

Soon after these contacts with the Malaxi theli, pneumonia swept through village B. In an effort to avoid the sickness, which was seen as due to witchcraft, the yano was abandoned and the villagers spread out in the forest, living in temporary shelters. Missionaries and people from village C attempted to reach them, but their canoe capsized. Later it was discovered that the accident had happened close to where some members of village B were camping, but they were too sick and weak to cry out. The crude mortality rate in 1960 soared to 233 as a result of ten deaths, seven men and three women. Eight of the deaths were probably due to the infection transmitted by contact with the Malaxi theli or possibly the prospectors. The Malaxi theli, in turn, were in indirect although infrequent contact with Brazilian peasants through the trade route of Yanomami villages along the watershed of the Catrimani River.

Village B was desperate to find an explanation for their misfortune. In traditional Yanomami thinking, the spread of disease was due to witchcraft. The question was: Who was performing the witchcraft against village B? The conclusion centered on the newly contacted Malaxi theli. The men of village B had aggressively pursued sexual relations with Malaxi theli women during their visit and the infectious disease was seen as a logical response by the Malaxi theli shamans, who had sent their disease-carrying spirits. A group from village B canoed upstream to take their revenge on the Malaxi theli.

Somehow the Malaxi theli were able to defend themselves against the accusation of witchcraft. Instead, they turned the attention of village B to the Xili theli and convinced village B that the Xili theli were the culprits. There was enmity between the Malaxi theli and the Xili theli, who lived a two- to three-day journey to the northwest of the Malaxi theli village. Together the Malaxi theli and the group from village B attacked the Xili theli, killed five men, and took five women as captives, although one escaped before reaching the Malaxi theli village. The Malaxi theli retained one of the captives and the other three were transported down the Mucajaí to village B, where they were taken as wives and incorporated into the village.

This contact with the Malaxi theli was further strengthened in the same year when a man from village B obtained a wife from a Malaxi theli family, thereby creating affinal kinship ties between the two groups. He was not required to perform the customary period of service for the bride's family in her village but brought her immediately to village B. He was probably able to do this by gifts of trade goods obtained from the missionaries. The fusion of the surviving members of village A, the women captives, and the Malaxi theli marriage yielded a high in-migration rate of 144.

The population of village B fluctuated greatly during this phase. In 1957 it increased by 13 people due to the collapse of village A and the fusion of its survivors into village B. But decrease came in 1960 when the village suffered eight deaths due to the spread of pneumonia among a group with low resistance to it. However there was increase in the same year from the in-migration and marriage of four females, which not only mitigated some of the loss from the high mortality but also increased the percentage of females in the population to over 39 percent. During the Contact phase, in spite of the high mortality stemming from infectious disease, village B had reversed the previous downward trend of their numbers and had overcome any threat to their survival. This is contrary to the expectation of the Ribeiro model. It was due to internal and external in-migration. This case confirms a point noted in regard to village A: in considering the impact of contact experiences on indigenous groups, migration is as important as mortality, and in some cases more important, in the change of size of the population. At the same time, the level of population analysis—group, village, or faction—needs clarification in any discussion of tribal population dynamics.

## III. Linkage Phase, 1961–1981

The mission station was established in 1958 on the Mucajaí River near its confluence with the Kloknai stream. In late 1960 village B moved downstream to a newly constructed yano about 200 meters (220 yards) from the mission post. They wished to be closer to the source of trade goods and medical assistance. Otherwise, they feared that village C would obtain a monopoly on these services of the missionaries. Village B remained in this area until 1979. They began the Linkage phase with a population of 28 and by its end in 1981, the village had more than doubled to 65, which represented a high 4 percent growth rate. This section examines the reasons.

The crude birth rate rose to a very high 59.6. The total fertility rate was 8.9 live births for the average mother over her reproductive period, much the same as it had been in the Precontact phase. The major change from the two previous phases was a much better sexual balance in the population. Females constituted over 49 percent of the population by the end of the phase. Several factors were responsible for bringing about this balance. The female captives taken at the end of the previous phase were integrated into the population and bore children. The sex ratio of births was nearly balanced, with 45 percent of the births being female. The meant that as the years passed during this phase, the younger population was close to sexual balance while the older population was still in sexual imbalance. This can be seen in the percentage age-sex distribution for this phase in table 10.1.c. Finally, there was the out-migration of nine men and only two women, which further decreased the number of males relative to females in the village population.

There were 14 deaths in the 21 years of this phase. The crude death rate dropped to a relatively low 15.2. Two deaths were accidental, one from toxic food and the other from a lack of milk from a sick mother for her baby. There were three infanticides and two young men were presumed killed when they visited the Xiliana and never returned.

Three people died of pneumonia and one each from measles and malaria. In spite of intermittent contact, the infectious diseases did not take a heavy toll during this phase. In 1975 the first case of tuberculosis appeared in the village. The patient was a visitor from village C, an Aica in-migrant who died a short time later. Although both malaria and tuberculosis made their appearance in this phase, most cases did not result in mortality because of treatment by the mission medical program. During this phase, the relative isolation of the Mucajaí group from the national society protected the village from heavy exposure to the sources of infection. These factors resulted in the lowest death rate for this village in any of the phases.

There was an external in-migration of a captive woman taken in a raid from a group living in the Ajarani River watershed. The details of this raid are discussed in chapter 11 about village C, which organized the raid. There were six male and six female in-migrations for marriage. Four of these were external in-migrants from the Malaxi theli, as kinship ties with this group continued to expand. The first external out-migration from this village took place in 1980 when a young man married and remained among the Malaxi theli. Out-migration slightly exceeded in-migration because of the exodus of a number of males to other Mucajaí villages. The crude net migration rate was −4.3.

This phase saw the population explode at a 4 percent rate of increase. The population more than doubled from 28 at the beginning of the phase to 65 at the end. The population dynamics were almost the exact opposite of what they had been in the Precontact phase. Fertility was very high, primarily due to attaining a balanced sex ratio in this phase. This balance was brought about by the in-migration of a number of women of reproductive ages in this and the previous phase along with the out-migration of a number of young men for marriage and other reasons. Mortality dropped to the lowest level of all the phases owing to the protection provided by the semi-isolation of the Mucajaí villages from the national society as well as to the efforts of the missionaries' medical program. The rate of natural increase was a very high 4.4 percent, although the negative net migration slightly reduced this to a 4 percent rate of total increase.

## IV. Brazilian Phase, 1982–1995

In this phase the village's population decreased significantly, from 65 at the beginning of 1982 to 37 at the end of 1995 for a –4.2 percent rate of total decrease. This decrease wiped out a considerable portion of the increase of the previous phase. An examination of the components of change explains the decrease.

Group fertility remained high with a crude rate of 54.3. However, there was some change in the fertility structure. The total fertility rate dropped to 6.5 from 8.9 live births over the female reproductive period. There was significant decline was in the age 15 to <20 group, as can be seen in the age-specific rates. The main reason was the rise in the age at first marriage and consequent rise in the age at first birth, which was 17.4. During this phase this village was dominated by descent category D, 55.4 percent of the population. The percentage for the younger generation was even higher, as a number of the other descent categories would be female spouses and their relatives. With a number of Yanomami brothers and sisters (parallel cousins), marriage was delayed until a suitable spouse could be found. There was some compensation for the decline in individual female fertility by an increase from 18.5 percent to 22.3 percent of reproductive women in the total population.

Mortality rose significantly from the previous phase to a high crude rate of 37.7. In 1979 village B moved away from the yano close to the mission station to a location on the Kloknai stream about an hour's journey to the north of the Mucajaí River. In 1993 after several deaths, the village moved farther up the Kloknai to Kwis, a journey of three hours from the Mucajaí River. This was the area where the village had first lived in 1935–37 after fleeing Yekwana retaliation. After 1979 village B visited the mission station less frequently and made less use of the medical program. At the same time their medical needs increased as the morbidity from infectious diseases increased. Pneumonia, malaria, and tuberculosis were the most important.

Although this village was located in one of the more remote areas of the Xilixana region, a member of this village organized professional begging trips to Boa Vista, where a group wearing rags panhandled in the streets. Their efforts were successful in acquiring old clothing and various discarded Brazilian goods. Many of the deaths from unknown causes were probably due to infectious diseases.

In 1987 this village suffered the first casualty as a result of the miners' invasion of Yanomami territory as described in chapter 3. Several members of village B had in-migrated from the Malaxi theli in the early 1960s. In 1987 six men from village B were visiting their Malaxi theli relatives. This family group attacked a miners' camp to steal their guns. In the exchange of gunfire and arrows, at least six miners and four Yanomami were killed, including one of the visiting men from village B.

While the high mortality was important for the decline of the village population in this phase, the more important reason was the out-migration of 60 people from the village for a crude rate of 90.5. This was partially offset by in-migration of 21 people, for a net migration loss of 39 people or a −58.8 crude rate.

Over half of the out-migration was the fission in 1986 of 38 people in order to found village H. At that time, village B's population had reached 70 people. This meant that the traditional enclosed yano was becoming crowded. The demographic density created tensions and conflicts, which resulted in some factions leaving the village yano and building a new one.

These tensions manifest themselves in what the Yanomami call *notha wei*, meaning bad talk. It consists of gossip, scolding, or the use of loud language in an aggressive manner about any real or imagined behavior that the speaker deems unsatisfactory. Another problem arising from demographic density is *wãs thethe*, meaning noisy. The ordinary sounds of everyday family life, especially the children, become concentrated in the small confines of the yano so that the noise level becomes annoying. When the demographic density of the yano reached 70 people, the conflicts and high level of noise led to the fission of several factions from village B to found village H in 1986.

In-migration took place during this phase for many reasons. When fissioning took place in other villages, some people did not move to the new villages but in-migrated to village B, where they had relatives.

The population of village B had a high −4.2 percent rate of decrease during the Brazilian phase. The primary reason was the fission of over half the village in 1986 to found village H, an event occasioned by the crowded conditions of the yano. Another reason for the decrease was the high level of mortality due to infectious disease, partially as a result of decreased use of the mission's medical facilities and increased contact with Boa Vista.

## V. The Stages of Contact

A model of stages of contact based on the intensity of the contact was outlined in chapter 5. Following the initial contact with Brazilians in 1957 and with the missionaries in 1958, this village remained in only intermittent contact with the national society. Contrary to what the model would predict, the contact has been peaceful, with the exception of the incident with the miners while visiting the Malaxi theli. Also contrary to model, the village population would have increased if the fission of village H in 1986 had not taken place. The fusion was due to the effects of population increase. Two reasons stand out for this village being an exception to the model. The first is the quality of the missionaries' medical program. Ribeiro did not envision a service organization being able to cope effectively with the infectious diseases that accompany contact. The other factor is the areas village B used for gardens and hunting have not yet been invaded by Brazilians. The village remains one of the most traditional in the Mucajaí group.

## VI. Life Cycles of a Village over Time

An inspection of figure 10.1 shows that over sixty-six years, the population of village B can be thought of as having had three life cycles defined by abrupt and sizable changes of size of population in the years of fusion or fission. There is a cycle of decline ending in 1957 when the fusion with village A took place. This fusion initiated a cycle of growth until the fission of village H in 1986. There is another incomplete cycle since 1986.

Using such cycles as the unit of analysis and calling them life cycles, several questions arise. How long is the typical village life cycle? What is its rate of growth or decline? What is the typical size of village populations at the beginning and end of the cycles? Is it possible to derive a typology of these cycles that differentiates their demographic properties?

Guided by these questions, we can examine the cycles of village B and their properties. Classifying the individual years by cycles instead of historical phases puts greater emphasis on the quantitative structure of the population dynamics, rather than on the historical and ethnographic factors responsible for them. The first two cycles of village B illustrate contrasting phases of population decline and growth.

## A. A Cycle of Decline

The cycle of decline starts with the initial date of the demographic data in 1930 with a population of 33 and continues for 27 years to 1957, when the population had declined to 21, after which it was substantially altered by the fusion (in-migration) of village A. The most important factor for the decline of the population was the village's unbalanced sex ratio, which depressed group fertility to a very low 18.5 instead of an expected crude birth rate in the 40s or 50s. This is the lowest group fertility rate for any cycle in the study (table 18.1 is a comparative table showing the demographic values of all the cycles in the study). The cycle of decline for village B (cycle 2 in table 18.1) provides an opportunity to see how the sex ratio of the population impacts fertility.

## B. Sex Ratios of the Population

Figure 10.2 shows the annual sex ratios of village B's population during the cycles of decline and growth. The female percentage of the village population is used to express the sex ratio of the population. A variant form called the reproductive ratio is also used, showing the percentage of the village population consisting of females aged 15–44. This variant form is more acute for examining the impact of a population's age and sex structure on fertility.

Values of approximately 50 percent and 20 percent for the two sex ratios respectively express sexual balance for this type of population. Figure 10.2 shows the low levels of both ratios in the cycle of population decline, especially the reproductive ratio. Because of its impact on fertility, it was the major factor for the previously discussed situation of demographic crisis of this village.

In any one year for both ratios, a change from the previous year is the result of the differential between the male and female components of change—births, deaths, in-migrations, and out-migrations. This is a small population and consequently a single demographic event can make a noticeable change in the magnitude of the sex ratios. Beginning in 1942, there were three downward spikes (marked 1, 2, 3 in figure 10.2) in the reproductive ratio so that by 1947 it was only 4 percent. This is the lowest percentage for this ratio in any cycle of the investigation in which a village remained in existence (table 18.1). Each of the first two spikes represents a woman turning 45 years of age and therefore passing out of the reproductive population (but remaining in the sex ratio of the population). The third downward spike is the death of a woman in her 40s, which left a single reproductive female in the population.

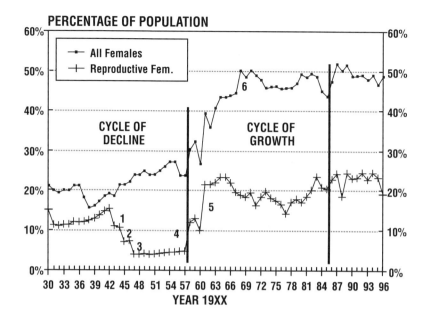

10.2. Sex ratios of Village B population.

Inspecting figure 10.2, it may seem anomalous that the sex ratio of the population is rising while the reproductive ratio is falling. Some of this is due to women reaching 45 years of age, as described. But more important in this case are the deaths and/or out-migrations of males. This increases the percentage of females in the population. It illustrates how some of these ratios can change without any gain or loss in the absolute number of females.

C. A Cycle of Growth (Cycle 5 in Table 18.1)

This is a 28-year cycle starting in 1958 after the fusion of village A into village B. It ended at the beginning of 1986 with the fission of several factions to begin village H. The cycle includes years in the Contact, Linkage, and Brazilian phases. In this cycle, village B reversed its demographic decline and grew to a total of 70 people just before the fission. The turnaround was primarily due to the reversal of the decline of the group birth rate, which reached a very high 53.4 for the cycle, overcoming a high death rate of 29.9 for the same cycle. The change from a low to high birth rate was primarily due to the population reaching sexual balance.

Figure 10.2 shows that in the cycle of growth, both ratios attained balance, although at different times. The reproductive ratio reached 20 percent early in the cycle, in 1961. It attained this balance with the help of two sharp upward spikes, which have been numbered 4 and 5. The same two spikes plus an additional one, 6, were required by the sex ratio of the population to attain the balance of 50 percent in 1969.

The fourth spike represents the fusion of village A into village B in 1958. Before the fusion, village B had no females ages 15–29, the most prolific ages within the reproductive period. There was a woman in her 40s in the 35–44 age category. She is represented in figure 10.2 by the string of 4 percent reproductive ratios in the latter part of the cycle of decline. Although village A's population was smaller and sexually unbalanced, it contributed three reproductive women aged 15, 18, and 33 to village B's population, which initiated the turnaround of the sex ratios for village B.

The fifth spike came in 1960 and brought balance to the reproductive ratio. Most of this spike involved the in-migration of the three captive women taken in the raid on the Xili theli. The remainder was due to more male than female mortality in the epidemic that preceded the raid. As can be seen from the graph, this combination produced the largest single jump (spike).

The sixth spike bringing balance to the sex ratio of the population occurred in 1967. This was due entirely to the chance loss of five males (three died and two out-migrated), which outweighed the death of a single female, the absence of female in-migration, and one birth of each sex.

The fluctuations of the sex ratios in the remaining years were mainly the chance outcomes of the sexual composition of the four components of population change. As can be seen from this analysis, the attaining of balance was not the result of a planned campaign on the part of village B but, for the most part, the result of chance events or decisions by individuals passing through their individual life cycles. The cycle illustrates the importance for a village and its factions of obtaining marriageable females in order to maintain themselves. If a village is composed of a single faction, or of multiple factions identified by the same descent category, or has a high level of female infanticide, it may incur the problem of a low reproductive and sex ratio of the population.

The reason for the low sex ratio of village B in 1930 lies in the period for which the demographic data are incomplete. This makes analysis of the question difficult. It is treated in a later chapter after more has been learned about the sex ratio of the population.

D. The Changing Sex Ratio and the Age-Sex Distribution

Figure 10.3 shows the percentage age-sex distribution of village B for each of the sixty-six years of the research period. It summarizes the analysis of

**POPULATION BY % AGE-SEX GROUPS**

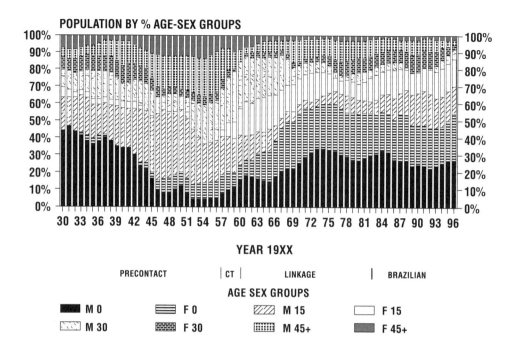

10.3. Village B age-sex distribution.

this chapter. Notice that there are no females in the younger age categories, 0–14, for the years 1930–32 and 1938–42 and, more important for fertility, in the age categories 15–29 for the years 1944–56, the years of the cycle of population decline. This contrasts with the relative size of these categories in the years of the two growth cycles dominated by the Linkage and Brazilian phases. The explosion in the female age 15 to <30 category can be seen beginning in 1957 with the fusion of the remaining population of village A. The falling fertility in the Precontact period and its high level in the Linkage and Brazilian periods can be seen in the relatively small and large percentages in the categories under age 15 for both sexes in these periods.

## VII. Summary: Sixty-six Years of a Village Population

The population dynamics of village B present a case history about the change of size of populations of Yanomami villages: a cycle of decline, a cycle of growth, and a final incomplete cycle. The Precontact and Brazilian phases were periods of population decrease although due to completely different population dynamics. The level of mortality in the Brazilian phase was higher than in the Precontact phase. The Contact phase had a slight increase of population in spite of the high mortality usually associated with first contact. The single period of substantial population growth was the Linkage phase, owing to the village's semi-isolation from Brazilian society, to the efforts of the missionaries' medical program, to the attainment of sexual balance in the population through in-migration of reproductive women and because of the progressive effect of a balanced sex ratio at birth.

# 11

# Village C

This was another of the three original villages living south of the Uraricoera River in 1930, a group who entered the Mucajaí watershed after the conflict with the Yekwana. At one point they built a yano and fields to the south of the Mucajaí River. After the epidemic of 1946, they retreated to the head-waters of the streams flowing into the Uraricoera. About 1953 they returned to the area where the Kloknai stream enters the Mucajaí River.

Village C always acted somewhat independently of villages A and B but maintained contact by visits, celebrations of the yaimo festival together, and by marital and trade exchanges. This village has had several names; the Alan bèk, Buxenawah bèk, and Bola bèk. The last means "the people of the rapids" which were near the village yano when this group first came to the Mucajaí River. The village still existed in 1999. Figure 11.1 shows the size of its population over a sixty-six-year span.

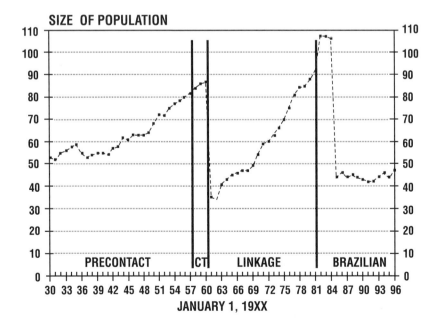

11.1. Village C population.

## I. Precontact Phase, 1930–1956

This was the largest of the three villages with 52 people in 1930, a substantial population for a Ninam yano. By the end of the Precontact phase the population had grown to 82 people (table 11.1.a,), a crude rate of total increase of 17.8 or 1.8 percent (table 11.1.b).

While the total fertility rate was a high 8.5, the crude birth rate was a moderate 33.2. The reason for the moderate group fertility was the same as seen in the two previous villages. Females constituted only 35 percent and the reproductive population only 12 percent of the village population.

But in addition to the imbalance in the sex ratio, many of its inhabitants were descended from a renowned shaman (descent category A), who had five wives in this village and one in village B. In 1930 at the beginning of the Precontact phase, about 34 percent of the village's population were descended through the male line from this shaman, and by the end of the phase in 1956, 51 percent. Among the population under twenty years of age, the proportion at the end of the phase was even higher, 62 percent. Therefore in addition to the shortage of females, the few who were present were frequently sisters or parallel cousins to the sons of the shaman. These conditions resulted in many polyandrous unions (Early and Peters 1990:104–8). Consequently, in spite of high individual fertility, the sexual imbalance and structure of kin relationships resulted in moderate group fertility.

The crude death rate was a high 20.8. Although the causes of many of the deaths are unknown, information is available about homicides. Two young sons of captive women were killed because the Mucajaí men who took their mothers as wives did not want them. This village suffered casualties during the Yekwana conflict. At the time of the Yekwana retaliatory raid with shotguns during the yaimo festival, the men from villages A and B were temporarily absent, as they had gone hunting. Only men from village C were present, along with the women and children from all the villages. The Yekwana killed four of the men, including the shaman. Also killed in the crossfire was a male infant, who was shot while in his mother's arms. In the same year there was an accidental homicide independent of the conflict.

Another significant mortality factor in this phase was ten infanticides, two males and eight females. In four of the cases, the father was not the husband. There were two cases in which the family had too many girls and two in which they apparently did not want any girls. Another infanticide was toward the end of a mother's reproductive period and she did not want another child. The reason for the remaining case is unknown.

## Table 11.1. Village C: Demographic Profile, 1930–96

### 11.1.a

| | 1930 | Precontact | 1957 | Contact | 1961 | Linkage | 1982 | Brazilian | 1996 |
|---|---|---|---|---|---|---|---|---|---|
| Population | 52 | | 82 | | 35 | | 107 | | 47 |
| Total Incr. | | 30 | | −47 | | 72 | | −60 | |
| Nat. Incr. | | 21 | | 0 | | 44 | | 13 | |
| Births | | 56 | | 12 | | 64 | | | |
| Deaths | | 35 | | 12 | | 20 | | | |
| Net Migration | | 9 | | −47 | | 28 | | −73 | |
| In-mig. | | 10 | | 4 | | 29 | | 1 | |
| Out-mig. | | 1 | | 51 | | 1 | | 74 | |

### 11.1.b — Crude Rates

| | Precontact | Contact | Linkage | Brazilian |
|---|---|---|---|---|
| Total Incr. | 17.8 | −149.0 | 55.3 | −77.5 |
| Nat. Incr. | 12.5 | 0 | 33.8 | 16.8 |
| Births | 33.2 | 38.0 | 49.2 | 43.9 |
| Deaths | 20.8 | 38.0 | 15.4 | 27.1 |
| Net Migration | 5.3 | −149.0 | 21.5 | −94.3 |
| In-mig. | 5.9 | 12.7 | 22.3 | 1.3 |
| Out-mig. | .6 | 162.0 | .8 | 95.6 |

### 11.1.c — Population: Age by Sex

| | 1930 | 1957 | 1961 | 1982 | 1996 |
|---|---|---|---|---|---|
| Population | 52 | 82 | 35 | 107 | 47 |
| Male | 36 | 51 | 22 | 54 | 25 |
| Female | 16 | 31 | 13 | 53 | 22 |
| % Female | 30.8 | 37.8 | 37.1 | 49.5 | 46.8 |

| % Age-Sex | Precontact | | Contact | | Linkage | | Brazilian | |
|---|---|---|---|---|---|---|---|---|
| | % M | % F | % M | % F | % M | % F | % M | % F |
| 0 | 22.1 | 11.9 | 21.1 | 17.7 | 16.5 | 23.8 | 29.5 | 20.5 |
| 15 | 21.8 | 6.3 | 12.4 | 5.7 | 13.4 | 14.9 | 9.6 | 14.1 |
| 30 | 15.4 | 5.8 | 16.2 | 5.4 | 10.4 | 6.0 | 9.0 | 8.5 |
| 45 | 5.9 | 10.7 | 13.0 | 8.6 | 9.2 | 5.8 | 4.4 | 4.3 |
| Total | 65.2 | 34.8 | 62.6 | 37.4 | 49.5 | 50.5 | 52.5 | 47.5 |

Table 11.2. Village C: Fertility Rates and Descent Categories

| Level of Analysis | Indicator | Age/ Sex | Phases | | | |
|---|---|---|---|---|---|---|
| | | | Precontact | Contact | Linkage | Brazilian |
| Village | Crude Birth | - | 33.2 | 38.0 | 49.2 | 43.9 |
| | Pf as % Pop. | 15–44 | 12.2 | 11.1 | 21.0 | 22.6 |
| Female Reproductive Population | Age-Specific Rates | 15 | 462 | 167 | 190 | 82 |
| | | 20 | 406 | 667 | 221 | 295 |
| | | 25 | 250 | 333 | 298 | 237 |
| | | 30 | 302 | 400 | 258 | 357 |
| | | 35 | 189 | 667 | 250 | 229 |
| | | 40 | 88 | - | 258 | - |
| | General | 15–44 | 272 | 343 | 234 | 194 |
| Avg. Female Total Fert. | | 15–44 | 8.5 | 11.2 | 7.4 | 6.0 |
| N Births | Total | | 56 | 12 | 64 | 34 |
| | | M | 29 | 5 | 30 | 17 |
| | | F | 27 | 7 | 34 | 17 |
| Village | % Descent Categories | | | | | |
| | A | | 40.8 | 50.7 | 43.0 | 43.7 |
| | B | | 4.9 | 5.0 | 11.6 | 8.0 |
| | C | | 5.9 | 3.5 | 3.3 | .9 |
| | D | | 16.2 | 18.9 | 8.5 | 5.3 |
| | E | | - | - | 2.2 | .7 |
| | F | | 7.5 | 4.1 | 3.3 | 2.1 |
| | Other/Unknown | | 5.9 | 1.8 | - | - |
| | External In-mig. | | 18.9 | 15.9 | 28.1 | 39.3 |
| | Total | | 100 | 100 | 100 | 100 |

While the levels of fertility and mortality in this phase resulted in a 12.5 (1.3 percent) rate of natural increase, a net migration rate of 5.3 brought the rate of total increase to 17.8 (1.8 percent). Most of the migration was due to the seven captives taken from the Mácu and Yekwana. Five of these were females of or near reproductive age, which helped to balance the sex ratios.

Village C had a substantial population of 52 people at the beginning of this phase and had increased to 82 by the end. In spite of the moderate level of fertility due to sexual imbalance and the structure of kin relationships, fertility surpassed mortality for a positive natural increase. The in-migration of captives offset the conflict losses and created the potential for sexual balance in the future. Had it not been for the losses during the Yekwana conflict and the infanticides, the mortality rate would have been extremely low.

Table 11.3. Village C: Mortality Rates

| Level of Analysis | Indicator | Age/ Sex | Precontact | Contact | Linkage | Brazilian |
|---|---|---|---|---|---|---|
| | | | | Phases | | |
| Village | Crude Death | | 20.8 | 38.0 | 15.4 | 27.1 |
| Age Groups | Age-specific Rates | 0 | 179 | 222 | 156 | 265 |
| | | 1 | 12 | 35 | 11 | 30 |
| | | 5 | 5 | - | 6 | 7 |
| | | 10 | 10 | 13 | 4 | - |
| | | 20 | 9 | - | 4 | 10 |
| | | 30 | 16 | - | 6 | 21 |
| | | 40 | 5 | 48 | 9 | 31 |
| | | 50 | 36 | 39 | - | - |
| | | 60 | 35 | 200 | 67 | 67 |
| | | 70+ | - | - | - | 333 |
| N Deaths | Total | | 35 | 12 | 20 | 21 |
| | | M | 18 | 5 | 12 | 8 |
| | | F | 17 | 7 | 8 | 13 |
| N Reasons | Infectious Disease | M | 1 | 2 | 8 | 5 |
| | | F | - | 3 | 4 | 9 |
| | Non-infect. Disease | M | 1 | - | 1 | 2 |
| | | F | - | - | - | 1 |
| | Infanticide | M | 2 | - | 1 | 1 |
| | | F | 8 | 1 | 3 | 3 |
| | Homicide | M | 7 | - | 1 | - |
| | | F | 1 | - | - | - |
| | Accidents | M | 1 | - | - | - |
| | | F | - | - | - | - |
| | Unknown | M | 6 | 3 | 1 | - |
| | | F | 8 | 3 | 1 | - |

## II. Contact Phase, 1957–1960

During the first part of this phase, villages B and C remained in the locations where they had been before the downstream trips. The establishment of the mission station in late 1958 caused both villages to move. The mission originally consisted of an airfield and two thatched buildings serving as residences for the three or four missionary personnel and as a dispensary. The small complex was located on the Mucajaí River just upstream from the confluence with the Kloknai stream, where the Mucajaí River divided to flow around four islands (Early and Peters 1990:32–34). During the late

Table 11.4. Village C: Migration Rates

| Level of Analysis | Indicator | Age/Sex | Precontact I | Precontact O | Precontact NM | Contact I | Contact O | Contact NM | Linkage I | Linkage O | Linkage NM | Brazilian I | Brazilian O | Brazilian NM |
|---|---|---|---|---|---|---|---|---|---|---|---|---|---|---|
| Village | Crude Rate | | 5.9 | 0.6 | 5.3 | 12.7 | 161.6 | -149.0 | 22.3 | 0.8 | 21.5 | 1.3 | 95.6 | -94.3 |
| | External | | 4.2 | - | 4.2 | 6.3 | - | 6.3 | 16.3 | - | 16.3 | - | 10.3 | -10.3 |
| | Internal | | 1.8 | 0.6 | 1.2 | 6.3 | 161.6 | -155.4 | 6.1 | 0.8 | 5.3 | 1.3 | 85.3 | -84.0 |
| Age Groups | Age-specific Rates | 0 | 5 | - | 5 | 8 | 163 | -154 | 23 | - | 23 | - | 85 | -85 |
| | | 15 | 13 | 2 | 11 | - | 175 | -175 | 30 | - | 30 | 5 | 98 | -93 |
| | | 30 | 3 | - | 3 | 29 | 147 | -118 | 19 | - | 19 | - | 96 | -96 |
| | | 45 | - | - | - | 15 | 162 | -147 | 10 | 5 | 5 | - | 148 | -148 |
| N Migration Total | | M | 10 | 1 | 9 | 4 | 51 | -47 | 29 | 1 | 28 | 1 | 74 | -73 |
| | | F | 5 | 1 | 4 | 3 | 32 | -29 | 15 | 1 | 14 | - | 38 | -38 |
| | | | 5 | - | 5 | 1 | 19 | -18 | 14 | - | 14 | 1 | 36 | -35 |
| Reasons: External Mig. | Marriage | M | - | - | - | 1 | - | - | 4 | - | - | - | 2 | - |
| | | F | - | - | - | 1 | - | - | 3 | - | - | - | 1 | - |
| | Captive | M | 2 | - | - | - | - | - | - | - | - | - | - | - |
| | | F | 5 | - | - | - | - | - | 1 | - | - | - | - | - |
| | Avoid Conflict | M | - | - | - | - | - | - | 6 | - | - | - | - | - |
| | | F | - | - | - | - | - | - | 4 | - | - | - | - | - |
| | Family | M | - | - | - | - | - | - | - | - | - | - | 1 | - |
| | | F | - | - | - | - | - | - | - | - | - | - | 2 | - |
| | Unknown | M | - | - | - | - | - | - | 1 | - | - | - | - | - |
| | | F | - | - | - | - | - | - | 2 | - | - | - | 2 | - |
| Reasons: Internal Mig. | Marriage | M | 2 | 1 | - | - | - | - | - | 1 | - | - | - | - |
| | | F | - | - | - | - | - | - | - | - | - | - | - | - |
| | Fission-Fusion | M | - | - | - | - | 32 | - | 2 | - | - | - | 35 | - |
| | | F | - | - | - | - | 19 | - | 4 | - | - | - | 30 | - |
| | Avoid Conflict | F | - | - | - | - | - | - | - | - | - | - | 1 | - |
| | Family | M | - | - | - | - | - | - | 2 | - | - | - | - | - |
| | Unknown | M | - | - | - | 2 | - | - | - | - | - | - | - | - |

Precontact phase, village C lived on the north side of the Mucajaí River. After contact with the Brazilians in 1957, they moved to the south side. The main yano was located about 130 meters (142 yards) from the river. They also had a secondary yano in some newer gardens about a three-and-a-half-hour walk farther south. When the missionaries arrived by canoe in 1958, villages B and C were having a yaimo festival at the latter location (Early and Peters 1990:8). In 1959 village C moved back to the north bank of the Mucajaí River to a location a few hundred meters from the mission. They wanted to satisfy their curiosity about the missionaries' way of life as well as to monopolize the missionaries' supply of trade goods and be near the dispensary.

Village C started this phase with a population of 82 people. Four years later, it had decreased to 35 for an extremely high 149 rate of total decrease. The components of change explain the decline.

Fertility continued moderate with a crude rate of 38, while the total fertility rate was a very high 11.2. (This was based on only 12 births.) Again the shortage of females and the Yanomami brother-sister relationships in the population were restraining group fertility in spite of high individual fertility. Females were only 38 percent and reproductive females only 11 percent of the village population during this phase.

There was a high crude death rate of 38, the same as the crude birth rate. As a consequence, there was no natural increase of the population during this phase. Although this village took part in the second and third down-stream trips to trade with the Brazilians, the trips resulted in few deaths. However in 1960 five people died from pneumonia acquired either from members of village B or from the Malaxi theli when they visited village C. There were three additional deaths that year, including one from snakebite.

At the beginning of this phase in 1957 village C had 82 people and by 1960 there were 87. The yano became crowded, causing the same kinds of problems seen in village B—excessive noise and gossip along with the conflict they generated. In 1960 these conditions led to the fissioning of 51 people, 59 percent of the village, to initiate village D. This fission is discussed in more detail in the next chapter as it gives insight into village factions and how they structure the fissioning process.

Again the population dynamics of this village are contrary to those predicted by the Ribeiro model. Until the fission in 1960, which was occasioned by population increase, the population increased rather than decreased. Important differences from the model were the peaceful nature of the contact, the absence of land invasions, and the protection provided by the missionary medical program.

## III. Linkage Phase, 1961–1981

During this phase, the missionaries and the Yanomami villages formed their own regional community in this remote area, partially isolated from other Yanomami communities and rural Brazil. Village C grew rapidly from a population of 35 to 107, an explosive 55.3 (5.5 percent) rate of total increase.

Group fertility rose, as shown by the high crude birth rate of 49.2. This rise was due to a balancing of the village's sex ratio, as seen in the increase of females to 50.5 percent and of reproductive females to 21 percent of the village population. The balance was brought about by a female majority in all four components of change. As the years passed, the younger population was coming into sexual balance while imbalance remained only among the older population. This can be seen in the age-sex distribution for this phase in table 11.1.c. The seven external in-migrants for marriage mitigated the problem of Yanomami brother-sister relationships between so many of the younger generation due to the dominance of descent category A.

There was a moderate crude death rate of 15.4. Infectious diseases, especially tuberculosis and whooping cough, were the primary causes. Tuberculosis was first diagnosed in 1966 by a Roraima physician in a young man who had been working on the Brazilian farms on the lower Mucajaí. The patient underwent treatment both at the mission and in Boa Vista and recovered. His mother was also treated in 1972 and recovered. In 1975 the incidence of tuberculosis appeared to increase. An Aica in-migrant to village D was discovered to have tuberculosis while visiting village B. He was moved to village C, where he was cared for by his aunt until he died. The aunt was also an Aica in-migrant, married to one of the village headman. She remarked on the similarity of her nephew's symptoms to those of her mother, who had previously died in an Aica village. The missionaries noticed that tuberculosis began to appear with greater frequency among families with marriage ties to the Aica and Palimi theli. Both of these groups had more frequent contacts with Brazilians, from whom they had contracted the disease.

Other sources of mortality were four infanticides, three by unmarried widows who rejected the infants because there was no male to provide food for them. There was a homicide in 1967; a hunter became separated from his party and met some unfriendly Aica. He killed several of the Aica but was shot with an arrow while fleeing.

In 1979 widespread sickness struck the village. There were two deaths, including one of the headmen. One faction of the village temporarily moved to two islands in the Mucajaí River. There was suspicion of witchcraft due to evil spirits sent by shamans from outside the Mucajaí group. The islands were considered a safer place to live during such times because the spirits bringing sickness cannot cross water. When the sickness subsided, this faction rejoined the rest of the village in the single yano on the mainland upriver from the mission.

There was substantial in-migration with a crude rate of 22.3 and almost no out-migration. In 1960 Peters, accompanied by a few Mucajaí men, visited the Palimi theli to help with the construction of a landing field for the Brazilian Air Force. The Palimi theli lived on the Uraricoera River northwest of the mission station, a six-day trip by land and water. As a result of this trip, village C people developed marital and exchange relationships with the Palimi theli. During this phase there were seven in-migrants for marriage from this group, four males and three females. A serious conflict arose within the Palimi theli community. Because of the affinal bonds created by the marriages, two Palimi theli families totaling ten people in-migrated to village C to escape the conflict.

The explosive growth of this phase was due to several factors. For the first time there was a high level of group fertility due to a balanced sex ratio and a declining incidence of Yanomami brother-sister relationships. The latter was due to the in-migration for marriage from the Palimi theli as well as from other Mucajaí villages. Mortality reached the lowest level of all the phases due to the partial isolation from Brazilian society and the medical efforts of the missionaries. In-migration more than offset the decrease from mortality. This phase was distinctive for village C in that group fertility and in-migration reached the highest levels of all the phases while mortality reached its lowest level.

## IV. Brazilian Phase, 1982–1995

Village C lived in several successive yanos in the vicinity of the mission station for a few years and then moved to a location a half-hour walk from it. In 1986 the village moved some distance up the Mucajaí River, a canoe trip of an hour and a half away. Sometime before the death of the village's headman, he advised his wife about the location of the village. They were not to return to the vicinity of the mission post because he believed that people became ill there. In 1984 the village fissioned. Following the fission, village C moved to an island in the Mucajaí River and remained there until 1991, when they built a new yano on the mainland about three hours upriver from the mission station.

Since that time, village C members have traveled to the mission station only to receive medicine or trade goods. The visits are usually hurried and specific, in contrast to the visits of villages E and G. Village C tends to be more traditional than some of the other Mucajaí villages. They have fewer manufactured goods. In the other villages women are not seen bare breasted among non-Yanomami, while the women of village C are less likely to use any covering. From a population of 107 at the beginning of this phase, there was a decrease to 47 at the end of the phase, a 77.5 (7.8 percent) rate of total decrease. Again, the components tell the story.

There was a slight decrease of fertility to a crude rate of 43.9, still a high level. Total fertility decreased to 6. The age-specific rates show that the drop was primarily in ages 15 to <20. The fertility histories indicate a rise in the average age of mothers at first birth to 20.8. A contributing factor is a continuing problem of the number of Yanomami brother-sister relationships due to descent from the previously mentioned shaman (descent category A). At the beginning of 1996, 66 percent of the population under 20 years of age were his descendants through the male lines. Marriage was hindered by other factors. There was a slight shortage of males relative to females in the sex ratio of the age 15 to 29 population, as seen in table 11.1.c. In this village, there was a strong-willed grandmother who did not want her granddaughters to leave the village. Every time a man from outside the village began bride service for one of the granddaughters, she made life so miserable for him that he would leave the village and find a wife elsewhere. The combination of these factors yielded the highest age at first birth in any of the villages.

The crude death rate rose to a high level of 27.1. Infectious diseases—pneumonia, malaria, tuberculosis, and dysentery—were the main problems. There were two infanticides. One was the child of a widow. The father of the other infant was not the husband of the mother and consequently he rejected the infant.

The main factor for the large decrease in this phase was out-migration. In 1984 the village population reached 104 people. Tensions from the excessive noise and gossip reached the point that all agreed a split was desirable. Sixty-five people, 63 percent of the village, fissioned and founded village G.

This was a phase of population decrease for village C. As a result of explosive growth during the previous phase, the population had become too large for the village yano. After the fission, there was continued high fertility, but growth of the village was slowed by high mortality from infectious diseases.

## V. Stages of Contact

Village C has had only intermittent contact with the national society, similar to that of village B. All contacts have been peaceful and the group has benefited from the missionary medical program. For these reasons and contrary to what would be expected in Ribeiro's model, including his alternative intermittent phase, the population has continued to increase. Up to 1999 there had been no invasion by Brazilians of the areas used for gardens and hunting. The traditional culture remained intact.

## VI. Village C and Its Life Cycles

Like village B, village C also had three life cycles, as seen in figure 11.1. There were two cycles of growth and an incomplete one of short-term duration. The two cycles of growth further illustrate the role of the sexual composition of a population for its growth.

### A. A Cycle of Growth (Cycle 4 in Table 18.1)

The first growth cycle of village C lasted thirty years from 1930 to 1959, including the Precontact and Contact phases of the village history. It began with a village population of 53 and ended with 86. As in village B (fig. 10.2) but to a much lesser extent, figure 11.2 shows that the first cycle was marked by sexual imbalance, which depressed fertility and helped to prolong the length of the cycle. During the cycle, females were 35.3 percent of the village population while the reproductive population comprised 12.1 percent. There was a downward trend in the ratio of the reproductive population with an average of about eight women a year during the last ten years of the cycle. Important in the decline was the chance occurrence of seven male and no female births for the years 1948 and 1949. In spite of the sexual imbalance, group fertility rate was 33, higher than the 18.5 of village B but significantly less that an expected rate in the 40s and 50s. This level of fertility overcame the 20.6 rate of mortality to make this a cycle of growth. When the population reached 87, there was a fission of 32 males and 19 females to form village D.

### B. Another Cycle of Growth (Cycle 6 in Table 18.1)

Following the fission, the second cycle of village C began with a population of 35 in 1961 and ended 23 years later when the population reached 105 and some factions fissioned to form village G. This cycle includes the Linkage phase and the first few years of the Brazilian phase. Since the cycle mostly reflects the conditions of the Linkage phase, it had an explosive 4.5

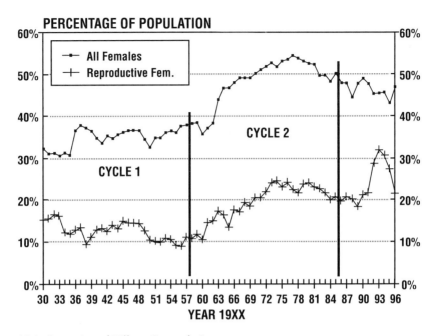

11.2. Sex ratios of Village C population.

percent rate of total increase. In the first part of the 1970s the village attained sexual balance. Figure 11.2 shows a jump in the female proportion of the population ratio in 1961. This was due to three male deaths offset by only one male birth, with no female births or deaths. From 1962 to 1966 there were seven female births and only two male ones, and during this same period there were four female in-migrants and only two males. The sex ratio of the population reached 50 percent in 1970 and has fluctuated around this level to the end of the research period.

C. A Short-Term Cycle (Cycle 9 in Table 18.1)

In the eleven years of this cycle, all within the Brazilian phase, the population has increased by only three people as high mortality restrained growth. The large jump in the sex ratio of the reproductive population to over 30 percent is due to the chance occurrence of three girls turning 15 years of age in 1991–92 while no women turned 45 in the same period.

## VII. Summary

Diversity of historical conditions gave rise to a diversity of population dynamics in each period in village C. This diversity is reflected in the changing age-sex distribution of the village population over the sixty-six years shown in figure 11.3.

In the Precontact phase the village had depressed group fertility along with high individual fertility. There was a shortage of females for marriage due to an unbalanced sex ratio, a problem intensified by the large number of Yanomami brother-sister relationships. However, the problem never threatened the village's survival as in village B. There was a moderate increase of the population in the Precontact phase as a result of fertility being higher than mortality, and net migration was positive owing mostly to the taking of captive women and their children.

High mortality was the demographic problem of the Contact phase, along with a continuing shortage of females. However, the level of mortality was relatively moderate compared to that in other contact situations. It did not outstrip fertility and consequently never threatened the continuation of the village.

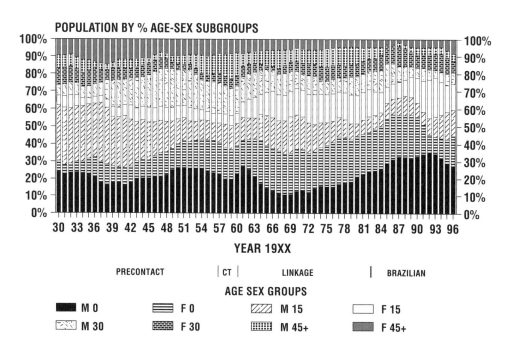

11.3. Village C age-sex distribution.

The Linkage phase saw the most favorable demographic conditions for growth and sexual balance of all the phases, with high fertility, low mortality, and significant in-migration, especially for marriage and refuge from Palimi theli conflict. The result was explosive growth and a balanced sex ratio as seen in figures 11.1 and 11.2.

The main problem of the Brazilian phase was high mortality from infectious disease. Although mortality rose to a high level, it was surpassed by high fertility to maintain natural increase.

These factors contributed to population growth in all the phases and by themselves would have resulted in a very large village of almost 160 people. A population of this magnitude would have been too large to sustain over an extended period because of the ecological pressures on a small area and limitations on the size of the closed yano. It also would have increased the problems arising from demographic density. Consequently village growth was regulated by the fissions of 51 people in 1960 and 65 people in 1983 to found villages D and G. In the following chapter we look more closely at the social structure of this village and these fissions.

# 12

# Village C: Factions and Fission

Village C having grown to 87 people at the beginning of 1960, the factional leaders decided there should be a fissioning because of the conflictive situations arising from the demographic density. This chapter is an examination of this fission and the social structure behind it. The discussion illustrates the roles of kinship, descent, and factional leadership, building on the chapter 4 introduction of these aspects of Yanomami culture.

## I. Inhabitants of Village C Prior to the Fission

Table 12.1 is a list of the inhabitants of village C at the time of the fission. They were divided into five factions (I to V) subdivided by family groups (the numbers after the roman numeral of the faction).

The table designates the headman or headmen (H) of each faction. As noted in chapter 4, this is a *primus inter pares* role, not one of defined authority. There were six of them, with faction I having two coheadmen. Of these factional leaders, five were brothers (factions I, II, III, V), sons of the renowned Ninam shaman (ID 87 in the Father column in table 12.1) killed in the conflict with the Yekwana. The table shows by an A in the descent column those who take their patrilineal descent category from this person, 55 percent (47/86) of the village population. Since it is the descent category of the dominant males of factions I, II, III, and V, these factions are identified with this patrilineal line. As previously noted, not everyone in the faction has this descent category since membership in a faction does not change an individual's descent category. All those with the same descent category in the same generation are Yanomami brothers and sisters to each other (siblings and parallel cousins). The table illustrates how the sexual imbalance in the village was not simply a question of an unbalanced sex ratio but also of the further restriction arising from the types of kin relationships within the unbalanced ratio.

The table also illustrates the importance of the female captives during the Precontact period for the population dynamics of the village. These captives have been marked with C before their identification number in the table.

**Table 12.1. The Factions and Families of Village C at the 1960 Fission**

| ID | Sex | Age | Descent | Father | Mother | ID | Sex | Age | Descent | Father | Mother |
|----|-----|-----|---------|--------|--------|----|-----|-----|---------|--------|--------|
| *Faction I, Family 1* | | | | | | *Faction II, Family 2* | | | | | |
| H1 | M | 47 | A | 87 | 100 | 44 | M | 33 | A | 36 | 37 |
| C2 | F | 46 | H | 99 | 99 | 45 | M | 40 | A | 90 | 37 |
| H3 | M | 44 | A | 87 | 100 | 46 | M | 34 | A | 90 | 37 |
| 4 | F | 33 | F | 91 | 19 | 47 | F | 37 | H | 99 | 99 |
| 5 | M | 27 | H | 99 | C2 | 48 | M | 6 | H | 99 | 47 |
| 6 | M | 25 | A | 3 | C2 | | | | | | |
| 7 | M | 17 | A | 1 | 4 | *Faction III, Family 1* | | | | | |
| 8 | F | 16 | A | 1 | 4 | H49 | M | 51 | A | 87 | 105 |
| 9 | F | 14 | A | 3 | C2 | 50 | M | 37 | A | 90 | 37 |
| 10 | M | 11 | A | 1 | 4 | 51 | M | 37 | A | 87 | 106 |
| 11 | M | 10 | A | 1 | 4 | C52 | F | 35 | H | 99 | C85 |
| 12 | F | 9 | A | 1 | 4 | 53 | M | 19 | A | 49 | C52 |
| 13 | M | 9 | A | 3 | C2 | 54 | M | 17 | A | 49 | C52 |
| 14 | F | 2 | A | 1 | 4 | 55 | F | 13 | A | 49 | C52 |
| 15 | M | 0 | A | 1 | 4 | 56 | M | 10 | A | 49 | C52 |
| 16 | M | 40 | A | 87 | 102 | 57 | F | 7 | A | 49 | C52 |
| | | | | | | 58 | F | 4 | A | 49 | C52 |
| *Faction I, Family 2* | | | | | | 59 | M | 0 | A | 50 | C52 |
| 17 | M | 44 | D | 92 | 103 | | | | | | |
| 18 | M | 30 | A | 36 | 37 | *Faction IV, Family 1* | | | | | |
| 19 | F | 50 | C | 93 | 104 | H60 | M | 49 | D | 97 | 103 |
| 20 | M | 30 | F | 91 | 19 | 61 | M | 45 | D | 98 | 107 |
| 21 | M | 13 | D | 17 | 19 | 62 | F | 30 | A | 83 | 108 |
| 22 | M | 10 | D | 17 | 19 | 63 | M | 16 | D | 60 | 62 |
| 23 | F | 7 | A | 18 | 19 | 64 | M | 14 | D | 60 | 62 |
| | | | | | | 65 | M | 12 | D | 60 | 62 |
| *Faction I, Family 3* | | | | | | 66 | F | 9 | D | 60 | 62 |
| 24 | F | 55 | C | 93 | 104 | 67 | F | 6 | D | 60 | 62 |
| 25 | M | 34 | B | 94 | 24 | 68 | M | 2 | D | 60 | 62 |
| 26 | F | 32 | B | 94 | 24 | 69 | F | 0 | D | 60 | 62 |
| 27 | M | 15 | A | 95 | 26 | 70 | M | 51 | A | 87 | 110 |
| 28 | M | 11 | H | 96 | 26 | | | | | | |
| 29 | F | 9 | H | 96 | 26 | *Faction V, Family 1* | | | | | |
| 30 | M | 5 | H | 96 | 26 | H71 | M | 51 | A | 87 | 100 |
| 31 | F | 2 | H | 96 | 26 | 72 | M | 43 | F | 98 | 109 |
| | | | | | | C73 | F | 36 | H | 99 | 99 |
| *Faction I, Family 4* | | | | | | 74 | M | 20 | A | 71 | C73 |
| 32 | M | 38 | B | 94 | 24 | 75 | M | 18 | A | 71 | C73 |
| 33 | F | 18 | A | 3 | C2 | 76 | M | 16 | A | 71 | C73 |
| 34 | M | 3 | B | 32 | 33 | 77 | F | 13 | A | 71 | C73 |
| 35 | M | 0 | B | 32 | 33 | 78 | M | 10 | A | 71 | C73 |
| | | | | | | 79 | M | 6 | A | 71 | C73 |
| *Faction II, Family 1* | | | | | | 80 | F | 3 | A | 71 | C73 |
| H36 | M | 55 | A | 87 | 100 | 81 | M | 0 | A | 71 | C73 |
| 37 | F | 56 | D | 88 | 101 | 82 | M | 65 | F | 98 | 109 |
| 38 | F | 22 | D | 89 | 24 | 83 | M | 64 | A | 87 | 110 |
| 39 | F | 18 | D | 17 | 19 | | | | | | |
| 40 | M | 7 | A | 36 | 38 | *Faction V, Family 2* | | | | | |
| 41 | F | 3 | A | 36 | 39 | 84 | M | 51 | H | 99 | 108 |
| 42 | F | 1 | A | 36 | 38 | C85 | F | 63 | H | 99 | 99 |
| 43 | F | 0 | A | 36 | 38 | 86 | M | 22 | H | 84 | C85 |

They are the wives of three of the six factional headmen (I, III, V) and the mothers of the majority of the younger generation of these factions.

## A. Faction I

This faction was led by two brothers (ID 1 and 3 in table 12.1—all individuals are identified in this way in the text to follow). They were in a group marriage with their two wives (2, a Mácu captive, and 4). A man unmarried at this time (16) stayed with this group but was not a family member.

Three other family groups belonged to this faction. Family I-2 was a polyandrous group composed of the primary husband (17), a secondary husband (18), the wife (19), and the children. The year following the fission, the primary husband died; the secondary husband became primary and the family remained with faction I. Family I-3 was centered around a widow (24) whose husband had died of pneumonia. Her daughter (26) had also lost her husband. Her son (32) was married to a daughter (33) of one of the coheadmen (3) of the faction and this family (I-4) remained with faction I. Due to these affinal bonds, the widowed mother (24) looked to faction I for assistance.

## B. Faction II

A polygynous family, this was led by the village shaman (36) with his three wives (37, 38, 39). The shaman status made this the most prestigious faction in the village. A son (44) of the shaman (36) and of the shaman's oldest wife (37) had married an in-migrating Palimi theli (47). She brought a young son (48) with her from a previous marriage. Her secondary husbands (45 and 46) were half brothers of the primary husband (44).

## C. Faction III

This faction was a single polyandrous family led by the primary husband (49) and the wife (52). The secondary husbands were a brother (51) and nephew (50) of the headman (49).

## D. Faction IV

Also a single polyandrous family led by the primary husband (60) and the wife (62), this faction included a secondary husband (61) and an older unmarried man (70) lived with the family. In spite of an age difference of forty-two years, he was betrothed to the oldest daughter (66). Such age differences are not uncommon in Yanomami unions (Early and Peters 1990:108–14; see appendix of the present work for a corrected version of table 9.3 on page 109 of that reference).

E. Faction V

This faction had two family groups. The first was a polyandrous family with a wife (73) who was captured from the Yekwana in 1935. There was a primary husband (71), who was headman of the faction, and a secondary husband (72). Two older men lived with the family, one a widower brother (83) of the headman and the other (82) a friend.

The mother (85) of the other family (V-2) in this faction was another Yekwana captive from the 1935 conflict. She remained a close friend of the captive mother (73) in V-1. Their friendship was an important bond integrating the two families into a single faction. The husband of family V-2 (84) died a year later. His widow (85) and son (86) joined family V-1. The son (86) began bride service for his future wife (77), the oldest daughter in the family V-1.

## II. Fissions

The fissioning from village C lasted about three years before the factional composition of the villages stabilized. It involved movement back and forth between the villages and an additional fission.

### A. The First Fission, 1960

During 1960 before the time of the fission, there were four births, seven deaths, and two in-migrations. The demographic density of the village yano had reached 86 people. The excessive noise, gossiping, and resulting conflict led to the fission (see description in chapter 10). Faction I, the largest, with its four families totaling 35 people, remained in the old yano. Factions II, III, IV, and V with 51 people occupied a new yano next to the old one. This was the beginning of village D. Factional membership had determined the composition of the fissioning group.

This arrangement turned out to be temporary. After a year, family I-1 led by the shaman (36) moved back to the old yano and rejoined village C. The exact reason for the move is unknown, although the desire of his two younger wives (38, 39) to be in the same yano as their mothers (24, 19) and siblings was an important influence. However, not all of family I-1 returned. The shaman's eldest wife (37) was growing old. He had put her aside when he took the younger wives (38, 39). The eldest wife (37) and her three grown sons (40, 41, 46) remained in village D, where they joined another son/ brother (50), who was the secondary husband of the polyandrous family comprising faction III. Upon the death of the headman (49) of faction III, this son (50) became its headman.

## B. Move of Village D

Village D was initially composed of factions III, IV, V, and half of II. The yano of village D remained next to the yano of village C for over a year. At that time, there was concern about the crowded conditions at the mission station, where the yanos of all three villages were now located. Game in the area was decreasing and sanitation was becoming a problem. The villagers began to discuss the difficulties, and the missionaries encouraged the people to spread out. The mission never had a policy of encouraging the Mucajaí people to live around the mission post. Villages B and C had moved of their own accord to the vicinity of the mission station because of their desire for trade goods and medical assistance. Neither of these required the villages to be located at the mission. But fear that one village might acquire a monopoly on the goods and services of the missionaries drew both of them. Village D decided to move downriver to where the Kloknai stream empties into the Mucajaí River, about a half-hour walk from the mission station.

## C. The Second Move of Village D and the Second Fission

Village D remained at the confluence of the river and stream for about a year. Then faction III found an area of fertile soils about 10 km (6 mi.) farther downriver and decided to move there. This was a journey of a half-day canoe paddle from the mission station. Factions IV and V at first did not wish to move this distance from the mission post and fissioned off from village D. Faction III, including a few new members from family II-1, moved downstream and became the only faction constituting village D. Factions IV and V built a new yano at the site where they had been living and initiated village E.

## D. Another Move

Factions IV and V stayed together as village E about a year. Members of faction IV had close friendship ties to faction III, which was in village D. They found these ties stronger than their desire to be a short distance from the mission post. Faction IV left village E and rejoined faction III in village D at their downriver location. The bonds between these two factions grew over the years as they entered into arrangements of exchanging their daughters as wives. This was possible as the headman (60) of faction IV was the only factional leader who had a different patrilineal descent category than the leaders of all the other factions (see table 12.1)

This left village E composed of a single faction, V. By this time, the husband of family V-2 (84) had died and his son (86) had begun bride service to the parents (71, 73) of V-1 to marry their eldest daughter (77). Upon the death of his father-in-law (71), the son-in-law (86) became the headman of the village and faction V.

Thus we can see how in the fissioning process the factions originally comprising village C founded new villages. Each of these factions continued with its own demographic history, in most cases increasing in size and then undergoing factional fissions while usually remaining in the village. There are some instances of factions losing members owing to deaths and marriages. These factions usually disbanded and their members joined other factions. The chapters to follow continue to describe the population dynamics at the village level, for the villages formed by fissioning, but these dynamics are partially determined by the population dynamics of the individual factions.

## III. Summary

This chapter is a case history illustrating the role of factions in social structure of tribal villages and the process of fissioning. We have presented a detailed picture of the composition of village C at the time of its first fission. The entire population by sex, age, and descent category is listed along with the faction to which each individual belonged. When fissions take place, the structure of factions and the role of kinship are brought to light. Understanding the outlines of the factions of village C will throw light on the accounts of the villages still to be described. All these villages except one (village H) originated directly or indirectly from the fission of village C in 1960.

# 13

# Village D

This village began in late 1960 by fission from village C. As described, at first the yano of the new village was next to the yano of village C. Around 1963, as also already noted, village D moved away from the mission post to build a new yano about a half-hour walk downriver from the mission post, where the Kloknai stream empties into the Mucajaí River. They stayed there for almost a year and then constructed the village yano about 10 km (6 mi.) farther downstream, where they found some fertile fields. They remained at this site until 1983.

## I. Factional Composition of the Village

As we saw in chapter 12, factions II, III, IV, and V with 51 people (fig. 13.1) were the original founders of village D. The fissioning process was spread

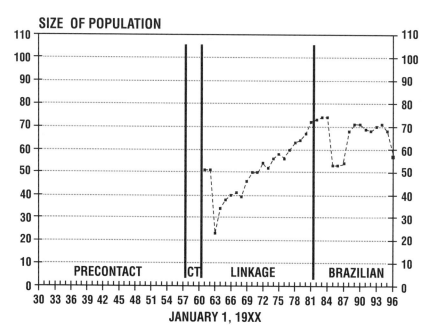

13.1. Village D population.

out over several years as factions moved back and forth between villages before settling in one of them. The year after the fission, half of faction II departed from village D and returned to village C. The following year factions IV and V fissioned from village D to form village E. But after a year, faction IV left village E and returned to village D. By 1964 village D was composed of 34 people, members of factions III and IV.

## II. Linkage Phase, 1961–1981

There was a total increase of 22 people for a crude rate of 20.5 (2.1 percent) during this phase (table 13.1.a, b).

Group fertility was high, as shown by a 44.6 crude birth rate. Total fertility was 6.9. There was a slight sexual imbalance. Females constituted 42.8 percent and reproductive females 18.6 percent of the village population.

Mortality was moderate with a crude rate of 18.6. Village D had established marital relations with the downriver Aica village, leading to the in-migration of a number of Aica. The Aica had been in contact with Brazilians for several decades and a number of them were suffering from tuberculosis; as mentioned, an Aica in-migrant from village D had spread tuberculosis to villages B and C. In 1975 a village D mother and daughter who were Aica in-migrants died. The missionaries treated other family members.

There was substantial in-migration and out-migration during this phase. Most of the out-migration from village D and some of the in-migration took place in the first few years while the fissioning process was stabilizing. Also important was the relationship of village D with the Aica village. The Aica came to the Mucajaí River to escape the increased disease associated with the Brazilian colonization of the lower Apiaú River (Ramos 1995:274 and see chapter 2, this volume). An Aica village, Flexal, was located downriver and developed marital ties with village D. There were six Aica in-migrants to village D during this phase.

There were also six in-migrants taken in a raid on the Hewakema, a Yanomami village on a tributary of the Ajarani River. An Aica brother-in-law of the headman of village D (49 in table 12.1) was killed by the Ajarani group in a raid on an Aica village. Sometime later a woman of village B died suddenly. A visitor from the Ajarani village claimed he had performed witchcraft that had killed her. He also insulted the people of village D. Some men from village D, assisted by relatives and friends from villages B, C, and E, decided to retaliate by raiding the Ajarani village. During the raid in 1968, the Mucajaí group killed eight men and seized four young women

Table 13.1. Village D: Demographic Profile, 1961–86

| 13.1.a | 1961 | Linkage | | 1982 | Brazilian | | 1996 |
|---|---|---|---|---|---|---|---|
| Population | 51 | | | 73 | | | 57 |
| Total Incr. | | | 22 | | | –16 | |
| Nat. Incr. | | | 28 | | | 18 | |
|   Births | | 48 | | | 46 | | |
|   Deaths | | 20 | | | 28 | | |
| Net Migration | | | –6 | | | –34 | |
|   In-mig. | | 26 | | | 19 | | |
|   Out-mig. | | 32 | | | 53 | | |

| 13.1.b. | | Crude Rates | | | | | |
|---|---|---|---|---|---|---|---|
| Total Incr. | | | 20.5 | | | –17.2 | |
| Nat. Incr. | | | 26.0 | | | 19.4 | |
|   Births | | 44.6 | | | 49.5 | | |
|   Deaths | | 18.6 | | | 30.1 | | |
| Net Migration | | | –5.6 | | | –36.6 | |
|   In-mig. | | 24.2 | | | 20.5 | | |
|   Out-mig. | | 29.8 | | | 57.1 | | |

| 13.1.c. | | Population: Age by Sex | | | | | |
|---|---|---|---|---|---|---|---|
| Population | 51 | | | 73 | | | 57 |
|   Male | 32 | | | 43 | | | 33 |
|   Female | 19 | | | 30 | | | 24 |
|   % Female | 37.3 | | | 41.1 | | | 42.1 |
| %Age-Sex | | %M | %F | | %M | %F | |
|   0 | | 23.7 | 19.8 | | 28.0 | 17.9 | |
|   15 | | 12.5 | 11.5 | | 15.2 | 11.7 | |
|   30 | | 8.3 | 7.1 | | 6.9 | 9.1 | |
|   45 | | 12.7 | 4.4 | | 7.4 | 3.7 | |
| Total | | 57.2 | 42.8 | | 57.5 | 42.5 | |

along with four of their children (Peters 1998:212–15). Six of the captives (two women and four children) came to village D, which organized the raid and one each went to villages C and E.

Fertility was high and mortality low for a 26.0 (2.6 percent) rate of natural increase. The departure of factions IV and V to found village E slightly offset the in-migration of Aica, the Ajarani captives, and several others for a negative net migration. During this phase village D gradually lessened visits to the mission post and use of the medical program owing to their gradual movement downriver.

Table 13.2. Village D: Fertility Rates and Descent Categories

| Level of Analysis | Indicator | Age/ Sex | Phases | |
|---|---|---|---|---|
| | | | Linkage | Brazilian |
| Village | Crude Birth | - | 44.6 | 49.5 |
| | Pf as % Pop. | 15–44 | 18.6 | 20.8 |
| Female Reproductive Population | Age-Specific Rates | 15 | 268 | 282 |
| | | 20 | 250 | 382 |
| | | 25 | 419 | 205 |
| | | 30 | 213 | 241 |
| | | 35 | 94 | 133 |
| | | 40 | 143 | 95 |
| | General | 15–44 | 244 | 238 |
| Avg. Female | Total Fert. | 15–44 | 6.9 | 6.7 |
| N Births | Total | | 48 | 46 |
| | | M | 26 | 24 |
| | | F | 22 | 22 |
| Village | % Descent Categories | | | |
| | A | | 50.5 | 53.5 |
| | B | | 2.3 | - |
| | C | | - | - |
| | D | | 24.6 | 29.2 |
| | E | | - | - |
| | F | | 1.6 | 1.8 |
| | Other/Unknown | | - | 1.3 |
| | External In-mig. | | 21.0 | 14.2 |
| | Total | | 100 | 100 |

## III. Brazilian Phase, 1982–1995

In 1983 the headman (49 in table 12.1) of village D died. The yano was burned after his death, according to Yanomami custom. At that time FUNAI was making a concerted effort to found posts among the Yanomami. One was established at Comara, 22 km (about 14 mi.) downriver from the mission station and 7 km (about 4.5 mi.) downriver from village D. This post was in contact with medical facilities in Boa Vista by air or by motorized canoe and road, the latter a two-day journey. FUNAI invited village D to relocate to Comara and assist in building an airstrip. Village D accepted and remained at the FUNAI post. This location gave them access to electricity and motorized boat transportation to Boa Vista.

Table 13.3. Village D: Mortality Rates

| Level of Analysis | Indicator | Age/ Sex | Phase | |
|---|---|---|---|---|
| | | | Linkage | Brazilian |
| Village | Crude Death | | 18.6 | 30.1 |
| Age Groups | Age-specific Rates | 0 | 63 | 186 |
| | | 1 | 30 | 67 |
| | | 5 | 21 | - |
| | | 10 | 5 | - |
| | | 20 | 12 | 7 |
| | | 30 | 8 | 19 |
| | | 40 | 22 | 27 |
| | | 50 | 25 | 25 |
| | | 60 | 22 | 85 |
| | | 70+ | - | 222 |
| N Deaths | Total | | 20 | 28 |
| | | M | 9 | 15 |
| | | F | 11 | 13 |
| N Reasons | Infectious Disease | M | 4 | 10 |
| | | F | 8 | 8 |
| | Non-infect. Disease | M | - | 1 |
| | | F | - | 1 |
| | Infanticide | M | 1 | - |
| | | F | - | 1 |
| | Homicide | M | 1 | - |
| | | F | - | - |
| | Accidents | M | - | - |
| | | F | 2 | 1 |
| | Unknown | M | 3 | 4 |
| | | F | 1 | 2 |

These events initiated a distinction within the Mucajaí population bloc. With this move, village D members recognized themselves as distinct from the other Mucajaí villages and only occasionally associated with the mission post. They called themselves the Comara people. The people of village D have more contact with Brazilians than do the other Mucajaí villages because of their closer proximity to FUNAI, the downriver Brazilian farms, and Boa Vista. Several Comara people have out-migrated to live among the Brazilians. Village D emulated the Brazilians by constructing small houses for individual families in place of the single yano. These houses were hooked up to the electrical supply of the FUNAI post. However in 1996,

Table 13.4. Village D: Migration Rates

| Level of Analysis | Indicator | Age/Sex | Linkage | | | Brazilian | | |
|---|---|---|---|---|---|---|---|---|
| | | | I | O | NM | I | O | NM |
| Village | Crude Rate | | 24.2 | 29.7 | −5.6 | 20.5 | 57.1 | −36.6 |
| | External | | 14.0 | 1.9 | 12.2 | 2.2 | 10.8 | −8.6 |
| | Internal | | 10.2 | 27.9 | −17.8 | 18.3 | 46.3 | −8.0 |
| Age Groups | Age-specific | 0 | 26 | 26 | 0 | 14 | 49 | −35 |
| | Rates | 15 | 35 | 39 | −4 | 32 | 52 | −20 |
| | | 30 | 24 | 24 | 0 | 13 | 67 | −47 |
| | | 45 | 5 | 33 | −28 | 29 | 87 | −58 |
| N Migration Total | | | 26 | 32 | −6 | 19 | 53 | −34 |
| | | M | 12 | 18 | −6 | 9 | 27 | −18 |
| | | F | 14 | 14 | 0 | 10 | 26 | −16 |
| Reasons | External Mig. | | | | | | | |
| | Marriage | M | 1 | - | | 1 | - | |
| | | F | 2 | 2 | | - | - | |
| | Captive | M | 2 | - | | - | - | |
| | | F | 4 | - | | - | - | |
| | Avoid Conflict | M | 1 | - | | - | - | |
| | | F | 1 | - | | - | - | |
| | Family | M | - | - | | - | - | |
| | | F | - | - | | - | - | |
| | Economic | F | - | - | | - | - | |
| | Unknown | M | 1 | - | | - | - | |
| | | F | 3 | - | | 1 | - | |
| Reasons | Internal Mig. | | | | | | | |
| | Marriage | M | 1 | 2 | | 7 | 8 | |
| | | F | - | - | | 4 | - | |
| | Fission-Fusion | M | - | 16 | | - | 10 | |
| | | F | - | 12 | | - | 10 | |
| | Avoid Conflict | M | - | - | | - | 4 | |
| | | F | - | - | | - | 5 | |
| | Family | M | 6 | - | | - | - | |
| | | F | 4 | - | | - | 1 | |
| | Unknown | M | - | - | | 1 | 3 | |
| | | F | - | - | | 5 | 1 | |

village D abandoned the houses at Comara and moved north to a stream about a half-hour walk from the FUNAI post. At this site the entire village once again resided in a single yano. Fear of disease was probably the main motive for the move and for decreased contact. During this phase village D has decreased in population from 73 to 57 for a –17.2 (–1.7 percent) rate of total decrease. Several factors are responsible for the decrease.

Group fertility has continued high with a crude birth rate of 49.5 and a total fertility rate of 6.9. During this phase mortality was very high with a crude death rate of 30.1 in spite of the assistance of FUNAI, which arranged transportation to Boa Vista for health care. Infectious diseases were the primary cause, as would be expected, because of the greater contact with Brazilians.

In late 1984 the two by now elderly headmen (50 and 60 in table 12.1) of factions III and IV decided to get away from Comara and relocate to a smaller and quieter community. Village D had a population of 75 people at that time. Assisted by members of village D, the headmen constructed a yano about three hours by canoe downriver from Comara and closer to the Aica village. This fission did not follow factional lines. Instead the two headmen were joined by 18 people, many of whom were originally in-migrants from other Yanomami communities, especially in-migrant Aica, who wanted to be closer to their Aica kin. This loss was partially offset by substantial in-migration to village D for marriage and various other reasons.

In summary, after village D moved to the FUNAI post at Comara, its population diminished. There was a high death rate, especially from malarial disease. The greatest loss was due to the fission of those who desired a village away from the FUNAI post or those who wanted to move closer to their relatives in Aica communities or to Brazilian sources of work.

## IV. A Village of Contrasts

The two phases of the existence of this village provide a case history of contrast. During the Linkage phase, the village first lived at the mission post, and then about 10 km (6 mi.) from it. During the Brazilian phase the village lived at the FUNAI post, which had only a few staff and a high turnover. While their contact with Brazilians could not be called permanent, their intermittent contact was more intense than that of the other villages. There was an increase from a moderate to a high death rate in the two phases. The case illustrates the impact on the mortality rate of increased Yanomami interaction with rural Brazil and the resulting infectious disease.

The high mortality combined with the fission of village F had led to a decrease in the population, which is in accordance with the contact model sketched in chapter 5. However the model sees the decrease as due to the high mortality, whereas in this village, out-migration due to fission was the more important factor.

# 14

# Village E

Village E fissioned from village D in 1963 when village D decided to move downstream to where they found better soil for their gardens. The members of village E, factions IV and V, wished to remain in the vicinity of the mission post. They constructed a new yano near the confluence of the Kloknai stream and the Mucajaí River. There were 22 people who were initially members of this village (fig. 14.1), but after a year, faction IV moved downriver and rejoined faction III in village D. At the beginning of 1965 village E was composed of faction V with 15 members, as shown in table 14.1.a.

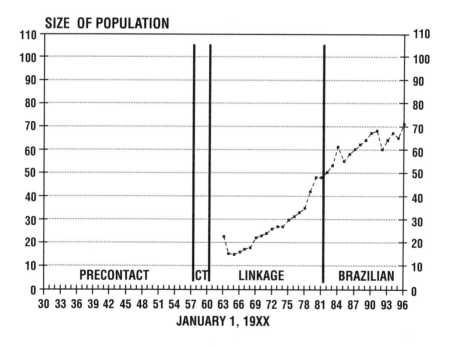

14.1. Village E population.

## I. Linkage Phase, 1964–1981

As the health of the headman (71 in table l2.1) of village E waned in the mid-1970s, his son-in-law (86) assumed the role of headman. He was extremely capable and an excellent diplomat. The proximity of village E to the mission post as well as the good relations of its headman with other villages made it an attractive community for in-migration. The population of village E had an explosive growth rate of 51.4 (5.1 percent) during this period. It would have been even higher were it not for the out-migration of faction D at the end of the first year of the village's existence.

Table 14.1. Village E: Demographic Profile, 1963–96

| 14.1.a | 1963 | Linkage | | 1982 | Brazilian | | 1996 |
|---|---|---|---|---|---|---|---|
| Population | 22(15) | | | 50 | | | 71 |
| Total Incr. | | | 28 | | | 21 | |
| Nat. Incr. | | | 22 | | | 26 | |
| Births | | 34 | | | 44 | | |
| Deaths | | 12 | | | 18 | | |
| Net Migration | | | 6 | | | −5 | |
| In-mig. | | 17 | | | 22 | | |
| Out-mig. | | 11 | | | 27 | | |

| 14.1.b | | Crude Rates | | | | | |
|---|---|---|---|---|---|---|---|
| Total Incr. | | | 51.4 | | | 24.3 | |
| Nat. Incr. | | | 40.4 | | | 30.1 | |
| Births | | 62.4 | | | 50.9 | | |
| Deaths | | 22.0 | | | 20.8 | | |
| Net Migration | | | 11.0 | | | −5.8 | |
| In-mig. | | 31.2 | | | 25.4 | | |
| Out-mig. | | 20.2 | | | 31.2 | | |

| 14.1.c | | Population: Age by Sex | | | | | |
|---|---|---|---|---|---|---|---|
| Population | 22 | | | 50 | | | 71 |
| Male | 13 | | | 29 | | | 44 |
| Female | 9 | | | 21 | | | 27 |
| % Female | 40.9 | | | 42.0 | | | 38.0 |
| % Age-Sex | | % M | % F | | % M | % F | |
| 0 | | 29.1 | 15.3 | | 33.3 | 19.8 | |
| 15 | | 13.7 | 14.1 | | 14.2 | 9.6 | |
| 30 | | 9.0 | 3.2 | | 4.6 | 8.1 | |
| 45 | | 8.9 | 6.7 | | 7.6 | 2.8 | |
| Total | | 60.6 | 39.4 | | 59.6 | 40.4 | |

Table 14.2. Village E: Fertility Rates and Descent Categories

| Level of Analysis | Indicator | Age/ Sex | Phases Linkage | Brazilian |
|---|---|---|---|---|
| Village | Crude Birth | - | 62.4 | 50.9 |
| | Pf as % Pop. | 15–44 | 17.3 | 17.7 |
| Female | Age-Specific | 15 | 375 | 291 |
| Reproductive | Rates | 20 | 520 | 328 |
| Population | | 25 | 200 | 91 |
| | | 30 | 364 | 409 |
| | | 35 | 667 | 346 |
| | | 40 | - | 227 |
| | General | 15–44 | 378 | 289 |
| Avg. Female | Total Fert. | 15–44 | 10.6 | 8.5 |
| N Births | Total | | 34 | 44 |
| | | M | 18 | 31 |
| | | F | 16 | 13 |
| Village | % Descent Categories | | | |
| | A | | 60.0 | 51.6 |
| | B | | - | - |
| | C | | - | .1 |
| | D | | 1.5 | 10.0 |
| | E | | - | - |
| | F | | 3.5 | 4.2 |
| | Other/Unknown | | - | - |
| | External In-mig. | | 35.0 | 34.1 |
| | Total | | 100 | 100 |

Group fertility was extremely high with a crude birth rate of 62.4 in spite of some sexual imbalance—females comprised 39.4 percent and reproductive females 17.3 percent of the village's population—and in spite of there being no female marriage partners for the older children, all of whom were male. Individual fertility was also high with a total fertility rate of 10.6. One reason for the high fertility was the in-migration to this small population of four females for marriage, including a captive taken in the raid on the Ajarani village. These women had children shortly after entering the group. Methodologically this means that prior to in-migrating, their person-years when not bearing children were not part of the denominators of the crude birth rate of this village. If they had been, the fertility rates would have been somewhat lower.

Table 14.3. Village E: Mortality Rates

| Level of Analysis | Indicator | Age/ Sex | Phases | |
|---|---|---|---|---|
| | | | Linkage | Brazilian |
| Village | Crude Death | | 22.0 | 20.8 |
| Age Groups | Age-specific | 0 | 206 | 159 |
| | Rates | 1 | 22 | 14 |
| | | 5 | 26 | - |
| | | 10 | - | - |
| | | 20 | - | 18 |
| | | 30 | - | - |
| | | 40 | - | 37 |
| | | 50 | 43 | - |
| | | 60 | - | 67 |
| | | 70+ | - | 158 |
| N Deaths | Total | | 12 | 18 |
| | | M | 6 | 15 |
| | | F | 6 | 3 |
| N Reasons | Infectious | M | 3 | 11 |
| | Disease | F | 1 | 1 |
| | Infanticide | M | 1 | 2 |
| | | F | 4 | 1 |
| | Homicide | M | - | 1 |
| | Unknown | M | 2 | 1 |
| | | F | 1 | 1 |

Group mortality was borderline high with a 22.0 crude death rate. Infant mortality was 206 and mainly responsible for the high group rate. Five infanticides accounted for all but two of the infant deaths. Some of the reasons were that an infant was born with a deformity; a female infant was born into the family who already had too many girls; and one infant was born to a family in which the mother did not think she could expect the father to support her and the child. Reasons for the other infanticides are unknown.

Tuberculosis was first detected in 1975. A Xiliana visitor who had worked for Brazilians and also had lived among the Palimi theli came to the village to receive treatment from the mission for his illness. It was found to be tuberculosis and the patient died the day before he was to be moved to Boa Vista for intensive treatment. Following this visit, several more cases were detected in the village.

**Table 14.4. Village E: Migration Rates**

| Level of Analysis | Indicator | Age/ Sex | Linkage | | | Brazilian | | |
|---|---|---|---|---|---|---|---|---|
| | | | I | O | NM | I | O | NM |
| Village | Crude Rate | | 31.2 | 20.2 | 11.0 | 25.4 | 31.2 | −5.8 |
| | External | | 14.6 | - | 14.6 | 10.4 | 8.0 | 2.4 |
| | Internal | | 16.5 | 20.2 | −3.7 | 15.0 | 23.1 | −8.1 |
| Age Groups | Age-specific | 0 | 25 | 21 | 4 | 15 | 20 | −5 |
| | Rates | 15 | 46 | 26 | 19 | 49 | 68 | −19 |
| | | 30 | 30 | 15 | 15 | 18 | - | 18 |
| | | 45 | 24 | 12 | 12 | 33 | 44 | −11 |
| N Migration Total | | | 17 | 11 | 6 | 22 | 27 | −5 |
| | | M | 10 | 7 | 3 | 15 | 16 | −1 |
| | | F | 7 | 4 | 3 | 7 | 11 | −4 |
| Reasons: External Mig. | | | | | | | | |
| | Marriage | M | 2 | - | | 7 | 3 | |
| | | F | 3 | - | | 2 | - | |
| | Captive | F | 1 | - | | - | - | |
| | Avoid Conflict | F | - | - | | - | 1 | |
| | Family | M | - | - | | - | 1 | |
| | | F | - | - | | - | 2 | |
| | Unknown | M | 1 | - | | - | - | |
| | | F | 1 | - | | - | - | |
| Reasons: Internal Mig. | | | | | | | | |
| | Marriage | M | 1 | 1 | | 2 | 2 | |
| | | F | 1 | - | | - | 3 | |
| | Avoid Conflict | M | - | - | | 1 | - | |
| | Unknown | M | 6 | 6 | | 5 | 10 | |
| | | F | 1 | 4 | | 5 | 5 | |

There was a high in-migration rate of 31.2, higher than the mortality rate. Village E befriended the Malaxi theli, the same group with whom village B had established marital relations. During this phase five Malaxi theli in-migrated to village E for marriage, along with two people from other Mucajaí villages and the single captive. In addition to the shortage of young females, village E also lacked diversity of descent categories: 60 percent of the village were in descent category A (table 14.2). In-migration was an absolute necessity for this village to survive. Most of the in-migrants came in the mid-1960s and, together with the natural increase, prevented any potential problem of survival for what had been a small village with an unbalanced sex and kin structure. Most of the out-migration was faction IV rejoining village D.

## II. Brazilian Phase, 1982–1995

The village abandoned the pattern of all its inhabitants living in a single yano. By 1994 there was a small yano in which the village headman (86) lived with his family, and nearby were five small rectangular houses in the Brazilian style, inhabited by four nuclear families and a single male. In addition there were two chicken houses, two outhouses, a leafed shed for the making of cassava, and a small storehouse, where one of the families placed their possessions when visiting elsewhere.

Fertility decreased from the previous phase but remained high with a crude birth rate of 50.9 and a total fertility rate of 8.6, the highest of all the villages. The high fertility was maintained in spite of the dominance of descent category A, carried by over half the village. The reason was the continuing high rate of external male in-migration.

Mortality remained borderline high with a crude death rate of 20.8, almost the same as in the previous phase. Infectious diseases—pneumonia, malaria, tuberculosis and dysentery—were the primary causes. This village took greater advantage of the medical services at the mission post than the other villages. Infant mortality decreased but remained a high 159. There were five infant deaths, two of which were infanticides. A female infant was rejected when the family thought they already had too many girls. A male child with a deformity was the other infanticide.

Members of this village also clashed with the miners. During this period four miners stole some sweet manioc root from a garden of one of the villagers. In retaliation five men from the village attacked the nearby miners' camp and killed four of them.

Village E had been in the same location since 1963 and game began to decline in the immediate vicinity. The men frequently hunted upriver near the Malaxi theli, among whom they had relatives. In 1992 a young man from village E was hunting with his older brother in this area. Suddenly the older brother was shot and killed by a miner. The younger brother immediately shot the miner and, still seeking revenge, organized a raiding party of Malaxi theli relatives, who killed five more miners (Peters 1998:217–19). There was a slight population loss due to a negative net migration. Marriage was an important reason for both in-migration and out-migration.

### III. A Village That Grew

Village E began as a faction of 15 people and was able to overcome the demographic problems of sexual and kin imbalance often characteristic of a small population. It grew in thirty-three years to a population of 71 at the beginning of 1996. In spite of substantial mortality and out-migration, this explosive growth was due to extremely high fertility and in-migration. Two capable headmen guided the village during these years and encouraged in-migration from the Malaxi theli and from the other Mucajaí villages. The proximity of the village to the mission was an important factor in attracting in-migrants.

This village had only intermittent contact with the national society throughout all the postcontact years. There has been no invasion of their subsistence areas by Brazilians. The village was an exception to the model of contact in that there were no very high death rates and the village population continued to grow during both postcontact phases. The peaceful nature of most contacts, the fact that their subsistence areas were not invaded, and the assistance of the missionary medical program were the key factors.

# 15

## Village F

This village was created by fission from village D in 1984. Village D had reached a density of 74 people and was located at the FUNAI post. The elderly headmen of factions III and IV (50 and 60 in table 12.1), wishing to move to a quieter location, selected a place downstream from Comara, a three-hour trip by canoe and close to the Aica village of Flexal.

### I. Brazilian Phase, 1985–1988

The village started off with a population of 20 people (fig. 15.1), a number of whom had previously in-migrated from the Aica villages and the northern Ninam (Xiliana); one was a Yekwana captive from the time of the con-

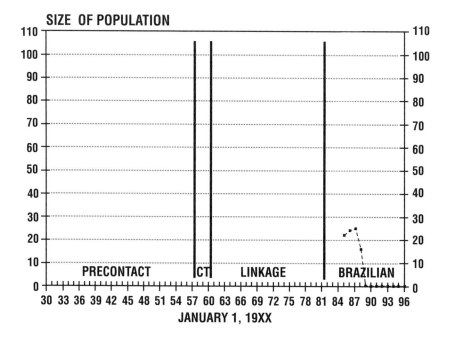

15.1. Village F population.

flict. The group was atypical in not having belonged to a single faction before fissioning. With such a small population, it was questionable how long the group could survive as an independent village. Table 15.1 shows the population dynamics of the village.

Group fertility was moderate with a crude birth rate of 34.5. The population was in sexual balance as females comprised 50 percent and reproductive women 20.7 percent of the village population. Mortality was extremely high with seven deaths in the small population, for a crude death rate of 92. Causes are unknown but probably involved infectious diseases. In 1988 the

Table 15.1. Village F: Demographic Profile, 1985–89

| 15.1.a | 1985 | Brazilian | | 1989 |
|---|---|---|---|---|
| Population | 20 | | | 0 |
| Total Incr. | | | −20 | |
| Nat. Incr. | | | −5 | |
| Births | | 3 | | |
| Deaths | | 8 | | |
| Net Migration | | | −15 | |
| In-mig. | | 5 | | |
| Out-mig. | | −20 | | |

| 15.1.b. | | Crude Rates | | |
|---|---|---|---|---|
| Total Incr. | | | −229.9 | |
| Nat. Incr. | | | −57.5 | |
| Births | | 34.5 | | |
| Deaths | | 92.0 | | |
| Net Migration | | | −172.4 | |
| In-Mig. | | 57.5 | | |
| Out-Mig. | | 229.5 | | |

| 15.1.c. | | Population: Age by Sex | | |
|---|---|---|---|---|
| Population | 20 | | | 0 |
| Male | 10 | | | 0 |
| Female | 10 | | | 0 |
| % Female | 50.0 | | | 0.0 |
| % Age-Sex | | % M | % F | |
| 0 | | 17.2 | 21.8 | |
| 15 | | 5.7 | 10.3 | |
| 30 | | 6.9 | 10.3 | |
| 45 | | 18.4 | 9.2 | |
| Total | | 48.3 | 51.7 | |

Table 15.2. Village F: Fertility Rates and Descent Categories

| Level of Analysis | Indicator | Age/ Sex | Phase Brazilian |
|---|---|---|---|
| Village | Crude Birth | - | 34.5 |
| | Pf as % Pop. | 15–44 | 20.7 |
| Female Reproductive Population | Age-Specific Rates | 15 | 333 |
| | | 20 | - |
| | | 25 | 1,000 |
| | | 30 | - |
| | | 35 | - |
| | | 40 | - |
| | General | 15–44 | 167 |
| Avg. Female | Total Fert. | 15–44 | 6.7 |
| N Births | Total | | 3 |
| | | M | - |
| | | F | 3 |
| Village | % Descent Categories | | |
| | A | | 48.3 |
| | B | | - |
| | C | | - |
| | D | | 4.6 |
| | E | | - |
| | F | | - |
| | Other/Unknown | | - |
| | External In-mig. | | 47.1 |
| | Total | | 100 |

two elderly headmen (50 and 60) who had initiated the village died from infections. The village yano was burned and the community dispersed.

Initially the small population was augmented by five in-migrants from outside the Mucajaí communities. This meant that more than 50 percent of the village's population had been born outside the Mucajaí group. When the community dispersed, most of the villagers fused with the downriver Aica village of Flexal. A number of them had Aica relatives there. Two of the out-migrants went to live in Brazilian communities where they had often worked. Only three remained within the Mucajaí group by moving to other Mucajaí villages.

This is another case history of a village attempting to function with a small population. It survived only four years, during which time it suffered high mortality. When the headmen died, the community disbanded. Like the village from which it fissioned, village F was atypical among the villages in its frequency of contact with Brazilians.

Table 15.3. Village F: Mortality Rates

| Level of Analysis | Indicator | Age/ Sex | Phase Brazilian |
|---|---|---|---|
| Village | Crude Death | | 92.0 |
| Age Groups | Age-specific Rates | 0 | 333 |
| | | 1 | 375 |
| | | 5 | - |
| | | 10 | 56 |
| | | 20 | - |
| | | 30 | - |
| | | 40 | - |
| | | 50 | - |
| | | 60 | 286 |
| | | 70+ | 250 |
| N Deaths | Total | | 8 |
| | | M | 4 |
| | | F | 4 |
| N Reasons | Unknown | M | 4 |
| | | F | 4 |

**Table 15.4. Village F: Migration Rates**

| Level of Analysis | Indicator | Age/ Sex | Brazilian | | |
|---|---|---|---|---|---|
| | | | I | O | NM |
| Village | Crude Rate | | 57.5 | 229.9 | −195.4 |
| | External | | 57.5 | 183.9 | −143.4 |
| | Internal | | - | 46.0 | −46.0 |
| Age Groups | Age-specific | 0 | - | 147 | −147.0 |
| | Rates | 15 | 214 | 500 | −357.0 |
| | | 30 | 67 | 200 | −133.0 |
| | | 45 | 42 | 208 | −208.0 |
| N Migration Total | | | 3 | 20 | −17 |
| | | M | 1 | 9 | −8 |
| | | F | 2 | 11 | −9 |
| Reasons: External Mig. | | | | | |
| | Avoid Conflict | M | 1 | - | |
| | | F | 2 | - | |
| | Fission-Fusion | M | - | 9 | |
| | | F | - | 7 | |
| Reasons: Internal Mig. | | | | | |
| | Fission-Fusion | M | - | - | |
| | | F | - | 4 | |

# 16

# Village G

The villages discussed in the last three chapters all fissioned directly or indirectly from village C in 1960, leaving it with a population of 35 people. After that time, the population of village C continued to grow so that by 1984, there were 105 people in the village. Once again the demographic density resulted in conflicts owing to the noise and gossip in the yano. Sixty-five villagers fissioned to found village G. The fissioning took place along factional lines. At the time of the first fission of village C in 1960, faction I with their two coheadmen (1, 3 in table 12.1) had remained as village C while the other factions initiated village D. By 1984 the two coheadmen had died. Faction I had grown and splintered (factional fission) into two sepa-

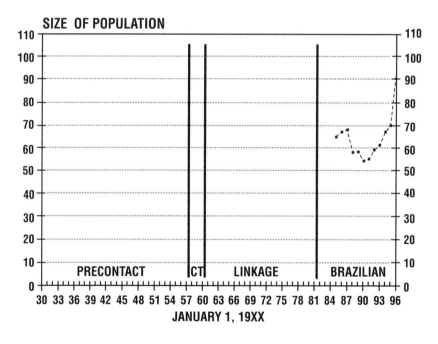

16.1. Village G population.

Table 16.1. Village G: Demographic Profile, 1985–96

| 16.1.a | 1985 | Brazilian | | 1996 |
|---|---|---|---|---|
| Population | 65 | | | 94 |
| Total Incr. | | | 29 | |
| Nat. Incr. | | | 19 | |
| Births | | 34 | | |
| Deaths | | 15 | | |
| Net Migration | | | 10 | |
| In-mig. | | 25 | | |
| Out-mig. | | 15 | | |

| 16.1.b | | Crude Rates | | |
|---|---|---|---|---|
| Total Inc. | | | 39.8 | |
| Nat. Incr. | | | 26.1 | |
| Births | | 46.6 | | |
| Deaths | | 20.6 | | |
| Net Migration | | | 13.7 | |
| In-mig. | | 34.3 | | |
| Out-mig. | | 20.6 | | |

| 16.1.c. | | Population: Age by Sex | | |
|---|---|---|---|---|
| Population | 65 | | | 94 |
| Male | 35 | | | 47 |
| Female | 30 | | | 47 |
| % Female | 46.2 | | | 50.0 |
| % Age-Sex | | % M | % F | |
| 0 | | 21.2 | 18.9 | |
| 15 | | 9.4 | 19.5 | |
| 30 | | 11.5 | 6.2 | |
| 45 | | 8.0 | 5.4 | |
| Total | | 50.0 | 50.0 | |

rate factions based on descent from one or the other dead coheadmen. Both factions remained in the village at the time of the factional fission. In 1984 the fission took place along these factional lines. The descendants of one of the deceased headman (3) along with the descendants of families I-2, I-3, and the returned portion of II-1, fissioned and initiated village G.

At the time of this fission, village C abandoned the old yano and moved upstream to an island in the river. Village G also moved upstream and constructed their yano on a neighboring island, about a ten-minute canoe paddle from village C. When village C returned to the mainland around 1991, village G moved downstream to two small islands. Here the village abandoned the traditional pattern of a single yano for all inhabitants. On

Table 16.2. Village G: Fertility Rates and Descent Categories

| Level of Analysis | Indicator | Age/ Sex | Phase Brazilian |
|---|---|---|---|
| Village | Crude Birth | - | 46.6 |
| | Pf as % Pop. | 15–44 | 25.7 |
| Female | Age-Specific | 15 | 158 |
| Reproductive | Rates | 20 | 226 |
| Population | | 25 | 157 |
| | | 30 | 235 |
| | | 35 | 200 |
| | | 40 | 77 |
| | General | 15–44 | 194 |
| Avg. Female | Total Fert. | 15–44 | 5.3 |
| N Births | Total | | 34 |
| | | M | 17 |
| | | F | 17 |
| Village | % Descent Categories | | |
| | A | | 23.2 |
| | B | | 19.6 |
| | C | | - |
| | D | | 19.2 |
| | E | | 1.2 |
| | F | | 1.9 |
| | Other/Unknown | | .1 |
| | External In-mig. | | 34.8 |
| | Total | | 100 |

one island there were three rectangular family houses and two dwellings for teenagers. On the other island there were three rectangular houses in Brazilian peasant style, each with a nuclear family; the headman lived in one of these houses.

## I. Brazilian Phase, 1985–1995

Village G began with 65 people (table 16.2.a), a large population for a new village. At the beginning of 1996 after eleven years of existence, it had 94 people, a high 39.8 (4 percent) rate of total increase (table 16.1.b).

The crude birth rate was a high 46.6 while the total fertility rate a moderate 5.3, the lowest rate for all the villages in this phase. The age-specific

Table 16.3. Village G: Mortality Rates

| Level of Analysis | Indicator | Age/ Sex | Phase Brazilian |
|---|---|---|---|
| Village | Crude Death | | 20.6 |
| Age Groups | Age-specific Rates | 0 | 235 |
| | | 1 | 14 |
| | | 5 | - |
| | | 10 | - |
| | | 20 | 9 |
| | | 30 | - |
| | | 40 | 15 |
| | | 50 | 49 |
| | | 60 | 82 |
| | | 70+ | - |
| N Deaths | Total | | 15 |
| | | M | 10 |
| | | F | 5 |
| Reasons | Infectious | M | 7 |
| | Disease | F | 2 |
| | Infanticide | M | 3 |
| | | F | 2 |
| | Unknown | M | - |
| | | F | 1 |

fertility rate for the age 15 to <20 category was a moderate 158, which appears to be the main reason for the moderate total fertility. The average age at first birth rose to a high 19.8. One reason was a shortage of males among those ages 15 to <30 (see table 16.1.c).

The crude death rate of 20.6 barely falls into the high range. Infectious diseases were the main causes of death. There were eight infant deaths for a high infant mortality rate of 235. Five of these were infanticides; two because the infants had deformities, one because the husband was known not to be the father, one because the family had too many girls, and one for which the reason is unknown.

There was positive net migration, primarily due to the arrival in 1995 of a large family from village D escaping a conflict situation. Substantial in-migration and out-migration for marriage offset each other. At the beginning of 1996 the village had grown to 94 people, who were divided among five factions and no longer in a single yano. During that year and the next,

**Table 16.4. Village G: Migration Rates**

| Level of Analysis | Indicator | Age/ Sex | Brazilian | | |
|---|---|---|---|---|---|
| | | | I | O | NM |
| Village | Crude Rate | | 34.3 | 20.6 | 13.7 |
| | External | | 4.1 | - | 4.1 |
| | Internal | | 30.2 | 20.6 | 9.6 |
| Age Groups | Age-specific | 0 | 27 | 17 | 10 |
| | Rates | 15 | 52 | 29 | 23 |
| | | 30 | 23 | 16 | 7 |
| | | 45 | 31 | 21 | 10 |
| N Migration Total | | | 25 | 15 | 10 |
| | | M | 14 | 9 | 5 |
| | | F | 11 | 6 | 5 |
| Reasons: External Mig. | | | | | |
| | Marriage | M | 1 | - | |
| | | F | - | - | |
| | Family | M | - | - | |
| | | F | 1 | - | |
| | Unknown | M | - | - | |
| | | F | 1 | - | |
| Reasons: Internal Mig. | | | | | |
| | Marriage | M | 7 | 7 | |
| | | F | 3 | 5 | |
| | Fission-Fusion | M | - | - | |
| | | F | - | - | |
| | Avoid Conflict | M | 5 | 1 | |
| | | F | 5 | - | |
| | Unknown | M | 1 | 1 | |
| | | F | 1 | 1 | |

after the end of the demographic data, it appeared that the village had begun another fission. One faction remained on the islands in the Mucajaí River about an hour-and-a-half canoe paddle upriver (west) from the mission. The largest faction had moved two and half hours north into the forest, where the village had previously built gardens. Two factions had moved to houses they constructed at the mission station. At the time of writing, it was not clear whether these would be temporary or permanent moves.

This village had high fertility and in-migration, which resulted in a high 4 percent rate of total increase despite high mortality in which infanticide played a substantial role. For a group still in intermittent contact with Brazilians, this is contrary to what would be expected under the contact model in chapter 5. Once again the important factors were relative isolation from Brazilians, no invasion of subsistence territory, and the medical program of the missionaries.

In spite of the community's intermittent contact, two individuals maintain political ties with wider efforts by the Yanomami to confront their problems of social change. A Palimi theli in-migrant to the village was raised as a child in a Brazilian home and speaks fluent Portuguese. He is periodically employed by FUNAI and nongovernmental organizations as a translator. He keeps the Xilixana and Palimi theli informed about political and economic events in Roraima and their impact on the Yanomami. He has also assisted the headman of village G in regional meetings of Yanomami headmen in Boa Vista and of indigenous leaders in Brasília.

# 17

# Village H

In the Precontact period village B faced a demographic crisis: its population had declined to 21 people and there was one reproductive woman in her forties in the group. As we have seen, fusion with village A in 1957, the female captives from the Xili theli, and in-migration from the Malaxi theli in the early 1960s reversed the trend and prevented the crisis. By 1986 the population of village B had grown to 70 people and they were experiencing the previously described problems of conflict arising from demographic density. Thirty-eight people fissioned from village B to start village H (fig. 17.1). Although village B was one of the Precontact villages, this was the first fission from village B because its rate of population growth was slower than in the other villages.

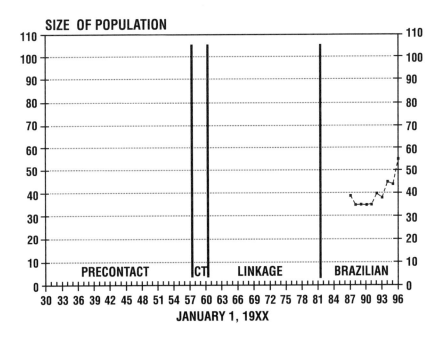

17.1. Village H population.

**Table 17.1. Village H: Demographic Profile, 1987–96**

| 17.1.a | 1987 | Brazilian | | 1996 |
|---|---|---|---|---|
| Population | 39 | | | 56 |
| Total Incr. | | | 16 | |
| Nat. Incr. | | | 5 | |
|   Births | | 13 | | |
|   Deaths | | 8 | | |
| Net Migration | | | 11 | |
|   In-mig. | | 19 | | |
|   Out-mig. | | 8 | | |

| 17.1.b | Crude Rates | | |
|---|---|---|---|
| Total Incr. | | 42.8 | |
| Nat. Incr. | | 13.4 | |
|   Births | 34.8 | | |
|   Deaths | 21.4 | | |
| Net Migration | | 29.5 | |
|   In-mig. | 50.9 | | |
|   Out-mig. | 21.4 | | |

| 17.1.c | Population: Age by Sex | | |
|---|---|---|---|
| Population | 39 | | 55 |
|   Male | 22 | | 33 |
|   Female | 17 | | 22 |
|   % Female | 43.6 | | 40.0 |
| % Age-Sex | % M | % F | |
|   0 | 28.9 | 13.5 | |
|   15 | 19.1 | 15.0 | |
|   30 | 5.5 | 5.2 | |
|   45 | 6.8 | 5.9 | |
| Total | 60.4 | 39.6 | |

Initially village H built the new yano a few yards away from that of village B, which at that time was on the Kloknai stream about an hour's walk north of the Mucajaí. In 1989 village H moved to an island about halfway between the site of village B and the mission post. They said the island location would protect them from disease-carrying spirits, which do not travel over water. In October 1991 the relatively young headman of the village died. The yano was immediately abandoned and the village moved back to the vicinity of village B on the mainland.

The following year, 1992, was extremely dry. The yield from the gardens was meager. At that time to the north on the Uraricoera River, FUNAI constructed a post at an airstrip abandoned by miners. FUNAI assisted the

**Table 17.2. Village H: Fertility Rates and Descent Categories**

| Level of Analysis | Indicator | Age/ Sex | Phase Brazilian |
|---|---|---|---|
| Village | Crude Birth | - | 34.8 |
| | Pf as % Pop. | 15–44 | 20.2 |
| Female | Age-Specific Rates | 15 | 130 |
| Reproductive | | 20 | 211 |
| Population | | 25 | 286 |
| | | 30 | 571 |
| | | 35 | - |
| | | 40 | - |
| | General | 15–44 | 188 |
| Avg. Female | Total Fert. | 15–44 | 6.0 |
| N Births | Total | | 13 |
| | | M | 8 |
| | | F | 5 |
| Village | % Descent Categories | | |
| | A | | 34.1 |
| | B | | - |
| | C | | 22.0 |
| | D | | 26.0 |
| | E | | - |
| | F | | 13.0 |
| | Other/Unknown | | - |
| | External In-mig. | | 4.9 |
| | Total | | 100 |

villagers with gifts of food and encouraged them to settle at the post. The people of village H saw this as an opportunity to obtain a monopoly on the trade goods, especially clothing, that would be distributed at the FUNAI post. The move took about ten months. The villagers moved between the two locations because manioc and other plants required time to move and mature. Although all the Mucajaí villages have moved a number of times, this was the first village to move away from the Mucajaí region permanently since contact. Village H still maintains contact with the Mucajaí villages, especially village B and somewhat with village E, with whom they have kinship ties. Even though this village has been located on the Uraricoera for three years of the demographic research period, it is included here as part of the Mucajaí group. In the nine years of the research period that this village

Table 17.3. Village H: Mortality Rates

| Level of Analysis | Indicator | Age/ Sex | Phase Brazilian |
|---|---|---|---|
| Village | Crude Death | | 21.4 |
| Age Groups | Age-specific Rates | 0 | 308 |
| | | 1 | 69 |
| | | 5 | - |
| | | 10 | - |
| | | 20 | - |
| | | 30 | - |
| | | 40 | - |
| | | 50 | 77 |
| | | 60 | - |
| | | 70+ | 333 |
| N Deaths | Total | | 8 |
| | | M | 4 |
| | | F | 4 |
| Reasons | Infectious Disease | M | 3 |
| | | F | - |
| | Non-infect. Disease | M | - |
| | | F | 1 |
| | Infanticide | M | 1 |
| | | F | 1 |
| | Unknown | M | - |
| | | F | 2 |

has been in existence, it has grown from 39 to 55 people, or a high 42.8 (4.3 percent) rate of total increase (table 17.1.a, b).

The crude birth rate was a moderate 34.8 and the total fertility rate was 6.0. The age-specific fertility rate for 15 to <20 years was low because the age at first birth had risen to 19.1 years. The reason is unknown. The crude death rate was a high 21.4, with mortality concentrated in the early years of life. Of the eight deaths, six were children, including four infants in the first year of life and two in the second year. There were two infanticides, one because of deformity; the reason for the other is unknown.

There was heavy in-migration, as shown by the crude rate of 50.9. Seven people came for marriage. The location at the FUNAI post made the village attractive to in-migrants. Also the location on the Uraricoera places village H closer to the Palimi theli and Xiliana, a setting that may affect alliance and migration patterns in future years. These factors probably account for

Table 17.4. Village H: Migration Rates

| Level of Analysis | Indicator | Age/ Sex | Brazilian | | |
|---|---|---|---|---|---|
| | | | I | O | NM |
| Village | Crude Rate | | 50.9 | 21.4 | 29.5 |
| | External | | 2.7 | - | 2.7 |
| | Internal | | 48.2 | 21.4 | 26.8 |
| Age Groups | Age-specific | 0 | 51 | 25 | 26 |
| | Rates | 15 | 39 | 16 | 23 |
| | | 30 | 71 | 24 | 47 |
| | | 45 | 66 | 22 | 33 |
| N Migration | Total | | 19 | 8 | 11 |
| | | M | 10 | 3 | 7 |
| | | F | 9 | 5 | 4 |
| Reasons: External Mig. | | | | | |
| | Marriage | M | 1 | - | |
| Reasons: Internal Mig. | | | | | |
| | Marriage | M | 2 | - | |
| | | F | 5 | 1 | |
| | Avoid Conflict | M | - | 3 | |
| | | F | 1 | 3 | |
| | Unknown | M | 7 | - | |
| | | F | 3 | 1 | |

most of the cases listed as migrations for unknown reasons in table 17.4. Marriage and a family group returning to village B because of a conflict within village H were important factors for out-migration.

Village H is another case history of a village living at a FUNAI post. The contact here is more intense than in the other villages, but given the few and changing personnel of this isolated FUNAI post, it remains an intermittent contact. This village has also had an increase of population, contrary to expectation under the contact model. The main factor has been heavy in-migration because of location, resulting in the unusual situation that the rate of net migration was higher than the rate of natural increase. Natural increase was slowed by high mortality and only moderate fertility.

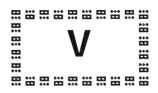

# Synthetic Views

# 18

# The Villages Compared

Following from examination of the eight Mucajaí villages as case studies of the history, social structure, and population dynamics of Yanomami villages, we now compare the findings from the individual cases to understand some common patterns in the population dynamics.

## I. The Need for Classification

The database provided annual information about the size of the population and its four components of change for each of the eight villages, whose duration of existence varied from four to sixty-six years and populations ranged from 11 to 108 people. For many purposes of analysis, yearly data are too discriminate, cumbersome, and volatile when small numbers are involved. There was a need for a classification to group the individual years.

The importance of fissions and fusions in determining the sizes of the village populations can be used as a basis of classification. They mark points of radical demographic restructuring since they can involve more than half of a village population. The common pattern involved a village starting by fissioning from another, growing substantially over a period, then in a single year undergoing fissioning as one faction or several moved out, bringing about a sharp decline of its population. Then the village commenced to grow once more. This pattern gives rise to a series of life cycles for a village. The graphs of the yearly size of the population of each village clearly illustrate these cycles. In chapter 10, the case history of village B, we introduce the concept of village cycles as a synthetic way to view the diachronic cases, and several of these cycles are described for villages B and C. Viewing the diachronic data in this manner emphasizes the quantitative patterns of the demographic data themselves rather than the historical factors influencing the components of change.

## II. The Cycles: A Comparative View

In the first part of this chapter we use these village life cycles as the unit of analysis and compare their demographic characteristics. A cycle begins with the size of a village population the year after it has been through a fission or fusion or been newly founded by a fissioning group. The cycle ends with the size of that same village at the end of the year before it goes through another fission or fusion. In instances in which the fissioning process took several years to work itself out, as happened to villages D and E, the beginning of the cycle is when the transition was completed.

Several kinds of village cycles can be distinguished using demographic and methodological criteria.

The main classification involves examining the sizes of the village populations at the beginning and end of the cycles to see if they are cycles of overall population growth or decline. We then analyze the components of change for these cycles to determine their relative importance in the two types of cycles.

Cycles of growth or decline can be subdivided into several other classifications. One is methodological. Village cycles defined as the time between two fissions, two fusions, or a combination of the two are called complete cycles. Since it can take twenty or more years for a complete cycle to unfold (table 18.1), it is difficult to obtain data about an entire cycle. In this study with a sixty-six-year time series, there are only four complete cycles. Incomplete cycles are limited by the dates of the demographic research period but were in existence either before or after these dates. The data on incomplete cycles of considerable length can give additional insight into the cycles of growth or decline.

Another subclassification of the cycles depends on the size of their beginning population (P1). Table 4.1 in chapter 4 shows that Yanomami villages of about twenty people or fewer are unusually small. This implies a demographic problem for villages of this size, which this classification helps to examine.

Another classification is villages with sexual unbalance. For this classification we examine the beginning sex ratios of the cycles to see how closely they approximate the 50 percent rule of thumb for the sex ratio of the population and 20 percent females of reproductive age for the reproductive sex ratio of the population. Large deviations from these norms indicate a particular type of demographic problem.

Table 18.1 presents the demographic characteristics of thirteen cycles derived from the case histories. The table distinguishes cycles of population decline (cycles 1–3) and growth (cycles 4–8) along with their demographic properties. There is a separate classification for five incomplete cycles (9–13) that are of relatively short duration as they were still developing at the end of the research period. Three of them had a small increase at that time,

# Table 18.1. Demographic Profiles of the Cycles

| | Decline | | | Growth | | | | | Incomplete—Short Term | | | | |
|---|---|---|---|---|---|---|---|---|---|---|---|---|---|
| Cycle # | 1 | 2 | 3 | 4 | 5 | 6 | 7 | 8 | 9 | 10 | 11 | 12 | 13 |
| Village | A | B | F | C | B | C | D | E | C | D | G | B | H |
| Type Cycle | I | I | C | I | C | C | C | I | I | I | I | I | I |
| Year Begin | 1930 | 1930 | 1985 | 1930 | 1958 | 1961 | 1964 | 1964 | 1985 | 1985 | 1985 | 1987 | 1987 |
| Year End | 1957 | 1956 | 1988 | 1959 | 1985 | 1983 | 1983 | 1995 | 1995 | 1995 | 1995 | 1995 | 1995 |
| # Years | 28 | 27 | 4 | 31 | 28 | 23 | 20 | 32 | 11 | 11 | 11 | 9 | 8 |
| Hist. Phases | P,C | P | B | P,C | C,L,B | L,B | L,B | L,B | B | B | B | B | B |
| **Population** | | | | | | | | | | | | | |
| Begin Pop. | 11 | 33 | 20 | 53 | 33 | 35 | 34 | 15 | 44 | 53 | 65 | 33 | 39 |
| End Pop. | 0 | 21 | 0 | 86 | 69 | 107 | 74 | 71 | 47 | 57 | 94 | 37 | 55 |
| Total Incr. | -11 | -12 | -20 | 33 | 36 | 72 | 40 | 56 | 3 | 4 | 29 | 4 | 16 |
| **Crude Rates** | | | | | | | | | | | | | |
| CTIR | -27.1 | -15.8 | -252.9 | 18.0 | 29.1 | 46.9 | 36.1 | 34.8 | 6.2 | 5.6 | 39.8 | 11.3 | 42.8 |
| CNI | -2.5 | -10.6 | -57.5 | 12.4 | 29.9 | 29.7 | 27.1 | 34.1 | 18.5 | 22.3 | 26.1 | 14.2 | 13.4 |
| CBR | 22.1 | 18.5 | 34.5 | 33.0 | 53.4 | 45.6 | 47.9 | 55.3 | 47.4 | 50.1 | 46.6 | 59.5 | 34.8 |
| CDR | 24.6 | 29.0 | 92.0 | 20.6 | 23.6 | 15.9 | 20.8 | 21.3 | 28.8 | 27.9 | 20.6 | 45.3 | 21.4 |
| CNM | -24.8 | -5.3 | -172.4 | 5.7 | -0.8 | 17.2 | 9.0 | 0.7 | -12.4 | -16.7 | 13.7 | -2.8 | 29.5 |
| CIR | 7.4 | 2.6 | 57.5 | 6.2 | 15.7 | 19.2 | 14.5 | 27.7 | 2.1 | 25.1 | 34.3 | 34.0 | 50.9 |
| COR | 32.0 | 7.9 | 229.9 | 0.5 | 16.5 | 2.0 | 5.4 | 27.0 | 14.4 | 41.8 | 20.6 | 45.3 | 21.4 |
| **Sex Ratios** | | | | | | | | | | | | | |
| Begin %Pf | 36.4 | 21.2 | 45.5 | 32.0 | 30.3 | 37.1 | 38.2 | 33.3 | 50.0 | 41.5 | 46.2 | 51.5 | 43.6 |
| End %Pf | 0.0 | 23.8 | 0.0 | 38.3 | 43.5 | 48.5 | 44.6 | 38.0 | 46.8 | 41.4 | 50.0 | 48.6 | 40.0 |
| d | -36.4 | 2.6 | -45.5 | 6.3 | 13.2 | 11.4 | 6.4 | 4.7 | -3.2 | -0.1 | 3.8 | -2.9 | -3.6 |
| Begin %Pf 15–44 | 18.2 | 15.1 | 13.6 | 15.1 | 12.1 | 14.3 | 11.8 | 13.3 | 20.4 | 20.8 | 20.0 | 24.2 | 20.5 |
| End %Pf 15–44 | 0.0 | 4.8 | 0.0 | 10.3 | 20.3 | 19.8 | 16.2 | 15.5 | 21.3 | 20.7 | 25.5 | 18.9 | 23.6 |
| d | -18.2 | -10.3 | -13.6 | -4.8 | 8.2 | -4.5 | 4.4 | 1.2 | 0.9 | -0.1 | 5.5 | -5.3 | 3.1 |

P = Precontact, C = Contact, L = Linkage, B = Brazilian, Pf = Female Population, d = Difference.

but their populations were fluctuating. Cycle 13 was similar until 1995, when there was a sizable increase due to the internal in-migration of two large family groups.

## III. Cycles Beginning with Small Populations

Villages A, E, and F (cycles 1, 3, and 8 in table 18.1) began with small initial populations of 11, 15, and 20 respectively. These contrast with the initial populations of 34, 65, and 39 for villages D, G, and H. The question is whether the small villages can survive as independent communities or will disband and fuse with other communities. Their continuance is problematical for several reasons.

Maintaining subsistence for such small groups can be questionable. Successful hunting can be sporadic, and consequently the kill is always shared with all the community. The smaller the number of hunters, the greater is the uncertainty factor. Also the fewer the gardens, the more difficult it usually is to recover from the ravages of insects and diseases. Another threat is mortality. A fatal attack of infectious disease or a fatal raid, especially if key members of the community die, can make the community unviable. Another problem is retention of members. Usually these small villages contain a single faction composed of a single family. This means all the young people are brothers and sisters to one another. The males usually out-migrate for their period of bride service to their in-laws. Their return following this period is problematical. The females remain for the period of bride service of their husbands, but their residence after this period is also problematical.

The populations of villages A and F (cycles 1 and 3) were unable to generate sustained growth. Both villages suffered the deaths of their headmen. The skills of the headmen are essential in coping with the problems faced by these villages and become a crucial element in their continuance. The combination of reduced numbers and the loss of the ability of the headmen brought about the survivors' decisions to disband the villages. Village A fused with village B, while the majority of village F out-migrated and fused with the Aica village of Flexal. As seen in its case history, village F lasted only four years. Village E (cycle 8) is an example of a village starting with a small population of 15 people but succeeding in growing. Its headmen were respected by all the Mucajaí communities, and its location near the mission with the medical and trading facilities made the village attractive to in-migrants, with a consequent high rate of growth.

## IV. Cycles of Population Decline

This classification includes two cycles (cycles 1 and 3) of villages with small initial populations unable to sustain themselves. The other case of a declining population, village B (cycle 2), probably would have disbanded had it not been for the in-migration from (fusion) of village A when that village ceased to exist. In all three cases, the population decline was the result of low or moderate fertility being unable to overcome the high mortality. In all three cases fertility was held down because of sexual imbalance in the population structure.

## V. Cycles of Population Growth

All of the growth cycles (4, 5, 6, 7, 8) in the study began with varying degrees of sexual imbalance, which the villages were able to overcome by in-migration and by allowing the impact of the sex ratio at birth to take effect. As a result, most cycles attained high fertility. Mortality was borderline between moderate and high. With the exception of cycle 4, the mortality rates were dampened by the favorable conditions during the Linkage phase. Overall, these were cycles of growth because of favorable levels of all four components: high fertility and in-migration, the positive factors in population growth, and only marginally high mortality and low out-migration, the negative factors.

## VI. Demographic Limits to the Size of Village Populations

An examination of the cycles in table 18.1 indicates that there are lower and upper limits to the size of village populations. The table confirms the rule of thumb of a population of about twenty people or less as a small size village. Below this limit, a village usually goes out of existence and its surviving population fuses with an already existing village.

The initial populations of the other villages were larger. For the cycles in the earlier years of the research period for which initial size is known (cycles 5–7), the initial populations were 33, 34, and 35. In later years the initial populations of the villages were 33, 39, 44, 53, and 65 for an average of 46.8 (cycles 9–13).

At what density do the village populations become too large and fission due to the problems of conflict arising from the crowded conditions? Cycles 4, 5, 6, and 7 indicate that fission takes place when the village populations living in a single yano reach somewhere between 70 and a little more than 100 people. The exact figures were 86, 69, 107, and 74 for an average of 84.

This is confirmed by the surveys of Yanomami villages in Table 4.1. There is no magical number at which fissioning takes place, as social, political, and psychological factors also enter into the decision, especially involving the headmen of the factions. As some villages change to a settlement pattern of individual families occupying Brazilian-style houses, it will be interesting to see how this affects fissioning arising from demographic density. Fissioning at almost any size of population may take place for reasons other than the problems arising from demographic density.

## VII. Lengths of the Cycles

The three complete cycles of growth (5, 6, 7) of villages with sizable initial populations lasted 28, 23, and 20 years respectively. The length of a cycle depends not only on the rates of total increase during the cycle but also on the size and sexual balance of the initial population. All three of these villages had an initial problem of sexual imbalance, which lengthened their cycles to various degrees. Although village E (cycle 8) had a high rate of total increase, the length of its incomplete cycle was 32 years, the longest of both complete and incomplete cycles. The reason was the small size (15) of its initial population.

## VIII. Villages with Sexual Imbalance

There was a shortage of females relative to the number of males at the beginning of cycles 1, 2, and 4 in the Precontact period and continuing in cycles 5, 6, 7, and 8 into the Contact period. Two main problems were created by this imbalance. For males, there was the problem of finding a marriage partner. But the more difficult problem was maintaining the group level of fertility high enough to overcome the level of mortality and thereby maintain the demographic stability or natural increase of the community.

The marriage problem resulted in a high percentage of polyandrous unions (Early and Peters 1990:105–8). The most prevalent form was fraternal polyandry. Some unions involved three or four men. The secondary husbands were not complacent about their situation and, as soon as possible, entered into unions in which they became the primary husbands. When sexual balance was achieved in these communities, monogamy became the predominant form of marital union.

The marriage problem created by the unbalanced sex ratio was further aggravated in some villages by the dominance of a single descent category, which meant the presence of many Yanomami brother-sister relationships (siblings and parallel cousins) between the members of the community. This created the necessity for marriages with other villages both within and out-side the Mucajaí bloc while the preference was for intravillage marriage.

The polyandrous unions and marriages outside the village did not solve the problem of low group fertility and its role in overcoming high mortality. Group fertility in the villages was increased by three means: external in-migration of reproductive females; the automatic mechanism of the sex ratio of births; and to some extent by external male in-migration.

In the Precontact and Contact phases, the taking of female captives was important for altering the fertility levels of villages B and C. The other means were encouraging the in-migration of females for marriage and the retention of Mucajaí females after an in-migrating husband's period of bride service. Not until 1983 did the first Mucajaí female out-migrate from the group (external migration) for marriage purposes. The Xilixana families were able to persuade the families of females from external villages to forgo the custom of the male performing bride service in those villages. Important for the persuasion were gifts of trade goods and the availability of medical services from the missionaries. These same two attractions kept male exter-nal in-migrants for marriage in the Mucajaí villages after they finished their period of bride service.

As is noted in the village histories, some villages were dominated by a single descent category, which meant that many of the younger generation were Yanomami brothers and sisters (parallel cousins) to each other, with marriage prohibited between them. This in turn delayed the age at first marriage, thereby lowering total fertility. This was especially true of village A, dominated by descent category E, and village C, dominated by descent category A, in the Precontact period. And this, in addition to the shortage of women, was why the period of isolation from other Yanomami groups was a difficult era for the Xilixana. In spite of the growth of category A in village C after contact, the effect of single-category dominance was offset by the growth of new descent categories from male external in-migration. The offsetting of the dominance of a single descent category by external male migration is especially seen in village E, which had the highest dominance of category A of all the villages. Village D had better balance in its descent composition because it was composed of two factions identified by different descent categories, so they could exchange marital partners between them-selves. Villages G and H are examples of villages with diversity in their descent composition.

Eight cases of prohibited marriages have been recorded. One was in 1963; there was village discussion about it, but it was allowed to stand. The remainder have taken place in the 1980s, half of them in village D at the FUNAI post. It may be that with the passage of time, ancestors closer in time are being taken as points of reference for determining descent categories. This divides a previous descent category into two or more categories, thereby lessening the number of parallel cousins and increasing the number of cross cousins.

Another factor in attaining sexual balance in the villages is the intrinsic tendency of populations to bring about sexual balance and maintain it. In figures 10.2 and 11.2, once the two sex ratios attained 50 percent and 20 percent respectively, the approximate values of sexual balance, they tend to level off and hover around these values. Migration and/or mortality with sex ratios different from those of the existing population simply speed up or slow down the intrinsic tendency.

This tendency gradually to bring about sexual balance is due to the sex ratio of births, which biologically is nearly balanced. No matter how large its sexual imbalance may be, a population will gradually attain sexual balance if the balanced sex ratio of births takes hold and continues year after year as each birth cohort works its way through the population's age structure. The sex ratios of deaths and migration may impede but usually do not overcome this intrinsic tendency.

The restoration of sexual balance in a population is illustrated in figure 18.1 by a model that holds all other variation still and shows only the impact of the sex ratio of births. It assumes that initially (year 0 on the x axis) there is a sexual imbalance of 80 percent males and 20 percent females in all age categories. Then year by year (x axis), propelled by the sex ratio at birth, the imbalance is replaced by a sexual balance of 50 percent and 50 percent for each consecutive single age group beginning with the first year of life. It takes 15 years before the 0 to <15 age category attains balance, as shown by the equal areas of the graph for the two sexes in the this age classification at the 15th year. During the population's first 15 years, the other age categories continue the 80 percent–20 percent imbalance. Once the 0 to <15 age category attains balance, the sex ratio of births continues to propel the balance year by year into the next age category. Once again it takes 15 years for this group to attain balance, as shown by the equal areas for the two sexes at year 30. The same pattern continues for the other two age categories. At the end of 60 years the entire population has reached sexual balance.

In actual situations, the idealized pattern of the model can be broken by the sex ratios of deaths, in-migration, and out-migration, which can affect the age distribution at any age. But the model shows how the underlying tendency of the sex ratio at birth is constantly a factor in the structure of a population. It was important in restoring the sexual balance of villages B

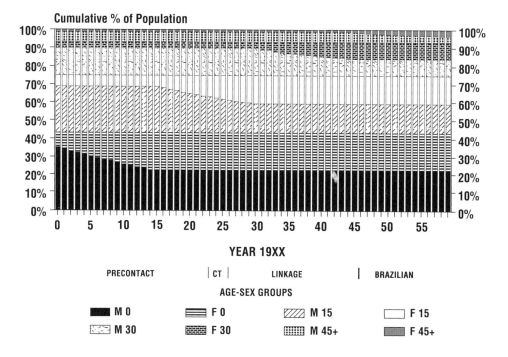

18.1. Effect of sexual balance of the sex ratio at birth.

and C following female in-migration. For the sake of simplicity, the model passes over the fact that the sex ratio of births usually shows a slight male predominance; but mortality in the early years also tends to have a slight male predominance, so that the effects frequently balance out in later childhood. There is also some question about the Yanomami sex ratio at birth, discussed in chapter 20.

## IX. Chance Occurrence as an Explanation Factor

In the discussions of the case histories, reference is made to chance occurrences. These chance occurrences, of which small-number volatility is one example, can become important factors in the magnitudes of the components of change. The various kinds of rational explanations for the magnitudes of the components may obscure the role of chance in the population dynamics.

An example of small-number volatility was seen in village F from 1985 to 1988 (chapter 15). There were three births in the 89 person years lived by this community, for a crude birth rate of 34.5 (table 15.1). This is moderate fertility. If there had been one less birth, the crude birth rate would have been 23.0, a rate difference of 11.5 and bringing it close to being labeled low fertility. Had there been one more birth, the crude birth rate would have risen to 46.0, which would have been called high fertility. Chance played a role in the number of births being three rather than two or four.

An example of a chance occurrence playing a significant role was in village C during the years 1948–49. As discussed in chapter 11, during these two years there were seven male and no female births. Figure 11.2 shows how this decreased the sex ratio of the population from 36.5 percent to 32.4 percent and the sex ratio of the reproductive population from 14.3 percent to a very low 10.3 percent. All the change was due to the chance occurrence of seven male and no female births, as deaths were evenly divided between male and female (one each) and there was no migration. Without this chance occurrence, the balancing of the sex ratios would have taken place sooner.

A further example of chance occurrence is a case of female sterility in village B during the Precontact phase, a period of low fertility due to a lack of reproductive females. The woman's reproductive years would have been a thirteen-year period, 1947 to the year of her death in 1959. If it is assumed that she would have had four children (based on spacing of three years), three of them during the Precontact period, the crude birth rate for this phase would have been 22.4 instead of 18.5. This would have mitigated the population decline of the phase.

Considering its possible role in all four components of population change, chance can play a significant role in the overall increase or decrease of a village population. It is possible that a village could go out of existence because of chance occurrences.

## X. Centers of Contact and Yanomami Population Dynamics

To compare the population dynamics of the villages from another point of view, the question can be posed: Were the varying distances of the Mucajaí villages from the centers of contact responsible for differential death rates and consequently natural increase or decrease of the populations? The phrase *centers of contact* is used here to designate places where nonindigenous groups maintain facilities to provide some type of public or religious service to indigenous groups. Historically missionary groups started many of these centers and it has been customary to call them missions. But with the passage of time and increased contact of tribal groups with the national society, many centers grow and become centers for governmental services, education, markets, and other enterprises. While the missionary function may remain important, it is frequently misleading to designate such places simply as missions.

## A. Centers of Contact among Venezuelan Yanomami

There has been discussion (Chagnon 1992:239–43, 1997:241–54) about the impact of Venezuelan centers of contact on the population dynamics of the Yanomami villages in the upper Orinoco region. The three main centers of contact are Ocamo, Mavaca, and Platanal, with Mavaca the largest of the three. At these centers there are buildings used for chapels, medical services, bilingual schools, Yanomami cooperatives, military posts (intermittently used), and malaria control. Mavaca had a small honey factory and a few small warehouses. To provide these services there are permanent nonindigenous personnel: Salesian priest(s), brother(s), and nuns; medical doctor(s) assisted by university medical students; and some nonindigenous employees connected with educational and medical work. Also there are trained Yanomami personnel who work with the various services. The centers contain small residences for these groups. In addition, the centers are the bases of operations for a floating population consisting of explorers, scientists, anthropologists, soldiers, government employees, Yekwana traders, and occasional tourists.

Chagnon (1997:244) has distinguished three types of villages by their degree of contact with these centers: (1) villages located at the centers of contact, where Yanomami have permanent contact with outsiders; (2) intermediate villages with intermittent contact with the centers; and (3) remote villages with no direct contact with the centers, only indirect or mediate contact because of contact with intermediate villages. Chagnon calculates that villages at the centers of contact and the remote villages suffered about a 5 percent and 6.5 percent loss of population respectively due to mortality, while the loss at the intermediate villages was around 20 percent. According to Chagnon, the rate is held down at the centers of contact by the availability of medical services and acquired immunity. The high rate for the intermediate villages is due to enough contact to be exposed to new diseases but insufficient contact to prevent villagers dying before they can get help. Chagnon gives no explanation for the low rate of remote villages.

A problem with Chagnon's methodology is the assumption that all the change in the size of the population or any age group is due to mortality alone, ignoring the other three components of change. His results are probably indicative of a mortality problem in the intermediate villages, but the extent of it cannot be indicated by the measures he uses. The claim for a low mortality rate for the remote villages raises some questions. Populations of this type usually have the least immunity and can experience epidemics of infectious disease contracted from intermediate villages. The case history of the high mortality in village B due to their relationship with the Malaxi theli in 1960 is an example. Also, Chagnon's data indicate that the mortality of these villages has been affected by Yanomami raiders using shotguns.

## B. Centers of Contact among the Mucajaí Yanomami

In Brazil there are two types of centers of contact at varying distances from the Mucajaí villages: missions and FUNAI posts. The Mucajaí mission post is small compared to the Venezuelan centers. The only permanent personnel are two or three missionaries, Brazilians or Americans. In the 1990s there were several buildings—three small residences, a medical dispensary, and two tool sheds. The first four have palm-slat sides with aluminum roofing. The mission is not strategically located as a stop-off point to another destination as far as the outside world is concerned except for miners using the Mucajaí River for access to the highlands. Consequently there was no floating population before 1987. It has been intermittent since that time.

In the case histories we have noted the various moves of the Mucajaí villages. A classification has been made of the years the villages have been located at various sites and their travel time from the centers of contact. This classification is analogous to Chagnon's classification of the Venezuelan groups but with important differences due to different circumstances. The categories are:

1. Villages located at the mission (B, 1961–79; C, 1959–79; D, 1961–62)
2. Villages located a travel time of a half hour to an hour and a half from the mission (B, 1980–82; C, 1980–91; D, 1963–83; E, 1963–96; G, 1984–96; H, 1986–91)
3. Villages located three hours or more from the mission (B, 1959–60 and 1993–96; C, 1991–96)
4. Villages located at FUNAI posts (D, 1984–96; H, 1992–96)
5. Village located two or more hours from FUNAI posts (F, 1985–88).

Table 18.2 presents the crude death rates of the villages classified by their location at or travel time from the centers of contact and by the historical

Table 18.2. Demographic Profiles of Mucajaí Villages by Travel Time from Centers of Contact

| | At Mission | ½–1½ hr. from Mission | 3 hr. from Mission | At FUNAI | 2 hr. from FUNAI |
|---|---|---|---|---|---|
| | Contact Phase | | | | |
| CNI | −13.6 | - | −84.0 | - | - |
| CBR | 54.2 | - | 33.6 | - | - |
| CDR | 67.8 | - | 117.6 | - | - |
| Person Yrs. | 148 | - | 60 | - | - |
| Villages | C | - | B | - | - |
| | Linkage Phase | | | | |
| CNI | 33.1 | 29.6 | - | - | - |
| CBR | 45.7 | 52.7 | - | - | - |
| CDR | 12.6 | 23.1 | - | - | - |
| Person Yrs. | 2,147 | 2,628 | - | - | - |
| Villages | B,C | B,C,D,E | - | - | - |
| | Brazilian Phase | | | | |
| CNI | - | 23.3 | 39.8 | 23.0 | −57.5 |
| CBR | - | 48.7 | 52.1 | 51.3 | 34.5 |
| CDR | - | 25.3 | 12.3 | 28.2 | 92.0 |
| Person Yrs. | - | 2247 | 327 | 956 | 76 |
| Villages | - | B,C,D,E,F,G | B,C | D,H | F |

phases, because of the different epidemiological situations of the villages in each phase. The death rates for the Contact phase show the differential impact of infectious disease as discussed in the case histories. It is not clear why the epidemic was so much greater in village B than in C. Distance from the mission does not appear to have been a major factor as the Malaxi theli visited both villages and the mission. There is a correlation in the Linkage phase of travel time from the mission and the crude death rate. In the Brazilian phase, the higher death rates at the FUNAI post and farther downriver at village F appear related to their more intense contact with the Aica and with Boa Vista. FUNAI, and later the Yanomami Health Service, transport Xilixana for treatment to Boa Vista rather than working at the posts due to the lack of trained personnel. The low rates of villages B and C appear to be related to lesser contact with Brazilians rather than to their distance from the mission.

## XI. Why Has Contact Remained Intermittent?

In the case histories of the Mucajaí villages, it was found that each village was still in intermittent contact with the national society. This raises a question: Why in spite of almost forty years of contact have the Mucajaí Ninam remained in intermittent contact? Why have they not entered into permanent contact, as would be predicted by Ribeiro's model?

The external reasons are that no ranchers or agriculturists have invaded and taken possession of Xilixana territory; no mineral ore worth mining has been found in the middle Mucajaí area; and there is no pressing need for Xilixana labor—Brazilians can obtain labor from savanna Indians and landless peasants. Further, government presence has been confined to FUNAI posts, where constant changes in personnel, their small number, and their lack of knowledge of the Ninam language decrease the intensity of this contact; and the middle Mucajaí area is not on any transportation route that would invite outside visitors.

Internally, due to fear of disease, the decision in the middle 1970s by the Mucajaí people themselves to restrict their contacts with Brazilians has prolonged the intermittent stage and muted the pressures for cash, manufactured goods, learning Portuguese, and the other factors of dependency leading to permanent contact. Even the missionaries have only intermittent contact with Brazilian society, as they live with the Mucajaí people and form part of the semi-isolated community. Their medical and trader roles mitigate the need of the Mucajaí people for more intense contact with the national society.

## XII. Summary

Three lines of inquiry are here explored to offer comparative perspectives of the eight case histories concerning the population dynamics of the Mucajaí villages. First we have distinguished and classified thirteen life cycles for the eight villages and have examined their demographic characteristics. Described next is how the sex ratio of births affects the sex structure of a population. Third is the question of the differential impact on the population dynamics of the villages' varying distances from the centers of contact. We end with an enumeration of reasons why the Xilixana, in spite of over forty years of contact, have remained in only intermittent contact. It has been a protracted intermittent period, as described by the alternative intermittent stage of Ribeiro's model in chapter 5, but one in which the population increased rather than decreased. We address some implications of this later.

# 19

## The Population Bloc

Moving the demographic imagination to a higher level of abstraction, we turn now to viewing the Mucajaí Yanomami as a single population, prescinding from the eight village populations that have been the focus so far. This is the level of abstraction employed in the previous volume (Early and Peters 1990). First, we present the demographic profile of the population bloc. The demographic rates presented in these tables can be considered as weighted averages of the values for the individual villages. The weights are the population sizes of the individual villages and consequently their differential contributions to the group values. An unweighted average would simply add the levels of the demographic variables for each village regardless of size (unweighted) and divide by the number of villages. The unweighted average reverts to the level of abstraction used in the preceding

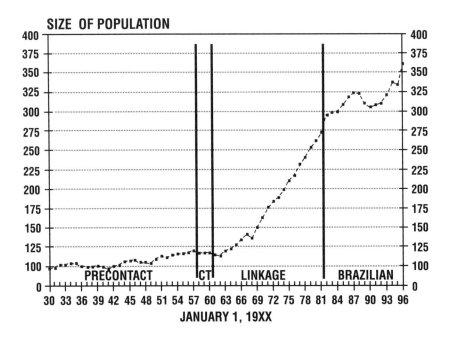

19.1. Mucajaí group population.

chapters by considering each village independently and as making an equal contribution to the group average. Both views can be helpful, depending on the analytical question being asked of the data. For purposes of summation and results based on a larger N, the group level as a weighted average is preferred.

## I. The Relative Importance of the Villages for the Group Profile

While considering the demographic profile for the entire group, it may be helpful to know the relative importance (weight) of each of the previous case histories for this profile. Table 19.1 shows the absolute and relative contributions of each village to the group population for the years at the beginning and end of each historical phase as well as the number of person years lived by each village during each historical phase. (The person years are the rounded figures of the annual midyear populations). For the Pre-contact and Contact phases, village C was clearly dominant, while in the other two phases, the village contributions were more evenly distributed.

In spite of the advantages of summation and decreased volatility because of the number of cases, viewing the Mucajaí Yanomami as a single population instead of as a series of village populations also has some disadvantages. It may conceal some unusual dynamics of individual villages because of their relatively small size. Because of the dominance of village C, the group population increased in both the Precontact and Contact phases. But this masks the population decrease and the demographic crisis in village B as well the collapse of village A. In the Linkage phase, the initial problematic situation of village E because of its small size is masked. In the Brazilian phase, the collapse of village F is lost. There are some population dynamics that take only place at the village level, fission and fusion being perhaps the most important. Viewing the Mucajaí population bloc as a single population or as eight individual village populations are two different ways of using the demographic imagination. Both views are important and they supplement each other.

## II. The Mucajaí Population and Its Components of Change

Figure 19.1 shows the growth of the Mucajaí population over the sixty-six-year period. Table 19.2 presents the quantitative levels of the components of change, while tables 19.3, 19.4, and 19.10 show in more detail fertility, mortality, and migration in the same manner as the tables for the individual villages. Both figure 19.1 and table 19.2 show the very different levels of

Table 19.1. Population and Person Years of Villages Comprising the Xilixana

Population (P) and Person Years (PY)

| Villages | | 1930 | Precontact | 1957 | Contact | 1961 | Linkage | 1982 | Brazilian | 1996 |
|---|---|---|---|---|---|---|---|---|---|---|
| Group | P | 96 | | 120 | | 114 | | 295 | | 361 |
| | PY | | 2,843 | | 468 | | 3,844 | | 4,420 | |
| A | P | 11 | | 17 | | - | | - | | - |
| | PY | | 398 | | 9 | | - | | - | |
| B | P | 33 | | 21 | | 28 | | 65 | | 37 |
| | PY | | 758 | | 118 | | 923 | | 663 | |
| C | P | 52 | | 82 | | 38 | | 107 | | 47 |
| | PY | | 1,687 | | 316 | | 1,300 | | 774 | |
| D | P | - | | - | | 48 | | 73 | | 57 |
| | PY | | - | | 26 | | 1,076 | | 929 | |
| E | P | - | | - | | - | | 50 | | 71 |
| | PY | | - | | - | | 545 | | 865 | |
| F | P | - | | - | | - | | - | | - |
| | PY | | - | | - | | - | | 87 | |
| G | P | - | | - | | - | | - | | 94 |
| | PY | | - | | - | | - | | 729 | |
| H | P | - | | - | | - | | - | | 55 |
| | PY | | - | | - | | - | | 374 | |

Village Populations and Person Years as Percentages of Total Group

| Villages | | 1930 | Precontact | 1957 | Contact | 1961 | Linkage | 1982 | Brazilian | 1996 |
|---|---|---|---|---|---|---|---|---|---|---|
| Group | P | 100% | | 100% | | 100% | | 100% | | 100% |
| | PY | | 100% | | 100% | | 100% | | 100% | |
| A | P | 11.5 | | 14.2 | | - | | - | | - |
| | PY | | 14.0 | | 1.9 | | - | | - | |
| B | P | 34.4 | | 17.5 | | 24.6 | | 22.0 | | 10.2 |
| | PY | | 26.7 | | 25.4 | | 24.0 | | 15.0 | |
| C | P | 54.2 | | 68.3 | | 33.3 | | 36.3 | | 13.0 |
| | PY | | 59.3 | | 67.5 | | 33.8 | | 17.5 | |
| D | P | - | | - | | 42.1 | | 24.7 | | 15.8 |
| | PY | | - | | 5.6 | | 28.0 | | 21.0 | |
| E | P | - | | - | | - | | 16.9 | | 19.7 |
| | PY | | - | | - | | 14.2 | | 19.6 | |
| F | P | - | | - | | - | | - | | - |
| | PY | | - | | - | | - | | 2.0 | |
| G | P | - | | - | | - | | - | | 26.0 |
| | PY | | - | | - | | - | | 16.5 | |
| H | P | - | | - | | - | | - | | 15.2 |
| | PY | | - | | - | | - | | 8.5 | |

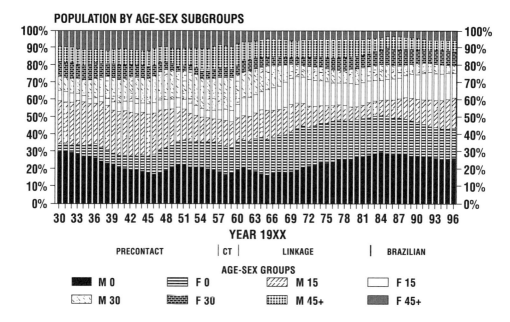

19.2. Mucajaí group age-sex distribution.

growth in each of the four historical phases. There was population decrease in the Contact phase, a slight increase in the Precontact phase, moderate growth in the Brazilian phase, and rapid growth in the Linkage phase. Natural increase or decrease were more important than net migration for the change of population size in all the phases. Table 19.2.c and figure 19.2 show the shifting composition of age-sex groups in the population over the sixty-six-year period. The figure indicates the relatively small proportion of females in the first two age categories during the Precontact phase for reasons discussed in the case histories. The gradual coming to sexual balance in the Linkage phase can be seen. The figure also shows the increasing percentage that children to the age of 15 are of the total population. In other words, the population is growing younger.

## III. Fertility (Table 19.3)

As detailed in the case histories, it is important to distinguish individual and group fertility since they are not necessarily correlated because of the age-sex structure of a population. In addition to the age-sex structure, fertility also depends on the distribution of descent categories. The dominance of

**Table 19.2. Mucajai Ninam: Demographic Profile, 1930–96**

| 19.2.a | 1930 | Precontact | 1957 | Contact | 1961 | Linkage | 1982 | Brazilian | 1996 |
|---|---|---|---|---|---|---|---|---|---|
| Population | 96 | | 120 | | 114 | | 295 | | 361 |
| Total Incr. | | 24 | | −6 | | 181 | | 66 | |
| Nat. Incr. | | 16 | | −12 | | 135 | | 87 | |
| Births | | 79 | | 14 | | 201 | | 210 | |
| Deaths | | 63 | | 26 | | 66 | | 123 | |
| Net Migration | | 8 | | 6 | | 46 | | −21 | |
| In-mig. | | 8 | | 6 | | 49 | | 21 | |
| Out-mig. | | 0 | | 0 | | 3 | | 42 | |

**19.2.b** — Crude Rates

| 19.2.b | Precontact | Contact | Linkage | Brazilian |
|---|---|---|---|---|
| Total Incr. | 8.4 | −12.8 | 47.1 | 14.9 |
| Nat. Incr. | 5.6 | −25.6 | 35.1 | 19.7 |
| Births | 27.8 | 29.9 | 52.3 | 47.5 |
| Deaths | 22.2 | 55.6 | 17.2 | 27.8 |
| Net Migration | | | | |
| In-mig. | 2.8 | 12.8 | 12.7 | 4.8 |
| Out-mig. | 0.0 | 0.0 | 0.0 | 9.5 |

**19.2.c** — Population: Age by Sex

| 19.2.c | 1930 | 1957 | 1961 | 1982 | 1996 |
|---|---|---|---|---|---|
| Population | 96 | 120 | 114 | 295 | 361 |
| Male | 69 | 78 | 71 | 159 | 202 |
| Female | 27 | 42 | 43 | 136 | 159 |
| % Female | 28.1 | 35.0 | 37.7 | 46.1 | 44.0 |

| % Age-Sex | Precontact %M | Precontact %F | Contact %M | Contact %F | Linkage %M | Linkage %F | Brazilian %M | Brazilian %F |
|---|---|---|---|---|---|---|---|---|
| 0 | 22.6 | 9.9 | 18.3 | 15.8 | 22.6 | 21.7 | 27.9 | 19.5 |
| 15 | 22.2 | 5.0 | 14.4 | 6.6 | 11.9 | 13.5 | 13.1 | 13.6 |
| 30 | 14.5 | 6.2 | 18.7 | 4.9 | 9.6 | 4.7 | 6.9 | 7.9 |
| 45 | 9.7 | 10.0 | 12.9 | 8.2 | 10.2 | 4.9 | 7.2 | 4.0 |
| Total | 68.9 | 31.1 | 64.4 | 35.6 | 54.3 | 45.7 | 55.1 | 44.9 |

Table 19.3. Mucajaí Ninam: Fertility Rates and Descent Categories

| Level of Analysis | Indicator | Age/ Sex | Precont. | Contact | Link. | Brazil |
|---|---|---|---|---|---|---|
| | | | | Phases | | |
| Group | Crude Birth | - | 27.8 | 29.9 | 52.3 | 47.5 |
| | Pf as % Pop. | 15–44 | 11.2 | 11.5 | 19.2 | 21.5 |
| Female | Age-Specific | 15 | 422 | 140 | 279 | 189 |
| Reproductive | Rates | 20 | 382 | 500 | 285 | 291 |
| Population | | 25 | 241 | 286 | 327 | 206 |
| | | 30 | 250 | 345 | 274 | 300 |
| | | 35 | 194 | 364 | 194 | 225 |
| | | 40 | 97 | - | 172 | 78 |
| | General | 15–44 | 248 | 259 | 272 | 221 |
| Avg. Female | Total Fert. | 15–44 | 7.9 | 8.2 | 7.7 | 6.4 |
| N Births | Total | | 79 | 14 | 201 | 210 |
| | | M | 41 | 7 | 104 | 116 |
| | | F | 38 | 7 | 97 | 94 |
| Village | % Descent Categories | | | | | |
| | A | | 31.5 | 42.7 | 43.8 | 40.5 |
| | S | | 2.9 | 3.6 | 4.6 | 4.5 |
| | C | | 6.4 | 4.5 | 4.3 | 3.1 |
| | D | | 18.3 | 22.3 | 18.1 | 22.8 |
| | E | | 6.4 | 5.1 | 1.3 | .3 |
| | F | | 10.7 | 6.8 | 4.8 | 3.2 |
| | Other/Unknown | | 10.9 | 3.6 | - | .3 |
| | Ext. In-mig. | | 13.0 | 11.5 | 23.2 | 25.1 |
| | Total | | 100 | 100 | 100 | 100 |
| Villages | Crude Rates | | | | | |
| A | | | 22.6 | 0.0 | - | - |
| B | | | 18.5 | 16.9 | 59.6 | 54.3 |
| C | | | 33.2 | 38.0 | 49.2 | 43.9 |
| D | | | - | - | 44.6 | 49.5 |
| E | | | - | - | 62.4 | 50.9 |
| F | | | - | - | - | 34.5 |
| G | | | - | - | - | 46.6 |
| H | | | - | - | - | 34.8 |

descent category A meant that there were difficulties finding marriage partners with a different descent category.

The total fertility rate as a measure of individual fertility was high in all the phases although there was some decline in the Brazilian phase. Table 19.3 shows that traditional Yanomami fertility is about eight live births over the reproductive span. This figure is confirmed by the total fertility rate of 7.9 found by Schkolnik (1983:116) in a study of ten villages in the Parima

Highlands with a population of 653. It is also confirmed in a survey of Venezuelan Yanomami by Neel and Weiss (1975:32), who found a pregnancy rate of 8.1. If fetal mortality were subtracted from this rate, it would probably approximate the findings of this study and of Schkolnik.

The fertility decline in the Brazilian phase appears to be due primarily to later age at first marriage. The reasons for this are not fully understood. It may be due partially to problems of sex ratios and descent categories. The deteriorating health conditions of this period are probably an additional factor.

In contrast to individual fertility, there is distinctive variation in group fertility as shown by the difference between the crude birth rates for the first two phases and the last two. The low levels of the Precontact and Contact phases were due to a shortage of females in the population (table 19.2) and the prevalence of Yanomami brother-sister relationships. Table 19.4 also shows the variation among the village crude rates. The clustering of the values in each of the four historical phases validates the usefulness of the historical classification to discriminate the data.

The level of the crude birth rate for the Mucajaí Linkage phase is also confirmed by Schkolnik's (1983:115) rate of 55.2 for the Parima bloc. This has been classified as a Linkage phase study because the ten villages were in a region where the services of New Tribes missionaries were available but remote from Venezuelan rural society and the centers of contact.

## IV. Levels of Mortality (Tables 19.4, 19.5)

Table 19.4 shows that this component of change had the most variation of the four components across the historical periods, and consequently it is the major factor for the variation in natural and total increase. The rate was at an extremely high level in the Contact phase; was less but still at a high level in the Brazilian phase; was high in the Precontact phase but less than in the Brazilian phase; and became moderate in the Linkage phase. From a health viewpoint, the rates clearly show the favorable conditions of the Linkage phase and the unfavorable conditions of the Brazilian phase. The mortality levels of the Brazilian phase are higher than in the Precontact phase in spite of Precontact deaths from conflict and infanticide and when the Yanomami had no access to any western health services. The mortality level of the Linkage phase is confirmed by Smole's (1976:74) crude death rate of 17.0 from the same Parima highland villages as Schkolnik's study and derived from missionary registers.

The age structure of mortality in table 19.4 is expressed by age-specific mortality rates, as was done for the individual villages. But at the group

**Table 19.4. Mucajaí Ninam: Mortality Rates**

| Level of Analysis | Indicator | Age/ Sex | Phases Precont. | Contact | Linkage | Brazil |
|---|---|---|---|---|---|---|
| Group | Crude Death | | 22.5 | 55.6 | 17.2 | 28.1 |
| Age Groups | Age-Specific Rates | 0 | 177 | 167 | 129 | 200 |
| | | 1 | 12 | 28 | 15 | 44 |
| | | 5 | 6 | - | 11 | 3 |
| | | 10 | 13 | 27 | 5 | 5 |
| | | 20 | 12 | - | 10 | 12 |
| | | 30 | 17 | 50 | 7 | 9 |
| | | 40 | 13 | 70 | 10 | 25 |
| | | 50 | 22 | 125 | 12 | 28 |
| | | 60 | 38 | 164 | 40 | 94 |
| | | 70+ | - | - | 15 | 220 |
| N Deaths | Total | | 64 | 26 | 66 | 124 |
| | | M | 34 | 15 | 35 | 68 |
| | | F | 30 | 11 | 31 | 56 |
| N Reasons | Infectious Disease | M | 1 | 10 | 17 | 33 |
| | | F | 1 | 7 | 13 | 21 |
| | Non-infect. Disease | M | 3 | 2 | 1 | 7 |
| | | F | - | - | - | 5 |
| | Infanticide | M | 2 | - | 4 | 6 |
| | | F | 11 | 1 | 9 | 10 |
| | Homicide | M | 8 | - | 5 | 2 |
| | | F | 2 | - | - | - |
| | Accidents | M | 2 | - | 1 | 2 |
| | | F | - | - | 3 | 2 |
| | Unknown | M | 18 | 3 | 7 | 18 |
| | | F | 16 | 3 | 6 | 18 |
| Villages | Crude Rates | | | | | |
| A | | | 15.1 | 266.6 | - | - |
| B | | | 29.0 | 84.4 | 15.2 | 37.7 |
| C | | | 20.8 | 38.0 | 15.4 | 27.1 |
| D | | | - | - | 18.6 | 30.1 |
| E | | | - | - | 22.0 | 20.8 |
| F | | | - | - | - | 92.0 |
| G | | | - | - | - | 20.6 |
| H | | | - | - | - | 21.4 |

**Table 19.5. Mucajaí Ninam: Life Table Values by Sex and Historical Phase**

| Indicator | Age | Precontact | | | Contact | | | Linkage | | | Brazilian | | |
|---|---|---|---|---|---|---|---|---|---|---|---|---|---|
| | | T | M | F | T | M | F | T | M | F | T | M | F |
| Life Exp.(e) at Birth | 0 | 39.8 | 45.2 | 35.8 | 29.1 | 39.8 | 22.3 | 46.3 | 46.9 | 46.5 | 35.4 | 36.4 | 33.2 |
| Probability dying (q) in Interval | 0 | 177 | 49 | 316 | 143 | - | 286 | 129 | 115 | 144 | 200 | 190 | 223 |
| | 1 | 45 | 46 | 44 | 105 | - | 157 | 59 | 25 | 94 | 162 | 113 | 230 |
| | 5 | 31 | 44 | - | - | - | - | 54 | 87 | 19 | 14 | - | 36 |
| | 10 | 122 | 112 | 156 | 239 | 144 | 357 | 51 | 55 | 48 | 50 | 60 | 37 |
| | 20 | 110 | 134 | - | - | - | - | 95 | 66 | 121 | 113 | 122 | 106 |
| | 30 | 156 | 177 | 92 | 402 | 403 | 400 | 67 | 75 | 56 | 88 | 99 | 79 |
| | 40 | 118 | 105 | 133 | 519 | 602 | - | 94 | 86 | 114 | 219 | 302 | 111 |
| | 50 | 195 | 243 | 150 | 769 | 732 | 833 | 116 | 153 | - | 249 | 307 | 142 |
| | 60 | 322 | 127 | 523 | 901 | 984 | 800 | 334 | 447 | 167 | 641 | 635 | 659 |
| | 70+ | 1,000 | 1,000 | 1,000 | 1,000 | 1,000 | 1,000 | 1,000 | 1,000 | 1,000 | 1,000 | 1,000 | 1,000 |
| % Surviving to Age (l) | 0 | 100 | 100 | 100 | 100 | 100 | 100 | 100 | 100 | 100 | 100 | 100 | 100 |
| | 1 | 82 | 95 | 68 | 86 | 100 | 71 | 87 | 89 | 86 | 80 | 81 | 78 |
| | 10 | 76 | 87 | 65 | 77 | 100 | 60 | 78 | 79 | 76 | 67 | 72 | 58 |
| | 30 | 60 | 67 | 55 | 58 | 86 | 39 | 67 | 70 | 64 | 56 | 59 | 50 |
| | 50 | 44 | 49 | 43 | 17 | 20 | 23 | 56 | 59 | 53 | 40 | 37 | 41 |

T = Total Group, M = Male, F = Female.

level there are more cases, so that a life table can be calculated although it is still based on a relatively small number of cases. The life table (table 19.5) is a probability model from which the life expectancy at birth is frequently taken as the summary indicator of the level of mortality expressed by the whole table.

The life expectancies for the group in the four phases show the same relationships as the crude death rates. Between the sexes there are ten- and sixteen-year differentials of life expectancy in the Precontact and Contact periods respectively. Part of this is due to preferential female infanticide, especially in the Precontact period, and also the volatility of small numbers, especially in the Contact period, for which a number of age classifications have no data. In the Linkage and Brazilian periods the sex differentials almost disappear. In the Brazilian phase, male life expectancy is even lower than it was in the Contact period of initial epidemics.

## V. Reasons for Mortality

Determining a cause of death without an extensive medical examination can frequently be difficult in industrial societies. Among tribal groups such as the Yanomami the difficulties are multiplied immensely. The basis for the classifications of the causes used in the mortality tables is explained in chapter 8.

### A. Unknown Causes

In table 19.6 absolute numbers of the causes of death from the last part of table 19.4 are converted into rates per 100,000 population, a convention frequently used for expressing mortality rates. Around 25 percent of the mortality in three of the phases falls into the unknown category and prevents tight analysis. However deaths due to accidents and homicides are well known and probably no deaths from these sources are included in the category of unknown causes. As discussed in chapters 6 and 7, there is also a good enumeration of infanticides. Therefore, most of the unknown causes are infectious or non-infectious diseases.

### B. Infectious Diseases

The wide range of diseases involved is discussed in chapter 8. As shown in tables 19.4 and 19.6, these diseases were responsible for the majority of the deaths in three of the four phases. An indeterminate portion of the deaths from the unknown category probably should be added to these to obtain the full picture. These diseases usually arise either directly from human contact or indirectly through the mediation of insects. Therefore any substantial

Table 19.6. Mucajaí Ninam: Causes of Death per 100,000 Population

| Cause of Death | Precontact | Contact | Linkage | Brazilian |
|---|---|---|---|---|
| Infectious Disease | 70 | 3,632 | 858 | 1,516 |
| Non-infectious Disease | 176 | 427 | 52 | 204 |
| Infanticide | 457 | 214 | 338 | 385 |
| Homicide | 352 | - | 104 | 23 |
| Accident | 35 | - | 78 | 45 |
| Unknown | 1,126 | 1,282 | 286 | 611 |
| Total | 2,216 | 5,556 | 1,717 | 2,783 |

increase of demographic density that involves exposure to new diseases increases mortality from this source. The Precontact phase had a low rate of infectious disease, but any inference from this figure is hindered by the high percentage of unknown causes. The infectious diseases are the most important factor in Yanomami mortality after contact. The findings here are confirmed in a survey of Venezuelan villages by Chagnon (1972:258) and by Eguillor (1984:51–53) for the concentration at Mavaca.

For the Mucajaí group, four deaths from malaria during the twenty-one years of the Linkage period were noted. But beginning with the Brazilian period in 1982, malaria was frequently noted as a reason for death. In a period of several months in 1990–91, there was an epidemic in which one third of Mucajaí population was down with malaria and six died. The missionary staff was pushed to exhaustion trying to cope with the epidemic, and some became victims themselves. A health survey from 1975–77 showed that there were twenty-two cases of tuberculosis in the population; a similar survey in 1992 showed twenty-seven cases.

There appears to be a pattern of infectious diseases contracted directly or indirectly from the national society. The early encounters usually involve measles and pneumonia. In time, these are supplanted in dominance by malaria and tuberculosis. The latter are lingering pathologies, the effects of which are played out over time. They weaken the health of their hosts, opening the way for the ravages of other diseases. This has happened in the Brazilian period, causing the elevated crude death rate. Malaria and tuberculosis were present in many more cases than those in which death was directly ascribed to them. Because of their importance, malaria and tuberculosis are discussed in greater detail later.

C. Non-Infectious Diseases

Most of these cases were diagnosed at the hospital in Boa Vista or by FUNAI personnel when the missionaries were temporarily removed by the government. Cancer and cirrhosis appear in the registers for this period, although the missionaries have some doubts about the accuracy of these categories.

### D. Homicide

This category includes intentional and accidental homicides but excludes infanticides, which are treated separately. The high rate of homicide in the Precontact phase primarily reflects the losses in village C during the conflict with the Yekwana. It is almost double an estimated 136 homicide rate for the Venezuelan Yanomami calculated from Chagnon's data for 1970–74 (Melancon 1982:33, 42). Among anthropological populations (Knauft 1987:464), it is surpassed only by the New Guinea tribes. In the other phases, the homicide rates are relatively low for an anthropological group. There was one accidental homicide in the Precontact phase, and two each occurred in the Linkage and Brazilian phases; these incidents are discussed in the case histories.

### E. Accidents

This category includes incidents of consuming poisonous berries, snake-bites, and being hit by falling limbs.

## VI. Malaria

Malaria was not endemic to the middle Mucajaí area until the arrival of miners in 1987. Since that time there has been a high incidence of the disease, which weakens its victims, who then become susceptible to other diseases. Some acquaintance with the miners and their work conditions helps one to understand the spread of malaria in the Yanomami area.

Many of the miners are from the underclass of eastern Brazil; poor, undernourished, and racked by various diseases. Before coming to Roraima, a number of them had worked in other gold rushes of the Amazon, where they contracted malaria. A gold mine frequently goes through a developmental process beginning with a manual stage (MacMillan 1995:43–44, 49). When an area yielding gold ore is discovered, a pit is dug in which the ore is loosened and scooped up with picks and shovels. The ore is mixed with large quantities of water and passed over a sluice box. The box is lined with sacking across which are placed horizontal wooden bars. The gold ore, being heavier than the water, sticks in the sacking and behind the bars, whence it is recovered. However, recovery is improved if mercury is used. Mercury is mixed with the sediment before this is moved through the sluice box. The mercury combines with the gold in the sediment, and the heavier amalgam of the two metals is easier to recover than gold alone. After the amalgam is recovered from the sluice box, it is placed in a metal dish where it is heated with a blowtorch to vaporize the mercury, leaving only the gold.

For those who can afford it, the operation becomes semi-mechanized. The miners use several different methods (Cleary 1990:6–22). In Roraima, use of hydraulic machines called *chupadeiras* was the more common method (MacMillan 1995:43; see also Schmink and Wood 1992:235–37). Two gasoline- or diesel-powered pumps with hoses were added to the operation. One pump turned the water source into high-pressure jets, which blasted out the sediment from the sides of the pit. The other pump and hose sucked up the muddy sediment and pulled it to the sluice box, where mercury was added before it passed through the sluice, and recovery was as in the manual operation.

The large amounts of water used with the pumps turn the pits into craters of slimy mud. O'Connor (1997:70) describes one that was seventy-five feet deep and compares it to looking down at a football stadium sunk into the earth. Descending into it, he found "a devastated lunar crater. Everything is awash in the light brown mud splattered from the riverbanks by the high-powered hoses. Two large tree trunks, recently torn from the earth, sit lopsided in front of me. A miner, eyes vacant, covered in dirt from head to toe, slowly wades through a pool of water, showing no recognition of our presence. . . . In the middle of the pit portable Yamaha generators sit vibrating continuously on wooden platforms. The tiny powerful machines drive the hydraulic pumps and give off a deafening noise permeating every corner of this devastated landscape." Waste mercury is sometimes salvaged before the firing. The remainder is dumped into the rivers or driven off as acid smoke to return later as acid rain.

Miners already infected with malaria and working in these conditions are frequently bitten by anopheles mosquitoes, transmitting the malaria parasite to the mosquitoes. To escape the blazing equatorial heat, the miners frequently work at night, the feeding time for mosquitoes. The infected mosquitoes spread over the region and bite other miners and Yanomami, thereby spreading malaria.

The landscape in a mining area is dotted by numerous pits. When the miners finish with a pit, the water remains and the pit is simply abandoned as is. The pools of water created by these work conditions provide an incubator for the mosquitoes. They breed in vast numbers and continue the cycle by biting and infecting more miners and Yanomami. While no one accuses the miners of deliberately transmitting malaria, it would be difficult to design a better environment for the spread of malaria than the work conditions of these gold mines. The elevated mortality levels of the Brazilian period, especially the infant mortality (table 19.5), are primarily due to malaria.

The results of this type of gold mining are an environment full of malaria-infecting mosquitoes; a rain forest wounded by the mining pits and by removal of trees; fauna driven off by the noise of the pumps; and rivers and streams choked with sediment polluted with mercury. For every ounce of gold extracted, there are nine tons of waste. For every gram of gold extracted, two cubic meters of sediment enter the watercourses (Sponsel 1997:103). The mercury released into the air and water is absorbed into the food chain, especially fish and fruits. Analysis of hair samples from fifteen Xilixana in 1990 showed an average mercury concentration of 4.13 micrograms of methylmercury per gram of hair, with one person above the acceptable World Health Organization limit of 6 micrograms (Castro, Albert, and Pfeiffer 1991:368–69).

## VII. Tuberculosis

Not only the miners but many of the Brazilian in-migrants to Roraima are from the poor underclass of eastern Brazil, people seeking to farm or have a small ranch. Coming from such a background, a number are in poor health and carry infectious diseases against which their constant exposure gives them some defense. When the Yanomami, without any previous exposure, work for these Brazilians, tuberculosis is frequently transmitted.

The infected Yanomami returns to his village and family. Here several Yanomami customs help to transmit the diseases to family members. When making *caxiri,* a fermented drink, a group of women chew sweet cassava to hasten fermentation and then spit it into a large trough, frequently an old canoe or, more recently, an aluminum pot. The mixture is then cooked and left to ferment. When the drink is served, whoever is serving it uses a gourd or pot as a dipper, which is continually filled and passed from person to person. Tuberculosis spreads readily under these conditions from any infected person who either helps with masticating the cassava or drinks from the communal pot or gourd. When any kind of food utensil is used, it is passed from person to person for use, allowing the infection to spread. Yanomami frequently spit on the dirt floor of the yano, the play area of children and dogs.

## VIII. Infanticide

Infanticide is the deliberate rejection and killing of an infant, usually immediately after the birth although sometimes it may take place several days later. The mother usually places a stick across the throat of the infant and applies pressure so that the baby chokes to death. The Mucajaí Yanomami do not practice infanticide beyond this period or pedocide. In tables 19.4 and 19.6 infanticide is treated as a category distinct from homicide because the Yanomami view infanticide as a terminal abortion, the same type of phenomenon as induced abortion, which was described in the previous volume (Early and Peters 1990:77).

The decision to kill the infant in most situations is made by the husband with or without the agreement of the mother, although various family members may express their opinion. Where there is no husband, especially in the case of widows, it is the decision of the mother reinforced by female and male residents in her yano. Infanticide can take place for a number of reasons, which are listed in table 19.7 for forty-four Mucajaí cases. The primary distinction in the table is between reasons that can apply to both sexes and reasons that apply only to female infants (also called preferential or deliberate or selective female infanticide).

### A. Spacing

This reason centers on the necessity to breast-feed infants. The main source of nourishment for the Yanomami infant is the mother's milk. This requires the infant to be breast-fed for at least the first two years of life. The Yanomami assume (as do many other groups) that the amount of a mother's milk is limited, so that a mother can properly breast-feed only one infant at a time. Therefore a pregnancy and birth following soon after the birth of a nursling who survives is seen as life threatening to the nursling. The new infant would compete for the mother's limited milk. Frequently such a pregnancy is aborted in the second month (Early and Peters 1990:77). But if there is no abortion at that time, the result is an infanticide at the time of birth, as happened in 5 percent of the Mucajaí infanticides. One of a pair of twins becomes an infanticide for the same reason. Usually a male or the stronger of the two infants is kept.

Another situation that can be included under spacing is the killing of the first infant of a young mother when she is around thirteen or fourteen years old. The Yanomami sometimes consider a young girl too immature to bear children. A pregnancy might result in injury to her lactating abilities or to the reproductive tract, which would cause trouble in future pregnancies. Again this is more often the occasion for an abortion, but sometimes it

Table 19.7. Frequency and Percentage of Infanticide by Historical Phase, Sex, and Reason

| | Precontact | | | Contact | | | Linkage | | | Brazilian | | | Total | | |
|---|---|---|---|---|---|---|---|---|---|---|---|---|---|---|---|
| | T | M | F | T | M | F | T | M | F | T | M | F | T | M | F |
| Infanticides | 13 | 2 | 11 | 1 | - | 1 | 13 | 4 | 9 | 17 | 7 | 10 | 44 | 13 | 31 |
| **Reasons—M or F** | | | | | | | | | | | | | | | |
| Spacing | - | - | - | - | - | - | 2 | - | 2 | - | - | - | 2 | - | 2 |
| Deformity | - | - | - | - | - | - | 1 | - | 1 | 5 | 3 | 2 | 6 | 3 | 3 |
| Support Problems | 4 | 1 | 3 | - | - | - | 6 | 3 | 3 | 3 | 1 | 2 | 13 | 5 | 8 |
| Unknown | 2 | 1 | 1 | - | - | - | 2 | 1 | 1 | 5 | 3 | 2 | 9 | 5 | 4 |
| **Reasons—F only** | | | | | | | | | | | | | | | |
| For this birth | 3 | - | 3 | 1 | - | 1 | 2 | - | 2 | 4 | - | 4 | 10 | - | 10 |
| For any birth | 4 | - | 4 | - | - | - | - | - | - | - | - | - | 4 | - | 4 |
| **Percentages** | | | | | | | | | | | | | | | |
| Infanticides | 100 | 16 | 84 | 100 | - | 100 | 100 | 31 | 69 | 100 | 41 | 59 | 100 | 30 | 70 |
| All Reasons | 100 | 100 | 100 | 100 | - | 100 | 100 | 100 | 100 | 100 | 100 | 100 | 100 | 100 | 100 |
| **M or F** | | | | | | | | | | | | | | | |
| Spacing | - | - | - | - | - | - | 15 | - | 22 | - | - | - | 5 | - | 6 |
| Deformity | - | - | - | - | - | - | 8 | - | 11 | 29 | 43 | 20 | 14 | 23 | 10 |
| Support Problems | 31 | 50 | 27 | - | - | - | 46 | 75 | 33 | 18 | 14 | 20 | 30 | 38 | 26 |
| Unknown | 15 | 50 | 16 | - | - | - | 15 | 25 | 11 | 29 | 43 | 20 | 20 | 38 | 13 |
| **F only** | | | | | | | | | | | | | | | |
| For this birth | 23 | - | 18 | - | - | - | 15 | - | 22 | 24 | - | 40 | 23 | - | 32 |
| For any F birth | 31 | - | 36 | - | - | - | - | - | - | - | - | - | 9 | - | 13 |
| % F only of all infanticides | 54 | | | 100 | | | 15 | | | 24 | | | 32 | | |
| % F only of all F infanticides | 64 | | | 100 | | | 22 | | | 40 | | | 45 | | |

results in an infanticide. We suspect that some of the cases classified as unknown in the Precontact period belong in the spacing category.

## B. Deformity

Any physical deformity in a newborn results in an infanticide, which accounted for 14 percent of the Mucajaí cases. The deformity may be something that industrial societies would consider a slight matter easily corrected by surgery, such as webbed fingers or toes. In the Yanomami view, any deformity is a possible sign of witchcraft. Life for a deformed person can be very difficult: the unfortunate is usually teased, taunted, and looked down upon. A further problem may arise because such a person may not be able to make the expected contribution to work in the garden, hunting and collecting in the forest, or food preparation. These various factors result in the practice of doing away with deformed infants.

## C. Support Problems

These are infanticides that take place because the mother does not expect support from the father to provide for the child. This reason accounted for 30 percent of the Mucajaí infanticides. If the continuance of a marriage is in doubt, a newborn may be rejected. Widows who become mothers frequently resort to infanticide. An angry husband will order an infanticide when his wife bears a child whom he knows cannot be his and the father(s) did not have the consent of the husband. The analogous case, although not infanticide, is the killing of the young captive children of a captive mother by her new husband.

## D. Unknown Reasons

There were nine cases or 20 percent of the infanticides in which the reason for the action was unknown. All have been included under the first classification, reasons that can apply to both sexes. Five were males. The fertility histories containing the four female cases have other surviving females in them, which eliminates the possibility of placing these cases under the classification of no females at any birth. But whether these female infanticides were preferential female infanticides for this birth only (explained in the next section) or whether they occurred for some other reason remains in question.

## E. Infanticide Restricted to Females

These are cases in which the infant is killed because of being female. This reason accounted for 32 percent of all infanticides. There is no possibility of an abortion in these situations because the sex of the infant is not known until birth. Female children are killed to quicken the possibility of another pregnancy and birth when parents hope for a male. We have distinguished two types of situations in which this logic is used, although the distinction may be overdrawn.

In the first situation, some men want only male children because of a desire to strengthen the family's subsistence position by providing hunters and protectors. A female is usually lost to her family of origin and becomes a member of her husband's family and faction unless the husband can be enticed to remain with the father-in-law after the period of bride service. This is the context when the word *valuable* is used in such ethnographic statements as "she was female and not valuable, so we killed her" and "females are considered to be less valuable" (Chagnon 1972:273). Families who take this logic to the extreme and kill all their female infants are rare, although this stereotype is sometimes derived from ethnographic literature lacking quantitative information about the reasons for infanticide. In the Mucajaí database, there were only two such families, all with children born either prior to 1930 or during the Precontact period. These two families account for the 9 percent of the infanticides in table 19.7.

The Yanomami consider the desire for only male children an extreme position. The strategic thinking behind this is not completely clear. Females are also valuable to a family, even if of lesser value than males. Daughters assist in the strenuous process of harvesting manioc and in peeling, grating, sifting, and baking it into bread, a staple in the Xilixana diet. A family needs daughters to give to other families in order to obtain wives for their sons. Also a father can pressure sons-in-law to remain after the period of bride service and join his faction.

In the majority of cases of preferential female infanticide (PFI), the families have surviving female children. They want the next birth to be a male and terminate the next infant if it is a female. If a male is born from the subsequent pregnancy, the family may accept females at later births. A fertility history illustrates this strategy in a family that had three preferential female infanticides. This was the birth order of their children by sex (M for male, F for female, I for infanticide): F, M, M, F, F, F, F-I, M, F-I, M, F-I, F. Some families want the first birth to be a male and terminate females at this stage until the arrival of a male. These are the more common situations in which the Mucajaí Yanomami practice preferential (deliberate, selective) female infanticide rather than the rejection of all female infants.

The rejection of all females may be not a different situation. Such an outcome may not be based on an a priori principle of no females. It may simply be the chance outcome of a fertility history in which the decision was made on a birth by birth basis but for which the final outcome at the end of the woman's reproductive cycle was the rejection of all female births. This is the reason why the distinction may be overdrawn.

In summary, the two most important reasons for infanticides are preferential female infanticide and situations in which male support of mother and child are considered doubtful, especially in the case of widows. These reasons contributed 62 percent of all the cases in the Mucajaí data and 77 percent of the cases for which the reason was known. In one of the few comparative studies that investigated the reasons for infanticide, Bugos and McCarthy (1984:510, 518, 519) found similar reasons among the Ayoreo, except preferential female infanticide. The most frequent reasons were support problems arising from marriage instability. Women need the economic contribution and protection of husbands to successfully raise children. Therefore, women without husbands or women who fear desertion will on occasion resort to infanticide. Preferential female infanticide was explicitly rejected by the Ayoreo.

## F. Missionaries and Infanticide

The missionaries know of four definite incidents when they were able to prevent an infanticide, three during the 1960s and one in 1987. One case was a male with a deformity later corrected by an operation. Another case was an initially rejected female. Still another case was the second twin in a difficult birth at which the missionaries assisted. Hearing family discussions prior to a birth about whether to keep a child, the missionaries would urge the family to keep the baby. But they do not know what weight their advice had or how decisive it was in the outcome.

## IX. Importance of Infanticide in Mucajaí Mortality

It is difficult to place the findings of this study in comparative perspective because of the dearth of quantitative studies about infanticide. Instead we probe the data and ask questions about the contribution of Mucajaí infanticide to the broader mortality structure. These questions are important for research about the role of infanticide in the rate of population growth of tribal societies.

Such questions involve several levels of mortality classification. Some are seldom used for lack of data and can be confusing because of conceptual and/or verbal similarity. As a preliminary guide, table 19.8 breaks group mortality down into categories pertinent for examining the contribution of infanticide to the overall mortality structure. Beginning at the left with total mortality and following the upper tier, the table shows categories asking progressively more specific mortality questions. The lower tier gives the

**Table 19.8. Table Decomposing Total Deaths by Categories Pertinent to the Analysis of Infanticide**

| | | | | | | Preferential Female |
| --- | --- | --- | --- | --- | --- | --- |
| | | | Infanticides | = | | + |
| | Infant Deaths | = | + | | | Male or Female |
| Total Deaths | = | | All Other Reasons | | | for Other Reasons |
| | + | | | | | |
| | Deaths at All | | | | | |
| | Other Ages | | | | | |

residual category and is shown simply to clarify what is excluded from the upper tier. With the conceptual clarification in table 19.8, table 19.9 shows the quantitative relationships of infanticide in the overall mortality structure.

A. Infanticides: Contribution of Preferential Female Infanticides to All Infanticides (Table 19.9, II)

The question begins at the upper right of table 19.8 and asks about the relationship of PFIs to all infanticides. The answer, 32 percent, was previously given at the bottom of table 19.7 and is repeated in table 19.9 (#7, Total) to link the tables. In qualitative terms, preferential female infanticide makes a substantial but not a majority or overwhelming contribution. Discussions in the literature sometimes assume that most infanticides in a culture take place for the same reason, and sometimes the assumed reason is preferential female infanticide. The analysis here should help clarify these kinds of questions and assumptions.

B. Infant Deaths: Contribution of Infanticides and Preferential Female Infanticides to All Infant Deaths (Table 19.9, III)

Infanticides contributed slightly over 50 percent of all infant deaths. Preferential female infanticides contributed 16.7 percent of all infant deaths, a significant but not a majority or overwhelming contribution.

C. Total Deaths: Contribution of Infant and Infanticide Deaths (Table 19.9, IV)

Infant deaths contributed 30.2 percent of the total deaths. From the infant deaths, infanticides contributed 15.8 percent and preferential female infanticides contributed 5.0 percent to the total deaths. Therefore preferential female infanticide is of moderate significance in the overall level of mortality.

Table 19.9. Mucajaí Infanticide: Relationships to Other Mortality and Sex Ratios at Birth

| | Precontact | Contact | Linkage | Brazilian | Total |
|---|---|---|---|---|---|
| **I. Absolute Numbers** | | | | | |
| 1. All Deaths | 63 | 26 | 66 | 123 | 278 |
| 2. Infant Deaths | 14 | 2 | 26 | 42 | 84 |
| 3. All Infanticides | 13 | 1 | 13 | 17 | 44 |
| 4. Preferential F Infanticide | 7 | 1 | 2 | 4 | 14 |
| 5. Live Births | 79 | 14 | 201 | 210 | 504 |
| 6. Person years | 2,843 | 468 | 3,844 | 4,420 | 11,574 |
| **II. % Composition of Infanticides** | | | | | |
| 7. PFI (4/3)* | 53.8 | 100 | 15.4 | 23.5 | 31.8 |
| 8. Others (100%-7) | 46.2 | - | 84.6 | 76.5 | 68.2 |
| **III. % Composition of Infant Deaths** | | | | | |
| 9. Infanticides (3/2) | 92.9 | 50.0 | 50.0 | 40.5 | 52.4 |
| 10. PFI (4/2) | 50.0 | 50.0 | 7.7 | 9.5 | 16.7 |
| **IV. % Composition of Total Deaths** | | | | | |
| 11. Infant Deaths (2/1) | 22.2 | 7.7 | 39.4 | 34.1 | 30.2 |
| 12. Infanticides (3/1) | 20.5 | .8 | 19.7 | 13.8 | 15.8 |
| 13. PFI (4/1) | 11.1 | 3.8 | 3.0 | 3.3 | 5.0 |
| **V. Some Components of Crude Death Rate** | | | | | |
| 14. Crude Death Rate (1/6) | 22.2 | 55.6 | 17.2 | 27.8 | 24.0 |
| 15. From Infant Deaths (2/6) | 4.9 | 4.3 | 6.8 | 9.5 | 7.3 |
| 16. From Infanticides (3/6) | 4.6 | 2.1 | 3.4 | 3.8 | 3.8 |
| 17. From PFIs (4/6) | 2.5 | 2.1 | 0.5 | 0.9 | 1.2 |
| 18. Percentage PFI of CDR (17/14) | 11.1 | 3.8 | 3.0 | 3.3 | 5.0 |
| **VI. Some Components of Infant Death Rate** | | | | | |
| 19. Infant Death Rate (2/5) | 177.2 | 142.9 | 129.4 | 200.0 | 166.7 |
| 20. From Infanticides (3/5) | 164.6 | 71.4 | 64.7 | 81.0 | 87.3 |
| 21. From PFI (4/5) | 88.6 | 71.4 | 10.0 | 19.0 | 27.8 |
| **VII. Hypothetical Sex Ratios** | | | | | |
| 22. Sex Ratio at Birth (SRB, T 19.3) | 48.1 | 50.0 | 48.3 | 44.8 | 46.3 |
| 23. SRB, infanticide removed (5-3) | 40.9 | 46.2 | 46.8 | 45.9 | 45.6 |
| 24. SRB, PFI removed (5-4) | 43.1 | 46.2 | 47.7 | 43.7 | 45.3 |

*The values in parentheses indicate previous lines used in calculation of the values in this line. Here line 7 is calculated by dividing line 4 by line 3.

D. The Decomposition of the Crude and Infant Death Rates (Table 19.9, V and VI)

So far table 19.9 has decomposed the Mucajaí mortality structure by percentages based on the absolute number of deaths as the simplest manner of expression. The same type of decomposition is done for the crude death rates and the infant mortality rates in sections V and VI. The percentages remain the same (see lines 13 and 18).

E. Sex Ratio at Birth: Impact of Infanticide (Table 19.9, VII)

In this section we examine hypothetical sex ratios at birth if one employs the contrary-to-fact assumption that the live births that became infanticides never existed. While an infanticide is a death after a live birth, some discussions about the sex ratio at birth ignore infanticides and address only the sex ratio of effective births; that is, of births of infants whom parents intend to nurture (see Early and Headland 1998:76–77). Line 23 shows what the effective sex ratio of births would be if all infanticides were removed from the sex ratio of demographic fertility (line 22). Line 24 shows the effective sex ratio if only preferential female infanticides were removed.

We showed in the previous chapter the importance of the sex ratio of births in restoring the sexual balance of a population once it has become unbalanced. When there is a shortage of females in the population and over half the infanticides are female, the impact of the sex ratio at birth is retarded in the process of restoring sexual balance. The difference between lines 22 and 23 of table 19.8 shows that the sex ratio of all Mucajaí infanticides depressed the effect of the sex ratio of births by 1.4 percent to around 8.3 percent in the historical periods.

## X. Migration (Table 19.10)

As has been noted, there is a change of level of abstraction when looking at the Mucajaí Yanomami as a single population rather than considering them as eight village populations. Confounding the two levels may lead to confusing results, as previously discussed regarding weighted and unweighted averages. Another consequence of the different level of abstraction is changing the boundaries for determining migration. When considering the Mucajaí Yanomami as a single population bloc, there is only migration between the Mucajaí bloc and external groups, either other indigenous groups or rural Brazilians. The internal migration between villages is lost by this abstraction since there is only one population. Consequently migration for the population bloc is not the weighted average of all village migrations but the weighted average of external migration into or out of the group.

# Table 19.10. Mucajaí Ninam: Migration Rates

| Level of Analysis | Indicator | Age/ Sex | Precontact | | | Contact | | | Linkage | | | Brazilian | | |
|---|---|---|---|---|---|---|---|---|---|---|---|---|---|---|
| | | | I | O | NM | I | O | NM | I | O | NM | I | O | NM |
| Group | Crude Rate | | 2.8 | - | 2.8 | 12.8 | 0.0 | 12.8 | 12.8 | .8 | 12.0 | 4.8 | 9.5 | -4.8 |
| Age Groups | Age-Specific Rates | 0 | 3 | - | 3 | 13 | - | 13 | 12 | 1 | 11 | 2 | 5 | -3 |
| | | 15 | 4 | - | 4 | 30 | - | 30 | 22 | 2 | 20 | 12 | 16 | -4 |
| | | 30 | 3 | - | 3 | 9 | - | 9 | 10 | 0 | 10 | 3 | 9 | -5 |
| | | 45 | - | - | - | - | - | - | 2 | - | 2 | 4 | 14 | -10 |
| N Migration Total | | | 8 | - | 8 | 6 | - | 6 | 49 | 3 | 46 | 21 | 42 | -23 |
| | | M | 2 | - | 2 | 1 | - | 1 | 20 | 1 | 19 | 13 | 18 | -5 |
| | | F | 6 | - | 6 | 5 | - | 5 | 29 | 2 | 27 | 8 | 24 | -16 |
| Reasons | External Marriage | M | - | - | | 1 | - | | 8 | 1 | | 10 | 5 | |
| | | F | - | - | | 2 | - | | 11 | 2 | | 3 | 1 | |
| | Captive | M | 2 | - | | - | - | | 2 | - | | - | - | |
| | | F | 6 | - | | 3 | - | | 6 | - | | - | - | |
| | Avoid Conflict | M | - | - | | - | - | | 7 | - | | 3 | - | |
| | | F | - | - | | - | - | | 5 | - | | 2 | 2 | |
| | Family | M | - | - | | - | - | | - | - | | - | 2 | |
| | | F | - | - | | - | - | | 1 | - | | 1 | 8 | |
| | Fission-Fusion | M | - | - | | - | - | | - | - | | - | 9 | |
| | | F | - | - | | - | - | | - | - | | - | 7 | |
| | Economic | M | - | - | | - | - | | - | - | | - | 1 | |
| | | F | - | - | | - | - | | - | - | | - | 3 | |
| | Unknown | M | - | - | | - | - | | 2 | - | | - | 1 | |
| | | F | - | - | | - | - | | 6 | - | | 2 | 3 | |

Table 19.10 shows the rates and absolute numbers of migration for the population bloc.

A. In-Migration

As indicated, external in-migration played a significant role in the Precontact, Contact, and Linkage phases, not only because of its magnitude but especially because of its age-sex composition. The entrance of females of or near reproductive age was crucial in balancing both the sex ratio of the population and the reproductive ratio. Without it, fertility would have re-mained depressed and possibly unable to withstand the high mortality from infectious disease characteristic of the Contact and Brazilian phases. Male in-migration was important for introducing a greater diversity of descent categories, thereby increasing the number of cross-cousin relationships.

B. Out-Migration

There was little or no out-migration in the Precontact, Contact, and Link-age phases. It is a distinctive characteristic of the Brazilian phase, where its magnitude is greater than that of in-migration, resulting in the only phase with a negative net migration. The increased out-migration primarily re-flects increased interaction with other Yanomami groups.

C. Reasons for Migration (Tables 19.10, 19.11)

Table 19.10 summarizes the reasons for in-migration and out-migration for all the phases. Marriage plus the female captives who were immediately incorporated as wives account for about 68 percent of all in-migration. The reasons for out-migration are varied. Marriage, especially marriage reci-procity with the Palimi theli and Malaxi theli, accounted for 20 percent. Family reasons are predominantly in-migrants for marriage who, after they become widows or widowers, return to their original groups. Out-migra-tion because of fusion represents the move to the Aica village of Flexal after the collapse of village F, a move strongly influenced by family ties.

D. Origins and Destinations of the Migrants (table 19.12)

The largest group contributing to in-migration was the Palimi theli, who established marital and trade relations with village C. This can also be seen in the corresponding out-migration to the Palimi theli. Village D established the same type of relationship with the Aica and villages B and E with the Malaxi theli. The cases listed as Brazilian in-migrants were three Yanomami who had been living with Brazilians prior to in-migration and whose origi-nal group is unknown. The out-migration to Brazilians represent a Mucajaí man who went to work permanently for Brazilians and a Mucajaí girl who

Table 19.11. Reasons for External Migration

| Reason | Number | | Percentage | |
|---|---|---|---|---|
| | I | O | I | O |
| Marriage | 36 | 9 | 42.9 | 20.0 |
| Captives | 21 | - | 25.0 | - |
| Avoid Conflict | 14 | 2 | 16.7 | 4.4 |
| Family | 11 | 12 | 13.1 | 26.7 |
| Fusion | - | 16 | - | 35.6 |
| Economic | - | 3 | - | 6.7 |
| Unknown | 2 | 3 | 2.4 | 6.7 |
| Total | 84 | 45 | 100 | 100 |

Table 19.12. Origins and Destinations of External Migration

| Group | Number | | Percentage | |
|---|---|---|---|---|
| | I | O | I | O |
| Yanomami Groups | | | | |
| Palimi theli | 18 | 8 | 21.4 | 18.2 |
| Aica | 16 | 19 | 19.0 | 43.2 |
| Malaxi theli | 14 | 6 | 16.7 | 13.6 |
| Ajarani | 10 | - | 11.9 | - |
| Xiliana | 9 | 1 | 10.7 | 2.3 |
| Xili theli | 3 | - | 3.6 | - |
| Sanumá | 1 | - | 1.2 | - |
| Other Groups | | | | |
| Yekwana | 6 | - | 7.1 | - |
| Brazilians | 3 | 9 | 3.6 | 20.4 |
| Mácu | 2 | - | 2.4 | - |
| Unknown | 2 | 1 | 2.4 | 2.3 |
| Total | 84 | 44 | 100 | 100 |

married a Brazilian and was later joined by her family to work for Brazilians.

## XI. A Graphical Summary (Figures 19.3. 19.4, 19.5, 19.6)

For a final look at the dynamics of the Mucajaí population bloc, the figures 19.3–19.6 present the annual crude rates of the components of change in both their individual and compound forms. These graphs lay out visually the dynamics of the population growth shown in figure 19.1 and table 19.2.

They also explain the changes in the age-sex distribution in figure 19.2. The graphs are the basic equation of chapter 8 in visual action. All the preceding chapters explain the variations shown in the graphs.

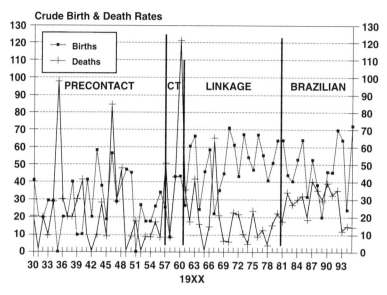

19.3. Mucajaí group annual crude birth and death rates.

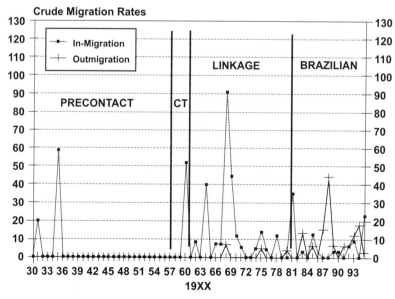

19.4. Mucajaí group annual crude migration rates.

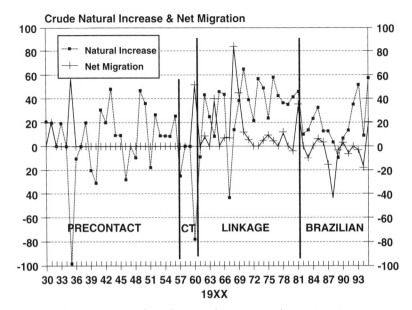

19.5. Mucajaí group annual crude natural increase and net migration rates.

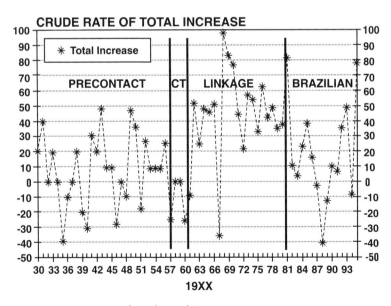

19.6. Mucajaí group annual crude total increase rate.

## XII. Shortage of Females in 1930

Why was there such a shortage of females in the Mucajaí population at the beginning of the research period in 1930? The question crops up in the first three case histories but treatment of it has been delayed for two reasons: first, the answer belongs in the period prior to 1930, for which the data are incomplete; and second, analysis of the question draws upon a number of elements presented in this and other chapters.

### A. The Problem

Tables 9.1, 10.1, 11.1, and 19.2 showed the age-sex distributions of the population bloc and villages A, B, and C at the beginning of the demographic research period in 1930. There was an imbalance in the sex ratios of the population bloc from age 0 to <30, or those born between 1900 and 1929. For age 0 to <15, the ratio is six males for every female, and in the age 15 to <30 group, the ratio is four males for every female. The imbalance is evident in all the village populations but especially in villages B and C. As previously discussed, this imbalance created for the males a problem in finding marriage partners and for the group the more serious problem of low fertility. If protracted, the low fertility could have been equaled or surpassed by the high mortality, resulting in population stagnation or decrease, as happened in villages B and C. An explanation frequently given for this shortage of females is the practice of preferential female infanticide (e.g., Ferguson 1995:352 and others, pers. comm.), although no demographic data are given to support the position.

### B. Demographic Structure of the Problem

To examine the problem, it is important to lay out and understand the demographic variables contributing to the sex ratio of a population. This ensures that all the pertinent variables are evaluated. The basic demographic equation seen in chapter 8 is at the heart of the structure. The shortage of females in a population depends on the combination of the sex ratios of the four components of population change; fertility, mortality, in-migration, and out-migration. For the problem at hand, the basic equation can be restated as follows:

$$P2 - P1 \text{ or } TI = \begin{cases} TIm = + Bm - Dm + Im - Om \\ \quad + \\ TIf = + Bf - Df + If - Of \end{cases}$$

(Here the symbols mean the same as in chapter 8, with the addition of m for male and f for female.)

Table 19.13 lays out the demographic structure of the variables constituting the sex ratio of a population at any point in time. In the table, the sex ratio of the later population, P2, (at the far right) is the point at issue. This sex ratio is determined by the sex ratio of the population at the beginning of the time period, P1 (far left), along with the sex ratio of the total increase (TI) during the interval. In turn, the sex ratio of total increase is determined by the four sex ratios of the elements of the basic equation listed in the table under TI. The sex ratio of infanticide is part of the sex ratio of deaths. The table decomposes the sex ratio of deaths into its components by age and then types of infant deaths and infanticides. The table shows the substantial number of variables that create the arithmetic maze standing behind the sex ratio of a population (P2). There are many possible magnitudes for these variables, including combinations of positive and negative values. These possibilities caution against attributing the sex ratio of a population or of large age segments to a single factor.

Table 19.13. Components of the Sex Ratio of a Population Following a Time Period and the Role of Preferential Female Infanticide

| Initial Population (P1) | Total Increase (TI) of Time Period | Resulting Population (P2) |
|---|---|---|
| P1 | + TI | = P2 |
| P1m + P1f (Sex Ratio) | + TIm + TIf (Sex Ratio) | = P2m + P2f (Sex Ratio) |
| | Components of the Sex Ratio of TI: | |
| | Bm + Bf | |
| | − | |
| | Dm + Df | |
| | Age 1–70, Dm + Df | |
| | Age −1, Dm + Df (infant deaths) | |
| | Df not infanticide | |
| | + | |
| | + Df infanticide | |
| | Df preferential | |
| | + | |
| | Df other reasons | |
| | Im + If | |
| | − | |
| | Om + Of | |

Table 19.14. Components of the Sex Ratio of the Xilixana Population at the End of the Precontact Period

| Initial Population (P1) Jan. 1, 1930 | | Total Increase (TI) of the Precontact Period | | Resulting Population (P2) Jan.1, 1957 |
|---|---|---|---|---|
| 96 | + | 24 | = | 120 |
| 69 P1m + P1f 27 | + | 9 TIm + TIf 15 | = | 78 P2m + P2f 42 |
| 28.1% Pf | | 62.5% Pf | | 35.0% Pf |

(51.9%) 41 Bm + Bf 38 (48.1%)

−

(54%) 34 Dm + Df 29 (46%)

Age 1–70, 32 Dm + Df 17 (34.7%)

+

Age −1, 2 Dm + Df 12 (85.3%) (infant deaths)

1 Df not infanticide

+

+ 11 Df infanticide

7 Df preferential

+

4 Df other reasons

(25%) 2 Im + If 6 (75%)

−

0 Om + Of 0

## C. Sex Ratio of the Population at the End of the Precontact Period

The Precontact period can be used as an example to understand these variables at work. Table 19.14 plugs the values for the Precontact period into the arithmetical maze of table 19.13. The absolute values are placed next to their symbols and percentage male or female in parentheses to the left or right of the absolute numbers.

There is a slight male dominance in the sex ratio of births with 48.1 percent female. This is far closer to balance than the 28.9 percent females in the sex ratio of the population for 1930. However, the tendency of the sex ratio of births gradually to bring about sexual balance of the whole population was mitigated by eleven female infanticides, seven of which were preferential female infanticides. The seven PFIs were 64 percent of the all female infanticides (table 19.7), 54 percent of all infanticides (table 19.9, line 7), 50 percent of all infant deaths (table 19.9, line 10), and 11 percent of all deaths (table 19.9, line 13). These are the highest percentages for any historical period except for the volatility of the single case in the Contact period.

But in spite of the relatively high preferential female infanticide in this period, the sex ratio of total increase for the same period was 62.5 percent female (table 19.14), which increased the percentage of females in the population from 28.1 percent at the beginning of the period to 35 percent at the end of it (table 19.14). In short, there was high preferential infanticide in a period in which the female percentage of the population increased. The reason is the role played by all the other variables in the arithmetic maze.

Important among these was the in-migration of six females, which in itself almost offset the seven cases of preferential female infanticide. Even if there had been no in-migration or out-migration during this period, the female natural increase would have been greater than that of males by 9 to 7 (table 19.14, births by sex minus deaths by sex). This analysis of the Precontact period confirms the importance of seeing the sex ratio of the population as being a multifactor phenomenon exemplified by the arithmetical maze of tables 19.13 and 19.14.

D. Sex Ratio of the Population in 1930

We can return to the original question of this section: Why was there a shortage of females in the population in 1930 as indicated by the 28.1 percent female population? Examination of the age structure of the population (table 19.2.c) shows that the shortage existed in ages 0 to <30. This suggests that the shortage began around 1900. The absolute numbers and sex ratios of ages thirty and more suggest near balance before that time.

The database for these years, even though deficient, lists four infanticides, three among families who rejected females at all births. Perhaps the strongest indication of female infanticides in this period is the paternity history of the renowned shaman from village B who died in the Yekwana conflict in 1935. From 1890 until the time of his death, he fathered twenty-three children (descent category A) by six wives: nineteen males and four females. This indicates that there may be some females missing in the data, probably individuals who died before maturity as females do not pass on descent markers and are more quickly forgotten. Some of these probably were females age one to fourteen who died of natural causes. Others may have been female infants who also died of natural causes. Some were probably female infanticides and some of these probably preferential female infanticides. Therefore preferential female infanticide probably played a role in the shortage of females in the 1930 population.

But the more pertinent question is: How important was preferential female infanticide in the overall structure of sexual imbalance? The answer depends on the values of all the other variables behind the sex ratio of the population, listed in table 19.13. The incompleteness of the database for these years prevents a definitive answer. But given the roles these variables played in the arithmetical maze for the 1930 to 1956 period (table 19.14), it is probable that they also played a role earlier, although with different magnitudes for the individual variables. This is confirmed by the history of the Mucajaí group discussed in chapter 2, revealing situations in which these other variables could have been in play. During this period there was conflict as well as marriage with other Ninam groups: the northern Ninam (Xiliana), Wehewe, Koliak, and Gilinai. Chagnon has cited the same type of contacts with the Yekwana. It is known that there was external in-migration and out-migration for marriage as three of the carriers of important descent categories were Xiliana in-migrants. There was armed conflict with these groups, which raises the possibility of losing women taken as captives. The conflicts could have involved accidental female deaths, as happened in the Yekwana conflict in 1935. There could have been migration of families to these other groups. Sexual imbalance could have arisen from the concatenation of these various factors. The possible role of chance variation in all four components, including small-number volatility, should also be kept in mind.

Therefore preferential female infanticide probably played a significant role in the shortage of females in this population in 1930, the beginning of the demographic research period. But in light of the complex demographic structure of the sex ratio of a population, the history of the group in the pre-1930 period, and the analysis of the role of preferential female infanticide in the Precontact period, there were probably additional factors, some of which were also significant. The sex ratio of a population is a multifactor problem encased in an arithmetic maze.

## XIII. Summary

In this chapter we have changed the perception of the Mucajaí Ninam from that used so far, considering them here as a single population instead of as eight village populations, and we have examined the overall structure of the four components of change in the size of a population. In the analysis of mortality, we have paid special attention to the role of infanticide in the population dynamics, especially preferential female infanticide. Finally, with the information obtained from this and the preceding chapters, we have attempted to throw some analytical light on the problem of sexual imbalance found in all three villages at the beginning of the demographic research period in 1930.

# Understanding the Yanomami

# 20

# The Anthropology of the Yanomami

In this research we have investigated eight villages comprising the Xilixana, a group of 361 Yanomami at the beginning of 1996. They are approximately 1.6 percent of the Yanomami population of twenty-two thousand and 3.6 percent of the Brazilian Yanomami population of less than ten thousand. Beginning around 1950, anthropologists, missionaries, filmmakers, and the captive situation of Helena Valero (1984) have produced a literature and visual record about this group. The literature leaves many unanswered questions, and some of it has provoked controversy. Up to this point we have refrained from these discussions to maintain unity in the presentation and to avoid distraction from the analytical points at issue. We turn now to placing the results of the preceding chapters into the wider context of other Yanomami studies to clarify some points as well as to raise some further questions. This discussion may be of greater interest to the specialist familiar with these studies than to the general reader, who may wish to proceed to the next chapter.

## I. The Formal Demography of the Yanomami

Table 4.1 is derived from the literature about the size of village populations. Field research about the four components of the basic equation for population change in other Yanomami communities has been sparse. Data are difficult to obtain and there has been a lack of demographic interest on the part of some ethnographers. In the previous volume we summarized and reviewed the available data (Early and Peters 1990:124–25). A significant omission from that summary was the work of Schkolnik (1983), which was unknown to us at that time. No significant new work in formal demography since then has come to our attention. Work using mathematical models and simulation was also summarized and reviewed in the previous volume.

How representative of other Yanomami groups is the formal demography of the Mucajaí villages and their four historical periods? In chapter 19 we examined the few comparative studies available and found similar values for fertility in two other regions. The fertility structure appears to have been stable over many years and could possibly be used as a model of tribal fertility. Mortality studies are particularly sparse. One confirmation of Mucajaí mortality for the Linkage period was found in the Parima Highlands. More demographic studies are needed to put this study in better perspective.

## II. The Social Organization of the Villages: Factions and Lineages

We have emphasized in chapter 4 the importance of the faction as the basic social unit within the village and described its relationship to the kinship system of the Yanomami. Our presentation differs in several ways from the discussions of Yanomami social organization by some ethnographers.

Perhaps the most influential discussion has been Chagnon's exposition in his textbook. From the experience of using his materials in teaching undergraduates, seeing their problems and trying to answer their questions, Early believes there is a basic confusion in the exposition. Chapter 4 is our attempt at a clearer presentation. There a distinction is made between two orders of phenomena: the logical categories of kinship classification and the actual communal (corporate) groups. We have taken care in the use of the words *categories of classification* and *group* to make the distinction clear. If the word *group* is used indiscriminately for both—that is, both for factions within a village and for patrilineal descent groupings—the communication becomes unintelligible. This has been the case in a significant portion of the Yanomami ethnographic literature. The problem may simply be semantic, but confusion at this level often indicates conceptual confusion as well. Some examples may clarify the problem.

### A. Chagnon

In describing the social organization of the village in the first and second editions of his text, Chagnon (1968:68, 1977:68) wrote:

> Local descent groups have three characteristics. First, membership in them depends on patrilineal descent. Hence the members all trace relationships to each other through males, and one can only be a member of the group if such a relationship exists. Second, members of the group must live in the same village. . . . Third, the group is corporate with respect to the function of arranging the marriages of the female members.

The first sentence gives the impression that these are the actual groups comprising the village, or the factions, to use the terminology of chapter 4. But the first characteristic is true only of the logical category of kinship classification, the lineage based on patrilineal descent. It is not a characteristic of all the members of a faction, although a faction is identified with the descent marker of the dominant agnatic members. If all members of a faction had the same patrilineal descent, husband and wife could not have married. Becoming a member of a faction does not change the category of one's patrilineal classification. In contrast to the first characteristic in the quote, the second and third characteristics pertain only to factions, not to the categories of descent—that is, to the lineages.

The text quoted described Yanomami social structure for the fifteen years in which the first and second editions introduced confusion to students trying to understand anthropology. The statement disappeared with the third edition. Instead this explanation appears in the third and subsequent editions (Chagnon 1983:127, 1992:140, 1997:140):

> Patrilineal descent defines as members of one *group*—called a patrilineal lineage . . . all those individuals who can trace descent through genealogical connections back to some male ancestor using only the male genealogical connections. . . . The general Yanomamö rule about marriage, insofar as it can be phrased in terms of a descent rule, is simply that everyone must marry outside of his or her own patrilineal *group*. The Yanomamö patrilineage is, therefore, an exogamic *group* [original emphasis deleted and a different one added].

All three uses of *group* in this statement refer to the lineages as logical concepts of kinship classification. They do not refer to the actual social groups (factions) comprising the village's social structure. But this passage appears in the context of social structure without any treatment of the faction. Therefore it implies that the kinship classifications are actual social groups, with much resulting confusion. While patrilinearity is a logical principle of social structure, it is not an actual social group comprising social structure.

## B. Lizot

Lizot offers an excellent description of factions (1988:554–58), which we find verified among the Xilixana. But Lizot at times uses "faction" and "lineage" in the same sense, which causes confusion. Although a faction is identified by the descent marker of the dominant males, "lineage" is more appropriate for the classificatory descent category. In a passage where faction would be the appropriate word, Lizot instead uses lineage (*linaje* in Spanish) and at the end appears to equate the two. In describing the interior ordering of the *shapono*, Lizot (1988:555 translated from Spanish) writes with our interpretations in brackets while the parentheses are his:

The different lineages [factions identified by lineage markers of the dominant males] occupy a delimited sector along with their allies in uxorial residence. Usually a man between 35 and 50 years of age is the headman of the lineage [faction] who is responsible for the collective affairs of his consanguineal relatives (brothers and sons) and of his allies (the husbands of his sisters and daughters) who live in the same sector and who are members of the faction he has established. Frequently the larger lineages [factions] fission into [two or more] factions.

## C. Ramos

The social structure of the Auaris Sanumá has been described by Ramos. She notes the terminology employed involves mere labels and not an attempt to fit reality to preexisting categories. The Sanumá have sib, subsibs, and lineages. Ramos (1979c:193; 1995:69, 71) is careful to describe sibs as classifications and not as actual corporate groups. But there appears to be ambivalence in Ramos's use of "lineage." At times she (Ramos 1979c:193; 1995:69, 71) uses lineage in the sense of faction by describing them as "localized social groups" and noting that "their greatest contribution is to provide a vantage point for political action of village leaders." But at other times she (Ramos and Albert 1977:74) states that lineages, like sibs, are not actual corporate groups. She (Ramos 1995:70) describes lineage members as spread over a number of villages. This implies lineages are categories of logical classification.

## D. Roots of the Problem

The problem of Yanomami lineages (frequently called "descent groups") arises from the indiscriminate use of the word *group* to describe two different but related phenomena: logical categories of descent classification versus actual social groups. It is a problem that goes beyond the Yanomami ethnographic literature. Anthropological textbooks, including the two most widely used in introductory courses in the United States (Kottak 1991:199; Haviland 1997:552), simply use the word *group* without discussing or distinguishing the two orders. This type of socialization in the discipline has led to much confused thinking and writing. Roger Keesing (1981:67–75, 212–27) saw this confusion and warned about it. Keesing (1981:214) wrote: "The anthropological literature is full of confusions about 'clans' and 'moieties' and 'lineages' and 'kindreds' where these distinctions between groups and categories . . . have been blurred or overlooked."

With regard to descent categories, Keesing (1981:227) wrote (somewhat violating consistent usage of "category" and "group"): "The descent group, which is only partly localized [in our terms, the descent category can be identified with a faction], and the local group, which is only partly based on descent [in our terms, not all members of the faction have the same patrilineal descent], are usually both important in different contexts—*and it is dangerously easy to get them confused* [emphasis added]." Once the distinction between categories of logical classification and actual social groups is made clear, as we have aimed to do in chapter 4 of the present volume, many communication problems regarding this aspect of Yanomami culture disappear.

## E. Consciousness of Categories of Classification

The fact that most Yanomami groups do not have a name for "lineage" raises a question: How conscious are the Yanomami of the category "lineage"—that is, a classified grouping of all those with the same descent category? The descent category (lineage) emerges out of the logic of the kinship system, but it appears to be taken for granted and simply applied to individuals. While the Xilixana know the descent category attached to each individual, they usually are not aware of all the individuals with the same descent category as a distinct grouping. Since the category is not an actual social group, and all those with the same descent marker in a village or in all the villages never come together as a group, there is no need to make a mental list of all with the same descent category. Upon reflection, especially when stimulated by the questions of an anthropologist, the Xilixana can compile such a list. But it is not a part of their everyday consciousness. The Sanumá may be an exception. Their sibs and subsibs have names and they appear to be a conscious logical grouping.

## III. Chagnon's War Theory

Primarily due to Chagnon's writings, the terms *war* and *warfare* are frequently applied to the armed conflicts among the Yanomami. There is a semantic problem about using these terms to describe Yanomami armed conflict. Sponsel (1998, especially 106–9) has pointed out how the terms exaggerate armed conflict among the Yanomami both as to its scale and intensity. The use of the term has been seized upon by some Brazilians as a justification to "pacify" the Yanomami while the real intent was to take their land.

## A. Frequency of Raids

Chagnon has emphasized the frequency of raids among the southwestern Yanomami in Venezuela south of the Orinoco River. He finds that these Yanomami "live in a state of chronic warfare . . . reflected in their mythology, values, settlement pattern, political behavior and marriage practices." He cites the case of a village that was raided approximately twenty-five times during a nineteen-month period (Chagnon 1968:1–3).

The Yanomami live in two countries, speak at least four different but related languages, and reside in villages which range from having no contact to permanent contact with the cultures of the nations in whose political territory they reside. While belonging to the same cultural family, the Yanomami are not a monolithic group. At times Chagnon presents some characteristics of the southwestern groups as if they applied to all Yanomami groups. Other Yanomami ethnographers have pointed out this problem (Ramos and Albert 1977:71, Taylor 1977: 91, Ramos 1979b:185–87).

The present study can contribute information about the frequency of raiding among the Yanomami. In the sixty-six-year period covered by the demographic part of this research, there were only five incidents: the conflict with the Yekwana in 1935, the attack by village B in company with the Malaxi theli on the Xili theli in 1960, the attack led by village D with Aica help on a Ajarani group in 1968, village C helping the Malaxi theli in a raid on the Dud theli in 1973 because of marital reciprocity, village C helping the Palimi theli in a raid on the Palahudi in 1978 for the same reason. Perhaps the ambush of the Mácu family in 1932 should be added to this enumeration. These findings are confirmed by the findings of Kenneth Taylor (1977:91), who spent 23 months of fieldwork in eight villages of the Auaris Sanumá. There were no raids during this period although he did hear about some later raids after his departure. The Yanomami do conduct deadly raids, but the stereotype of all Yanomami as engaged in chronic warfare is false and resented by the Yanomami themselves (see Salamone 1997:20).

## B. Sex Ratio at Birth

Chagnon sees *war* arising among the Yanomami as a result of fights about women. He found the conflicts rooted in a shortage of women, expressed by the sex ratio of the population. Chagnon (Chagnon et al. 1979:308–9) explained these unbalanced sex ratios as due to an average 129 sex ratio at birth (55.7 percent male and 44.3 percent female, see table 8.1). He gives the impression that the sex ratio at birth is the only or the major factor leading to the unbalanced sex ratios of the populations. However the sex ratio at birth is only one of the four sex ratios for each of the four components of population change (tables 19.13, 19.14). Once again, this is a situation of a four-variable problem being reduced to a single variable.

But independent of its relationship to the sex ratio of the population, there is a question about the reasonableness of the magnitude of a 129 sex ratio at birth. Demographers and biologists usually cite a 104 to 107 conventional sex ratio at birth (52 percent to 51 percent male, 48 percent to 49 percent female) for human populations (Shryock and Siegel 1973:196). Chagnon had previously claimed a high rate of preferential female infanticide based on a methodology that estimated Yanomami female infanticide by subtracting the expected sex ratio at birth from the 129 ratio his data showed for the Yanomami. Later, he thought the result exaggerated the amount of infanticide he encountered in his ethnographic experience. Therefore he suggested that the Yanomami had a higher than usual sex ratio at birth.

Data from the present study allow an examination of Chagnon's position. For the Mucajaí Yanomami, the sex ratios at birth expressed as male percentages for the four historical periods were 55.8 percent, 50 percent, 51.7 percent, 54.9 percent for a weighted average of 53.7 percent and an unweighted one of 53.1 percent. (In conventional form these sex ratios are: 126, 100, 107, 122 for weighted and unweighted averages of 116 and 113.) For these data, the average sex ratios at birth are higher than the rule of thumb but not as high as Chagnon's figure, although the level of the Precontact phase is close. Therefore the data from this study provide some support for Chagnon's suggestion. There is additional support for the idea behind Chagnon's suggestion. Two reviews of the literature on the sex ratio at birth (James 1987:721–52, 873–900; Chahnazarian 1988:214–33) have found that the ratios of U.S. whites are consistently higher than U.S. blacks, the ratios of Orientals are higher than those of whites with exceptions, and there is a difference between the ratios of the upper and lower extremes of social classes. None of these differences are very large. This literature also indicates that the underlying factors are biological although there are no definitive answers. Thus there is some support for maintaining that the sex ratio at birth for the Yanomami could be higher than the expected rule of thumb, but not of the magnitude suggested by Chagnon. There is a need for biological studies of the Yanomami.

## IV. *War* Theory of Divale and Harris

Chagnon's emphasis on the *war* characteristics of Yanomami culture stimulated Harris and Divale to develop a model to explain the origin and consequences of conflict among band and village groups with the following characteristics: low population density, virilocality, fraternal interest groups, and short distance raiding (Harris 1984:112). The chain of logic in the model begins with preferential female infanticide being responsible for a shortage of marriageable females expressed as an unbalanced sex ratio of the Yanomami population. This leads to conflict. As a result, there is a male superiority complex in the culture, which in turn devalues females and leads to preferential female infanticide. At this point, the logical chain repeats itself in a continuing circle. As a result of preferential female infanticide as well as the direct and indirect conflict casualties, Yanomami population growth is limited so that people live in an ecological balance with the resources of their environment.

The theory consists of ethnographic and demographic variables tied together by logic but with little quantified data to verify the attributed importance of the variables in the chain of logic. The Mucajaí research provides data to examine the importance of some of the posited relationships.

## A. PostMarital Residence

The question here is: Does Yanomami ethnography show them to be a virilocal group and thus covered by one of the four assumptions of the theory? The Sanumá faction has some distinctive characteristics not found in other Yanomami subgroups. In the other subgroups, the male lives with the girl's parents for a period of years to perform bride service. The length of time depends on the marriage agreement. At the end of this period, the family is free to remain or go elsewhere. But the Sanumá are matrilocal, not just for the period of bride service, but for the lifetime of the groom. Ramos (Ramos and Albert 1977:74) notes: "Although they [grooms] expect to go back at the end of the brideservice phase, which can last as long as 10 or 12 years, their inlaws do not admit of taking away wife and children. Thus from the point of view of a man's mother[-in-law] and father-in-law, he is a permanent resident of their village, from the moment he marries until death or divorce breaks the union." This means that although the Sanumá sibs and subsibs are defined by a patrilineal logic, and the headmen of the factions are males, the women are the focal points of bringing males into the factions by marriage and births. Dieter Heinen (Heinen and Illius 1996:554 and pers. comm.) says this gives women a greater role in the Sanumá factions than among the other Yanomami groups and believes it is one of the reasons for the lower level of disputes among the Sanumá. Based on language, social organization, and cultural inventory, Heinen believes that the Sanumá should not be considered as a Yanomami subgroup but as a distinct group related to the Yanomami.

Lizot (1988:540) has made a frequency count of the various possibilities of marital residence among the Venezuelan Yanomami north of the Orinoco River. Virilocality described 46.3 percent of the cases, remaining in the same community 36.1 percent, uxorilocality 11.1 percent and other arrangements accounted for 6.5 percent. Therefore in spite of the use of the Yanomami as the archetypical case in the theory about *war* in tribal societies, it appears they do not have one of the essential characteristics required by the theory in over 50 percent of the cases. Virilocality with its emphasis on male dominance was important to the logic of Harris's argument about the importance of preferential female infanticide.

## B. Preferential Female Infanticide and Population Increase

Harris (1984:111) maintains that preferential female infanticide slows population growth, and in this way contributes to a balance between the size of the population and the resources available to it. The concern here is only with the first part of the argument, the relationship between preferential female infanticide and population growth. There is no doubt that preferential female infanticide has a dampening effect on natural and consequently total population increase. But the question is: How important is it in restricting population growth? In the four historical periods, this study found that preferential female infanticide contributed 11.1 percent, 3.8 percent, 3.0 percent, and 3.3 percent of all deaths in each of the four historical periods respectively (table 19.8, line 13). This meant that they contributed 2.5, 2.1, 0.5, 0.9 to the crude death rates for the same periods (table 19.9, line 17) or to say the same thing in a different manner, they constituted 11.1 percent, 3.8 percent, 3.0 percent, and 3.3 percent of the crude death rates (table 19.9, line 18). These are not overwhelming contributions. The crude death rates in turn were only one of the four components determining the change in the size of the population for these periods.

If preferential female infanticides are subtracted from the deaths for each of the Mucajaí historical periods, the rate of total increase for the Precontact period would change from 8.4 to 13.0, for the Contact period from −12.8 to −10.7, for the Linkage phase from 47.1 to 50.5, and for the Brazilian phase from 14.9 to 18.8 (table 19.2). Preferential female infanticide was an impediment to growth of the Mucajaí population, but not as much as the shortage of females in the Precontact period and infectious disease after contact.

Infanticide was never practiced for the explicit purpose of slowing population growth. For this to be a reason, the decision about infanticide would have to be a group consideration rather than an individual one. All the Xilixana reasons are based on individual, not group, circumstances. This is confirmed by the Ayoreo study with its findings of individual rather than group decisions about infanticide (Bugos and McCarthy 1984:518–19). For the same reason, Dickemann (1984:437) also rejects infanticide as an important factor providing for an ecological balance between size of population and available resources.

## C. Preferential Female Infanticide and Unbalanced Sex Ratios of Population

The writings of Divale and Harris sometimes give the impression that the unbalanced sex ratio of the population is due exclusively to preferential female infanticide. Divale and Harris have no quantitative data about infanticide, much less about its sex ratio or the proportion provided by preferential female infanticide. Consequently at no time do they assign a weight to this factor in their purely conceptual model. In tables 19.13 and 19.14 the arithmetic maze behind the sex ratio of the population shows that it is improbable that preferential female infanticide is the dominant factor.

## D. Tribal *Warfare* Encourages Preferential Female Infanticide?

As a variant of the same argument, Divale and Harris posit a strong relationship between tribal *war* and preferential female infanticide. Lacking any data about PFI, they used a proxy variable. They compare the sex ratios of the age segment <15 years with the age segment >15 years for a series of populations. They divide the populations into three groups by their history of warfare. A total of 160 groups were enumerated before the cessation of warfare; 236 groups were enumerated five to twenty-five years after the end of warfare; and 165 more than twenty-five years after the end of warfare. The conventional sex ratios of the two age groups were 133 and 96 before the cessation of warfare. The sex ratios for both age groups were 133 in the first postwar period, and 104 and 92 respectively in the second postwar period. (These sex ratios translate as 57 percent and 49 percent in the war period, 57 percent in first postwar period, 51 percent and 48 percent in second postwar period. See table 8.1.) Preferential female infanticide is cited as the reason for the high male dominance of the sex ratio for ages <15 in the war period. This is shown by the distinctly lower level for the sex ratio of the >15 age group during the same period as well as the relatively small differences between them in the postwar periods.

Demographically this argument leaves much to be desired. Is the sex ratio of the population age <15 a satisfactory proxy variable for preferential female infanticide? The elements comprising the answer to this question are outlined in tables 19.13 and 19.14. Given that the sex ratio of a population or any of its age segments is the result of the sex ratios of the four component variables; given that deaths are only one of these four components; given that the female portion of the sex ratio of deaths includes the sex ratios for each individual age, of which the infant rate is only one; given that within the infant rate, the sex ratio of infanticide is only one portion of it; and finally given that preferential female infanticide is only one segment of all female infanticides, the linkage of the sex ratio of age <15 of a population as a proxy variable for preferential female infanticide becomes highly questionable. Such an argument could possibly be used as a vague hint, a faint suggestion, but by itself it has no probative value.

Even if it should be granted that the sex ratio of the age <15 group is a valid proxy variable, there are problems with the quality of the data themselves used by Divale and Harris to derive the sex ratios. Various questions have been raised about their validity and reliability (Hirschfeld, Howe, and Levin 1978:110–15; Lancaster and Lancaster 1978:115–17; Norton 1978: 665–67; Howe 1978:671–73). Divale and Harris (1978a:117–18; 1978b: 379–86; 668–71; Divale, Harris, and Williams 1978:379–86) have replied but, in our opinion, not always satisfactorily. Without getting into all the details, we would make a summary criticism: the acceptance of demographic data that, in a number of the sources when given, lack a sufficiently critical process to assess the reliability of the census enumerations. Given the difficulties of enumerating these types of populations, the critical process cannot be omitted or assumed.

## E. Sex Ratio and Shortage of Females

The shortage of females as depicted in Chagnon's arguments cannot be expressed simply by the sex ratio of the population. The conflicts arise from a shortage of marriageable females, not just females or mature females. The heart of the problem is a male problem of acceptable sexual access. Sufficient marriage partners (balanced sex ratio of the population) of itself does not necessarily solve this problem. Even if there is sexual balance among the mature portion of a population, there would probably still be a problem of acceptable sexual access as perceived by Yanomami males. Needless to say, this is not a specifically Yanomami problem.

With regard to the structure of sexual unions, polygyny can diminish the number of available female partners. But polygyny is usually restricted to shamans and other high status males who can afford it. Polygyny can be countered by polyandry, which was the predominant form of sexual union in the Precontact period (Early and Peters 1990:106). Neither of these aspects of the type of sexual union is necessarily expressed by the sex ratio of a population.

Other problems not expressed by the sex ratio of the population arise within the structure of marital unions themselves. The average Yanomami mother is pregnant or nursing for 92 percent of her reproductive years (Early and Peters 1990:51). There is an ideal postpartum taboo against sexual relations for an approximate two-year period. Restraint for this entire period is seldom practiced; it is more frequently limited to six months to a year. But restraint is required if women are pregnant or nursing for extended periods in a high fertility population. This can create a problem for the male and is one of the reasons for polygyny. None of this is expressed by the sex ratio.

Another problem within marriage is putting aside an older wife by divorce and acquiring a younger one or omitting divorce and turning the marriage into a polygynous one. Yanomami marriages can be marked by large differences in the ages of the couple (compare Early and Peters 1990:109 and the corrected table in the appendix to the present volume). Competition by older men for young Yanomami wives through the political dynamics of family and factions is not a rare occurrence.

To reiterate, all of these situations within marriage itself led to a perceived shortage of Yanomami women from the males' perspective, and this in turn can cause conflict. Yet none of these situations within the marital structure are reflected in the sex ratios of the mature segment of the population.

## F. Male Dominance

The literature has discussed the male supremacy complex among the Yanomami. Women's liberation is a concept quite removed from Yanomami culture. Description of the Yanomami as warlike and fierce focused consideration on these characteristics as the origin of the male supremacy complex. But as noted earlier in this chapter, the Xilixana have engaged in relatively few raids over a sixty-six-year period. Yet they illustrate the ideology of male supremacy. The Xilixana case cautions against exaggerating Yanomami conflict as *warfare* and as the only factor giving rise to this ideology. We believe there are other factors of equal and perhaps greater importance.

The ideology of male supremacy is not a generalized, free-floating element in Yanomami culture. It should be interpreted in terms of its institutional embodiment in the social structure. We have emphasized the importance of the family and faction in Yanomami social dynamics. These structural elements embody the male supremacy complex and where the complex manifests itself as a principle influencing the outcomes of decisions dominated by males, especially concerning marriage exchanges.

## V. Other Topics in the Yanomami Literature

While the argument of the *war* theory raised many topics discussed about the Yanomami, there are some additional subjects not intrinsically tied to the argument.

### A. Position of Women

Chagnon (1992:122) has described the condition of women among the southwestern groups as complete subjugation to males without voice in any decisions, as "pawns to be disposed of by their kinsmen" in marriage. Ramos (1979b:186) sees women of the Auaris groups as being in a different position. "Women are not dominated by men and their contribution to economic, social and political matters is substantial, and fully recognized by the male members of their society." The situation of the Xilixana approximates Chagnon's description but with less severity. Xilixana women make a substantial contribution to the community and older women speak up regarding village decisions. How much weight it carries is a different matter. The women tend to be subjugated by males and used as pawns in political maneuvering by the core agnates of the factions.

The status of Xilixana women has increased in the Linkage and Brazilian phases. Women have not been killed in anger or struck with firebrands by their husbands. In the early Linkage phase many earned money by sewing beaded aprons. A few have acquired money by working as domestics for the missionaries. In the Brazilian phase a few women grasped at independence by working in Brazilian homes for several months or becoming prostitutes for the miners.

### B. Size of Tribal Villages and Reasons for Fissioning

This study has found that Xilixana villages tend to fission when they reach between 70 and 100 inhabitants, the average being 85. The immediate reasons for fissioning usually were the social conflicts arising from the demographic density of the group living in a single yano. Some ecological theorists (for example, Harris 1984:125) have tended to see fissioning as a reaction to the shortage of game and fish in an area. But in the analysis here, unless a village is very large, shortages of game or fish in an area were usually met by movement of the entire village rather than by fissioning along factional lines.

Sponsel (1981:156–78) describes hunting among the Sanumá and much of his description is applicable to the Xilixana. Good (1989) analyzes hunting, trekking, and gardening by a Yanomami village in Venezuela. Much of his description also applies to the Xilixana except their treks are fewer and of shorter duration. He finds population growth of a village limited either by the impossibility for a larger group to sustain successful hunting while trekking or by the impossibility of distributing meat among all the factions with the resulting resentments. This can be an important source of conflict arising from demographic density. Our findings show that social conflicts independent of ecological considerations are also important immediate occasions for fissioning.

## C. The Ceremonial Dialogue (Yaimo)

Lizot (1994) has described and analyzed this intricate ritual among the Central Yanomami of southwest Venezuela. The ceremony is similar among the Ninam. Its purpose according to Lizot (1994:218) is to serve "both as an expression of conflicts and as a means of opposing them: by conjuring the threat of declared hostility, it restores peace." Lizot says that these ceremonies are rarely held among the population bloc but only with more distant communities with whom relationships are more problematical. But as mentioned in chapter 4, throughout the known history of the Xilixana, the ceremony was continually held among the Xilixana villages that constitute a population bloc. In addition, the ceremony was also held with the Malaxi theli, Palimi theli, and Aica groups with whom the Xilixana have marriage ties. Therefore among the Ninam, the ceremony is held within the population bloc and with those communities with whom they have marital ties. The ceremony is not only a means of expressing and calming actual or potential conflict but also an affirmation of the bonds unifying these groups.

## VI. Summary

This chapter initially attempted to place the findings of the Xilixana study into the wider context of Yanomami population studies. However, with the exception of some data from the Parima Highlands, few formal demographic studies based on fieldwork are available. The chapter then examined the problem of ethnographic descriptions of Yanomami social structure. This was followed by a discussion of some questions raised by the *war* theorists regarding the Yanomami. The chapter has attempted to show how demographic analysis can throw light on ethnographic questions. It has emphasized the importance of demographic measurement instead of using variables in a purely conceptual manner that can lead to concept twirling. This has been a problem not only of the anthropology of the Yanomami, but of many other groups.

# VII

# The Brazilian Yanomami
# in the Planetary Web

# 21

# Brazil and the World System

This research has been focused on eight Xilixana villages located in the Amazonian rain forest in the western part of the state of Roraima in Brazil. Knowledge gained from the case histories enabled us to clarify in the last chapter some points in the literature about the Yanomami and to raise some further questions. But the knowledge gained also has relevance to the ongoing situation of the Yanomami as they face a crisis of cultural change, and in some cases survival, resulting from their increasing contacts with the Brazilian nation. In the next chapter we examine the contact experiences of other Yanomami groups in Roraima and compare them with the experience of the Xilixana group. But to comprehend the Yanomami situation in Roraima more fully, it must be seen against the background of the northern Amazon basin, a region of Brazil closely linked to international markets and the world arena of politics and media. In brief, the Xilixana are a small nodule of the world system in which they are ultimately linked to all the other nodules, large and small.

We therefore present a sketch of Brazilian history and the nation's connections to the world system in order to illuminate the forces behind the contact experiences of the Yanomami groups in Roraima. Rather than peppering the chapter with citations, we simply offer our interpretation of the existing research, listing at the end of the chapter works that have influenced the presentation.

## I. The Amazon

Brazil is the third largest country in the world for contiguous land area, surpassed only by China and Canada. It is slightly larger than the continental United States and occupies half of the continent of South America. But considered as a nation rather than national territory, Brazil was effectively confined to the eastern part of the country until the middle of the twentieth century, when it began its westward expansion into the central region; much of the Amazon remained a remote area (see map 4). The eastern and central regions contain 90 percent of the country's population (map 5) but only 42 percent of its territory. While the Amazon Basin lies within the national boundaries of Bolivia, Peru, Ecuador, and Columbia, most of it is in Brazil, constituting 58 percent of the area of the country but with about 10 percent of its population, many of whom live along the Amazon River itself.

Spain relinquished all claims to the Brazilian Amazon and recognized those of Portugal by the treaties of 1750 and 1777. The Portuguese claims were established by explorers and traders who passed through the area but did not remain. The colony resisted the efforts of the British, Dutch, and French to encroach on its northern border. Although few Portuguese and Brazilians settled in the Amazon, they have remained sensitive to the integrity and defense of their Amazonian borders. Until 1964 foreign prospecting and investment were not allowed in the Amazon. The interior was occupied by various Indian groups living in a tribal world, which until the 1950s had only occasional contact with the Portuguese and Brazilians who have plied the main waterways as explorers, traders, collectors, missionaries, and slave hunters since the sixteenth century. We sketched in chapter 2 the Yanomami flight into the Parima Highlands to escape the slavers.

## II. Brazil's Determination to Industrialize

Brazil had been an agricultural colony and later a country producing raw materials for the export market, using the profits to finance imported capital and consumer goods. In the boom-bust world of commodity markets, sugar was the primary export in the sixteenth and seventeenth centuries, gold in the eighteenth, coffee and rubber in the nineteenth, and coffee in the early twentieth. Until 1930 a two-class system predominated. This system was based on large land holdings (latifundia) focused on the production of export crops by peasant labor in client relationship to the patron, the landowner. With the election of Getúlio Vargas as president in 1930, the stranglehold of the agrarian aristocracy was broken and the country began to undertake industrialization. Vargas pursued economic nationalism, and during the 1930s industry became the fastest growing sector of the economy. But the world depression of the 1930s, the capriciousness of world commodity markets, declining prices for raw materials relative to manufactured goods, and the drop in world trade during World War II all resulted in unemployment and poverty, expanding the underclass in the rural areas and creating one in the urban areas of the eastern regions. These experiences focused Brazilian determination to raise the rate of economic growth by industrializing to become a world power befitting the country's size.

In the latter part of the 1960s, the Amazon became important in Brazilian national policy as a major contributor to these aspirations and to the solution of the socioeconomic problems in other regions of the country. Implementing these aspirations defines the problematic circumstances under which much of the contact in the last part of the twentieth century took place in the Amazon between indigenous groups and Brazilians.

## III. The Problem of Inequity

The starting point of this industrialization was a social system marked by large inequities in the distribution of its economic and social benefits. All social systems contain structural inequities, but Brazil has been an extreme case. Beginning with its settlement as a Portuguese colony in 1532, Brazil has been influenced by a two-class system. This system was originally based on a plantation economy producing sugar using Indian slaves and, after their demise, African slaves. In spite of social changes over five centuries— independence from Portugal in 1822, abolition of slavery in 1888, establishment of democratic government in 1889, and industrialization (including agricultural industrialization) taking hold around 1930—Brazil's class structure continues to be marked by a great disparity of access to and benefits received from the country's resources. The small upper class dominating all socioeconomic institutions consists of both the old landed aristocracy, because agricultural exports have continued to be important, and the growing business elite, who became the masters of industry in place of the plantation or the sugar refinery. The emerging middle class was small and tied to the elite. Industrialization of agriculture terminated the minimal security provided to the peasant by the patron-client system of the countryside. Intermittent wage labor was substituted, giving rise to a rural proletariat. Many people poured into the cities to form an urban proletariat, symbolized by the famous favelas of Rio de Janeiro and São Paulo.

But throughout all these changes and in spite of the impressive annual rates of economic growth and the emergence of a small middle class, Brazil still carried the imprint of the colonial two-class system and had a huge imbalance in the distribution of its resources. As is seen in table 21.1, those with the highest 10 percent of Brazilian incomes received more than 45 percent of total income; the highest 20 percent, more than 60 percent. This is one of the most unequal income distributions in the world, according to a report by the World Bank (Skidmore 1988:284–86). About half the arable land is owned by only 1 percent of the landowners, while 3.1 million small farmers have only 3 percent of the arable land (Sponsel 1997:114). The inequality increased between 1960 and 1980 and continues to increase. Because of the large number in the lower class who survive outside the

Table 21.1. Percentage Distribution of Household and Individual Income by Income Rank of Population, 1960 and 1970

| Income Rank of Population | % Household Income | | | % Individual Income | | |
|---|---|---|---|---|---|---|
| | 1960 | 1970 | d | 1960 | 1970 | d |
| Bottom <10% | 1.4 | 1.2 | −0.2 | 1.2 | 1.2 | 0.0 |
| 10 to <20% | 2.4 | 2.4 | 0.0 | 2.1 | 2.0 | −0.1 |
| 20 to <30% | 3.6 | 3.2 | −0.4 | 3.0 | 3.0 | 0.0 |
| 30 to <40% | 4.6 | 4.1 | −0.5 | 3.8 | 3.6 | −0.2 |
| 40 to <50% | 5.6 | 4.9 | −0.7 | 5.0 | 4.4 | −0.6 |
| 50 to <60% | 7.2 | 6.0 | −1.2 | 6.2 | 5.6 | −0.6 |
| 60 to <70% | 8.1 | 7.7 | −0.4 | 7.2 | 7.2 | 0.0 |
| 70 to <80% | 13.1 | 10.8 | −2.3 | 10.0 | 10.0 | 0.0 |
| 80 to <90% | 14.6 | 16.6 | 2.0 | 15.2 | 15.4 | 0.2 |
| 90%+ | 39.4 | 43.1 | 3.7 | 46.5 | 48.0 | 1.5 |

Source: Skidmore 1988:286.

economy, economists distinguish between the formal and informal economy. In table 21.2, Weyland classifies the economically active population. The class system underlies the classification. Many of those in the last two classifications are the marginal lower class as well as being the informal sector of the economy; perhaps underclass is the more appropriate term. They probably constitute 30 percent to 40 percent of the economically active population.

A characteristic of the marginal sector of Brazilian society is its mobility. Wagley (1971:101) described this for the rural masses, but it also applies to urban marginals, many of whom are from rural backgrounds:

> People are loosely attached to the soil and are often seminomadic. The lack of land, the periodic droughts, and general poverty keep forcing rural Brazilians to migrate. They move seasonally from the arid *sertao* [backlands] to the sugar cane coastal strip, looking for harvest work.

Table 21.2. Percentage Distribution of Economically Active Population, 1985

| Economically Active Population | % |
|---|---|
| Professional, Shopkeepers, Businessmen | 10 |
| Workers, Employees | 38 |
| Urban Irreg. Employees + Informal Sector | 28 |
| Rural Poor—Peasants, Seasonally Employed | 24 |
| Total | 100 |

Source: Weyland 1996:52.

They go to the coffee fazendas of São Paulo and to the cities of the South seeking employment and often return after a year or more. Often they simply move about their own region vaguely hoping to improve their lot and to acquire a better *patrao* [patron]. People are attracted by such "boom crops" as babassu nuts and Brazil nuts; they also seek out localities where large building projects might provide employment.

Thus the inequities of the Brazilian class system produce a large marginal underclass of people who are seminomadic and prepared to pour into any region of the country, such as the Amazon, where there appear to be opportunities to alleviate their poverty.

## IV. Inflation

To hasten the industrialization of the country, in the 1950s the Brazilian government took an active role in the economy by a series of protective tariffs and exchange controls that favored industrialization. The government also reversed the previous policy of self-financing by profits from exports and turned to foreign investment and borrowing. Large loans were obtained from international monetary institutions. Multinational corporations were invited to take part in the development of the country's resources. Inflation began to take hold of the economy. By the early 1960s the distortions induced by inflation created serious economic problems. Servicing the growing international debt created a balance-of-payments problem, which in turn contributed to more inflation. As the inflation worsened, it became self-perpetuating due to the monopolistic positions of business firms, unions, and the government in the Brazilian economy. Under inflationary conditions and using their monopolistic positions, these institutions fought to increase their share of the national income by passing on their increased costs in the form of increased prices. In addition, governments, especially weak ones or those with little legitimacy, bowed to political pressures and refused to cut spending and slow industrialization. All this created an inflationary spiral.

The inflationary situation suffered further deterioration due to distant eruptions in the world system: oil crises in 1973 and 1979 when the Organization of Petroleum Exporting Countries (OPEC) quadrupled and doubled the price of oil respectively. Brazil lacked oil and imported 80 percent of its requirements at that time. High oil prices created havoc with the balance of payments and fueled more inflation. In the early 1980s there was a dramatic rise of interest rates in the United States, which impacted Brazilian debt service as it was tied to variable interest rates. This gave inflation another boost as the Brazilian balance of payments became even more problematical. Brazil was using two thirds of its export earnings just to pay for the interest and amortization of its foreign debt.

In the economy racked by inflation, costs were continually passed down the class structure until they reached the lowest sector, which could not pass them any further. This increased the already heavy burden of inequality on the marginal underclass. The desperate poverty, political and social unrest, repression, tortures, bloodshed, and killings that accompanied this economic turmoil have been described elsewhere.

## V. The Geopolitical View of the Military

The Brazilian military became alarmed by perceived threats to national security owing to the policies of President Joatilde Goulart in trying to cope with inflation and social inequality. In 1964 the military deposed the president and established a military dictatorship, which endured until 1985. The geopolitical thinking of the military was implemented at the policy and program levels during this period. After restoration of the democratic process in 1985, these views continued to provide a foundation for government action as the military remained influential in Brazilian politics. Insight into this worldview provides some additional background for understanding a number of government policies and programs that have structured the contact between Brazilians and indigenous groups in the Amazon.

The geopolitical views of the military have been driven by an emphasis on national security and on continuation of the effort to make Brazil an industrialized power. National security has been defined by perceived external and internal threats. The external threats have centered on the Amazon. Due to the vastness of the Amazonian rain forest and the wholesale destruction of rain forests in other areas of the world, the international community became greatly concerned about the rate of Amazonian destruction and its impact on world climate and resources. The Brazilian government has come under heavy criticism for its management of this resource and there have been calls for the internationalization of the Amazon, a direct affront to Brazilian sovereignty and international aspirations.

Other external threats arose from problems within the countries along Brazil's northern border: Colombia, Venezuela, Guyana, Suriname, and French Guiana. The Amazonian portion of Colombia had become an area of drug production ruled by drug lords and forces fighting the Colombian government. Venezuela had launched its own program of development of the upper Orinoco Basin, which includes its border with Brazil. Venezuela had also renewed its claim to a substantial portion of Guyana up to the Essequibo River. Armed conflict could endanger the integrity of the Brazilian border in that area. Marxist-leaning governments in Guyana and Suriname caused concern, especially with Cuba off their Caribbean coasts, and there was a frontier dispute with French Guiana.

The military also perceived internal threats to national security. The continuing wide disparity in land holdings and income and the advancing results of inflation had created the huge underclass in the eastern region of Brazil, especially the northeast. The urban unemployed and peasants who had lost their land roamed Brazil seeking to survive. This social unrest was a potential source of internal rebellion. Another perceived internal threat was the presence of the Amazonian indigenous groups. It was feared that they would attempt to establish independent Indian nations in the border areas. This fear applied especially to the Brazilian Yanomami, some with ties to the Yanomami across the border in Venezuela.

## VI. The Role of the Amazon

To control these possible threats and pursue economic development, the military—both during the period of their presidential dictatorships from 1964 to 1985 and by their influence in the elected governments after that period—developed a strategic plan tightly linking national security with the occupation and economic development of the Amazon, especially the northern Amazon Basin. The plan was elaborated into various policies and gradually implemented in a series of projects. These plans, policies, and projects have gone through a number of versions with various names. Originally they were based on a "Garden of Eden" vision of the Amazon—an unoccupied region of rich soil and fabulous mineral deposits (Commission on Development and Environment for Amazônia 1992:2–6). Historically the Amazon had been an appendage of Brazil, although jealously guarded from anyone else's possible occupation of it.

### A. Program of National Integration (PIN), 1970

In 1970 the already impoverished Brazilian northeast suffered a punishing drought. President (General) Emílio Médici made a visit, during which he realized that something drastic needed to be done. A previously existing program, Operação Amazônia, was expanded and called the National Integration Program (PIN), which Médici said was "the solution to two problems, men without land in the Northeast and land without men in Amazônia." Among its provisions was the building of a system of highways and airfields to provide access to the region. The Transamazon Highway from the east coast of Brazil to Peru was to be a major project, along with settlement of seventy thousand families along this corridor to occupy and develop the Amazon. The strategy of family colonization was later dropped and emphasis was placed on private, federal, and multinational corporations developing the agricultural, mineral, and timber resources of the region. The direct and indirect labor force required for these enterprises would become the occupiers of the Amazon. Other Amazonian roads were to be built: the north-south Cuiaba-Santerém Highway, opening up the middle of the states of Mato Grosso and Pará, and the east-west Northern Perimeter Highway through the region north of the Amazon River and linking the east coast of Brazil with Colombia and Peru.

Another project of PIN was an aerial reconnaissance of the Amazon using the latest techniques of radar technology to detect the presence of commercial minerals. In the early 1970s using American companies and their technology, this survey (Project RADAM) mapped the mineral resources of the Amazon. Important for the purposes here were the findings that Roraima was a state rich in minerals.

In brief, the Amazon was seen as the primary solution to Brazil's problems of inequality, of financing industrialization, of paying off the international debt, and of taming inflation. As Skidmore (1988:145) notes, "Difficult social problems—such as the misery in which one third of Brazil lived—would be solved not by nationalizing or redistributing the wealth or income of anyone else—but by finding *new* resources."

## B. Calha Norte Project, 1988

The continuation of these plans for the northern Amazon into the 1980s became known as the Calha Norte Project, the strategy for which can be summarized in five objectives:

1. To establish a military presence on the frontiers by building army garrisons and air force bases.
2. To encourage colonization of the Amazon, which would also act as a safety valve against the social unrest created by the urban unemployed and landless peasants from eastern Brazil.
3. To encourage the development of large-scale agribusiness, mining, and forestry.
4. To accomplish the above objectives, to build an infrastructure of roads, airfields, and telecommunications in the Amazon.

5. To provide governmental fiscal incentives and subsidized credit to businesses willing to invest in the Amazon.

The third and fifth objectives required international financing and organization to make them effective. These objectives would require large tracts inland of the border areas. This strategy linked national security and economic development as two sides of the same coin.

## VII. The Indigenous Populations

One of the fallacies of the Brazilian vision of the Amazon was seeing it as unoccupied. The Amazon was a tribal world of Indians who inhabited it long before the establishment of the Portuguese colony and Brazilian nation in the eastern and central sectors. The indigenous groups require relatively large tracts of land both for their foraging activities and to accommodate the periodic need to move villages to different areas to allow for recuperation of fatigued soils and depleted game. This meant that the indigenous groups were not constantly present on the land historically used and required for their subsistence. This characteristic of the tribal world aided the Brazilian illusion of unoccupied land.

The size of the indigenous population in Brazil at various historical periods is difficult to estimate. Hemming (1987:480) thinks that at the time of European colonization in the sixteenth century it was more than three and a half million. By 1760 the population was reduced to two million. By 1910 it had decreased to less than a million tribal Indians. Ribeiro (1967:110) estimated that by 1957 there were between 68,000 and 100,000, with 43,000 to 62,000 living in the Amazon. However, later United Nations and Inter-American Bank sources place the Indian population of the Brazilian Amazon at 213,352 (Commission on Development and Environment for Amazônia 1992:28).

Since colonial times there had been contact with Indians, which as noted was initially characterized by slavery. In the eastern and central regions, the contact usually ended with the elimination of Indians by disease or by killings, as seen in chapter 5. Was this to be the unspoken assumption about the Amazon being unoccupied in the second half of the twentieth century?

## VIII. Bibliographical Note

The sources in the following list have influenced the presentation of various topics in this chapter. Bearing in mind the writer's prayer—"Lord, deliver me from my enemies and those who interpret and quote me"—the list allows specialists to judge if we have been observant of the caution in this prayer. For those not acquainted with this material, the list suggests some sources that may be helpful in exploring the rich history of Brazil and its relation to its indigenous populations.

Geography: James and Minkel 1986

Social History and Structure: Conniff and McCann 1989, Poppino 1973, Scheper-Hughes 1992, Wagley 1971, Wood and Carvalho 1988.

Economy: Baer 1995, Merrick and Graham 1979, Weyland 1996.

Politics: Skidmore 1988.

Amazon: Commission on Development and Environment for Amazônia 1992, Davis 1977, 1988, Davis and Mathews 1976, Goodman and Hall 1990.

Indigenous Population: Hemming 1978, 1987, Ribeiro 1967.

Commissions or Reports on Indian Conditions: Ação Pela Cidadania 1989, 1990, Brooks et al. 1973, Cultural Survival 1979, Cultural Survival Quarterly 1989 (vol. 13, no. 1).

PIN and Calha Norte: Albert 1992, Allen 1992, Flavio Pinto 1989, Santilli 1989.

# 22

# The Yanomami in Roraima

The Brazilian conception of the Amazon and the resulting developmental policies, as influenced by Brazil's internal problems and their relationships to the world system, are the larger setting examined in the previous chapter. We now survey the impact of these policies on Brazilian activities in the eastern part of the state of Roraima and how these activities have fostered contact with the Yanomami in the rain forests of western Roraima. Our analysis of the consequences of this contact on the Yanomami villages begins with groups neighboring the Xilixana, and we then compare their contact experiences with the impact on the Xilixana themselves.

## I. Roraima

Located on the northern rim of the Amazon Basin, the state of Roraima (see maps 4, 5) is considered one of the more remote regions of the Amazon. Roraima's northern and western borders are the portions of the Pacaraima and Parima highlands where the watersheds drain east and south into the Rio Branco (see map 1). The portions draining north and west to the Orinoco River belong to Venezuela. Roraima's eastern border with Guyana is the beginning of the eastward-flowing drainage to the Rio Branco from the Pacaraima Mountains. Much of Roraima is covered by tropical rain forest, but the northeastern quadrant is savanna.

For years the state was inhabited by various Indian groups but sparsely occupied by Brazilians, most of whom lived in the savanna area as ranchers. During the rubber boom from 1850 to 1912, Roraima attained some importance as a food supplier for Manaus. Roraima's importance increased with the discovery of gold and other minerals beginning in the 1960s. Within Brazil's administrative structure, Roraima was a territory until 1991 when it achieved statehood.

Indians in the savanna are the Macuxi and smaller groups of Ingarico, Wapixana, and Taurepang. For several centuries there has been contact between these Indian groups and the Brazilians, leading to some assimilation. The forest area of the western part of the state is the homeland of approximately seven thousand Yanomami, about 33 percent of all Yanomami and 77 percent of the Yanomami in Brazil, the remainder living in the state of Amazonas, southwest of Roraima. Historically in Roraima there was little contact or communication between the savanna and the western forest areas, which remained an unknown region to Brazilians. Expeditions of initial exploration took place in the western sector until the 1950s.

The town of Boa Vista, located in the savanna on the Rio Branco, is the capital and economic center of Roraima. Boa Vista had a population of 67,000 in 1980 and grew to an estimated 163,024 in 1998, almost two thirds of Roraima's population. This growth was primarily due to Boa Vista becoming a center for the administration and servicing of mineral exploration and mining, for expansion of cattle ranching and agriculture, and for the growth of government agencies. It has become the transportation link for miners departing to and returning from mining sites throughout the state. Some of the characteristics of Boa Vista as the hub of economic activity in this frontier region are described in chapter 3. The city's population includes about eight thousand savanna Indians.

Traditionally the principal economic activity of Roraima was cattle ranching in the savanna. The state's first ranches were established by the Portuguese army around 1780. Ranchers were attracted to the savanna because it offered an extensive area of free grazing and a cheap labor force mostly provided by Macuxi Indians (MacMillan 1995:13–17). The development of ranching was historically limited by Roraima's distance from urban markets and its lack of transportation links to the rest of the Amazon and eastern Brazil. In the savanna there was also small-scale farming to provide for local food needs. Small-scale diamond mining began around 1912. Diamonds along with small deposits of gold were taken by placer mining from the principal rivers flowing through the savanna, the Maú, Cotingó, Suapí, and Quinó. Another activity was gathering and selling Brazil nuts. These various economic activities eventually brought Brazilians into contact with the Yanomami in the rain forest in the western part of the state.

## II. History of Yanomami Contact in Roraima

The Yanomami groups on the lower reaches of the Apiaú and Ajarani rivers have been in sporadic contact with Brazilian nut collectors since the last century. These same groups probably first came into contact with Brazilian ranchers and farmers in the 1940s. There were no Yanomami on the lower Mucajaí at that time.

As previously described, the first contact with missionaries was in 1958 when Robert Hawkins and Rod Lewis of the Unevangelized Fields Missions

(UFM, later to become MEVA) contacted the Palimi theli on the Uraricoera River and John Peters and Neill Hawkins contacted the Xilixana on the middle Mucajaí. In the same year Ernest Migliazza of the Baptist Mid-Missions took up residence among the Xiliana on the upper Uraricaá, a northern tributary of the Uraricoera.

The first known contact of Yanomami with miners was in 1960 on the upper reaches of the Uraricaá River, near the Venezuelan border, and on the upper reaches of the Mucajaí River, when four prospectors passed through villages B and C. Both of these contacts were with relatively small groups of transient miners. To this point, these sporadic contacts marked the slight interaction between the eastern part of Roraima and the Yanomami in the western part. The situation was about to change as the government's projected development of the Amazon reached Roraima.

Government efforts to stimulate economic activity in the northern Amazon region are described in the previous chapter. In Roraima, these efforts were embodied in two main projects, the construction of roads and, along these roads, the founding of agricultural colonies for in-migrants escaping the problems of eastern Brazil (see map 6).

Roads were constructed to connect Roraima with the rest of the Amazon and the nation and to provide access to the agricultural colonies and markets within the state. The road connecting Boa Vista with Manaus on the Amazon River, BR 174, was completed in 1974. At Manaus, this road joined the Pôrto Velho–Manaus Highway, giving access to the national road system. To the north of Boa Vista the road went to the border, connecting with the Venezuelan road system.

Another effort was initiating construction of the Northern Perimeter Highway, BR 210, which was to run parallel to the Transamazon Highway and connect eastern Brazil with Colombia and Peru. The thrust of BR 210 west from the town of Caracaraí on the Rio Branco brought it into an area traditionally occupied by Yanomami groups on the Ajarani and Catrimani rivers (see later discussion).

Along the newly built roads the PIN program also sponsored colonization projects, the goal of which was agricultural and cattle development. In-migrating settlers were provided with land and houses. They were promised an infrastructure of transport, health care, education, credit lines, and technical advice. Agricultural communities founded under this program (map 6) were Alto Alegre in 1978, Pad Anauá and other communities along BR 174 in 1979, Apiaú in 1981, and Confiança and the communities in the eastern area of BR 210 in 1982 (MacMillan 1995:17–23, 30). In-migrants from northeast Brazil, especially the state of Maranhão, predominated in the earlier communities while in-migrants from Rondônia predominated in the later communities. Most of the latter were originally from eastern Brazil before going to Rondônia.

However, most of the agricultural lands assigned to the colonists offered poor soils, and the infrastructure promised by the government never materialized. As a result of the poor returns from agriculture and cattle raising, the colonists turned to other activities to supplement their incomes. Some went seasonally to Rondônia to work in the rice fields; others went to the southern forest areas of Roraima to gather Brazil nuts; and some moved to Boa Vista or Manaus to seek employment in the informal sector. But most important for the Yanomami, some became part-time miners (*garimpeiros*) who began to prospect for gold along the lower reaches of the rivers of the western forest area.

In summary, as a result of the government's PIN program for the colonization and development of the Amazon, there were two sources of intrusion into forested area of western Roraima inhabited by the Yanomami; the westward extension of the Northern Perimeter Highway and the excursions of garimpeiros seeking gold to supplement their income in view of the inadequacies of the colonization projects. The following sections examine the effects of these contacts on various Yanomami communities.

## III. Contact Experience of the Southern Ninam (Aica)

(Taylor 1979:75–90, especially 75–76, 81, 88; Ramos 1979a:9–24; 1995:271–75)

The Yanomami groups comprising the southern Ninam lived in the area drained by the lower Apiaú and Ajarani rivers.

The Apiaú River lies south and southeast of the middle Mucajaí and empties into it farther downriver. The Yanomami in this rivershed, the Aica, live on the fringe of the western forest area. They have had sporadic contacts with nut gatherers for most of the twentieth century and with Brazilian farmers and ranchers since at least the 1940s. In 1959 Peters and a group of Xilixana men visited one of the Apiaú villages. The following year the two groups celebrated a feast at village C to initiate relations of alliance. The same year saw the first marriage between the groups with the in-migration of a widow and her young son to village C. This began a series of in-migrations from the Apiaú to the Mucajaí group. In 1960–61 the Consolatas, an Italian Catholic missionary group, established contact with a village on the lower Apiaú. At that time there were five villages with a total population of approximately 150 on the lower Apiaú.

In 1967–68 a measles epidemic broke out among the Yanomami in Brazil and Venezuela. Through unknown sources, it spread to the Apiaú area. The Apiaú Ninam suffered an estimated one hundred deaths. By mid-1975 there were only thirty Yanomami left on the lower Apiaú, a decline of 76 percent in about eight years.

Soon afterward, the survivors abandoned the Apiaú River valley. A few in-migrated south to villages in the Ajarani valley while others moved north and started a village, Flexal, on the lower Mucajaí River near the Brazilian ranches and farms. Later at the urging of FUNAI, they moved upriver to a site closer to the FUNAI post at Comara and village D. In spite of the presence of Yanomami in the Apiaú rivershed until at least 1975, the government in that year announced a previously prepared plan to clear cut two million hectares (almost five million acres) in Roraima as part of the Apiaú colonization program. This included the lower Apiaú rivershed. In terms of the model of intensity of contact discussed in chapter 5, the Apiaú groups appear to fall into the category of a population in intermittent contact, which became extinct. The extinction involved high mortality, but it also involved dispersal (out-migration). In 1992 Ramos flew over the lower Apiaú and saw nothing but reddish-brown skies from the smoke of settlers burning the forest.

To the south of the Apiaú is the Ajarani watershed, home of the Yawarib Yanomami. Migliazza's aerial survey of the area in 1970 showed twelve villages with an estimated population of four hundred. The Consolatas contacted the villages on the middle part of the river in 1960–61 and found a population of 145.

In September 1973 as part of PIN, the construction of the Northern Perimeter Highway began westward of the Rio Branco and approached the middle sector of the Ajarani River. There were 102 Yawarib in the area at that time, living in five villages. At kilometers 32 and 33 in an area already being colonized by Brazilians, the highway reached two small Yawarib villages of twenty and ten people respectively. With the arrival of the road, there were two deaths from pneumonia, two people moved away from the area, and one person is unaccounted for. (Ramos is the only writer to note population loss due to dispersal as well as deaths as a result of the contact experience).

In the latter part of 1973 the road reached two more Yawarib villages, Arapishi and Castanheira. Contact with the road workers was deadly; the crude death rates soared to 364 and 208 respectively. The villagers became disorganized and there were further losses due to dispersal. The Ajarani Yanomami were reduced to a remnant population of sixty-three people. In FUNAI's 1977 survey they reported that there were no Yanomami in the area. A Brazilian journalist remarked: "In truth there were no Indians. They were dead." Ramos (1995:275) summarizes their fate: "After losing many of their relatives, [the Yawarib] also lost their land to Brazilian colonists.

Now, consumed by alcohol, they live as a favor on the 'properties' of these new settlers. Epidemics prove once again to be efficient instruments for creating empty lands for white occupation."

There was another Yawarib village, the Nainashiuteri (Rainathauxiu-theri), on the upper Ajarani. In February 1974 they were raided by the Opikteri and four Nainashiuteri were killed. By mid-1975 seven more Nainashiuteri had died, evidently from diseases contracted on visits to the road. This left a small village of twenty-seven people, who dispersed. Some fused with the Opikteri village and the remainder with Yawarib in the middle Ajarani.

## IV. Experience of the Southern Yanomam

(Saffirio and Hames 1983:1–52; Saffirio 1985:36–106; 1986, 1996, and pers. comm.; Missão Catrimani 1995; Albert 1985, 1988, 1992; Ramos 1979a:24–30, 1995:273–74, 308; O'Connor 1997:161–213, 345–63)

Southwest of the Ajarani lies the Catrimani rivershed, where Yanomam is spoken. There were eight villages in the middle portion of this area in 1974. The ancestors of these villages had earlier experienced epidemics of measles as a consequence of being contacted by two expeditions of exploration, the Salathe expedition in 1929–30 and the Sotelo expedition in 1952. The deadly impact of the road project continued among these groups.

The Opikteri is a Yawarib group that had migrated to the Catrimani valley. In 1974 the road reached kilometer 135 near the Opikteri village. (A fission in 1976 led to a second Opikteri village at kilometer 132). Soon a measles epidemic erupted. While the Opikteri suffered, there were no deaths because they had been immunized by the medical program of the Catholic missionaries. Although spared death, the Opikteri suffered severe health problems the following year, including a major influenza epidemic and malnutrition. Ramos describes the deculturating effect of the road experience: "Most of the Opikteri turned to a life of what might be called 'roadside nomadism.' They spent their time going from one work camp to another, covering distances of 50 kilometers or more. They developed the technique of standing across the road, making a human barrier, to force drivers to stop in order to ask them for food, clothes or just a lift."

As the construction of the road continued, it arrived at kilometer 146 where the Wakathautheri lived near the Catrimani River and the Catholic mission run by the Consolatas. The Wakathautheri had assisted in the road construction since its inception in the western forest but were soon brought low by the infectious diseases construction crews carried. In the fifteen months from the first cutting of the trail for the road, the Wakathautheri suffered fifteen influenza epidemics, which in many cases escalated into more serious respiratory diseases. In 1974 a measles epidemic broke out, but as with the Opikteri, there were no deaths owing to the immunizations previously administered by the medical program of the missionaries. Malaria that had been endemic became epidemic.

This village has overcome the biological and cultural crises of initial contact. Its population increased from thirty-two people in 1967 to sixty-eight in 1981, due in part to the medical care and vaccinations by the missionary medical program. Ramos (1979a:30) notes:

> The Wakatauteri maintain their life style virtually unaltered. They made a very sharp contrast with the Yawarib as we saw them at Castanheira, and although they spend a great deal of time visiting the construction camps, they have not fallen into the undesirable situation in which the Opikteri found themselves. . . . Living with them in their temporary shelters and later in the big communal house was a reassuring experience which can only lead to praise of the missionaries' work. In spite of the enormous pressures from outside, they have succeeded in saving the Wakatauteri from the fate that trapped the Yawarib and the Opikteri.

In 1972 the mission was evaluated by a delegation from the Aborigines Protection Society (APS) of England, who had been invited by the Brazilian government to study the contact situation between indigenous groups and nationals. The visitors (Brooks et al. 1973:62) found that "nowhere could the inevitable processes of integration have been begun with greater tact and understanding towards the Indians."

These remarks from the 1970s have been confirmed by the subsequent population growth of this community. The biological danger from the road ceased in 1976 when the Brazilian government abandoned construction of the highway for financial and political reasons. Since that time, its use has become confined to the missionaries, FUNAI, and Catrimani villagers. Because of its location near the Catrimani mission with its medical and trader functions, the Wakathautheri community has continued to attract in-migrants from other communities in the Catrimani and Demini drainage areas. Several fissions have taken place. The population of this group in 1965 when they first settled near the mission was 28; in 1968 it was 32, by 1973 it reached 40, and in 1975 at the time of the measles epidemic, it was 46. It climbed to 61 in 1980, 68 in 1981, and in 1983 the first fission took place. The combined population of the two villages in 1985 was 93; in 1988 another fission took place; by 1995 the combined population of the original and fissioned villages was 129. This is a high 5.2 percent rate of annual growth in thirty years. In terms of the model of intensity of contact in chapter 5, the Wakathautheri are in intermittent contact with the national society. The contact has remained intermittent because of the termination of the highway and the provision of basic human services by the missionaries, obviating the need for Brazilian contact.

On a tributary of the Catrimani River, the Lobo de Almada, about a three-day walk north of the highway, lived three Yanomam communities: the Uxiutheri, Iropitheri, and Maxikopiutheri. Immunization and medical assistance were intermittent in these communities because of their distance from the mission. During a measles epidemic at the beginning of 1977, these villages lost 46 percent, 51 percent, and 30 percent respectively of their populations, an average of 44.8 percent. The epidemic started when a young boy from one of the communities had been transported over the road to the FUNAI Indian ward in the Boa Vista hospital. There he contracted measles but was released before the disease became manifest. He returned to his community and the epidemic began in these relatively isolated villages. This incident underlines the fact that epidemics can begin with a single infected carrier.

After the epidemic, the Uxiutheri and Iropitheri remained on the upper Catrimani for a time and then began a series of moves toward the highway to be closer to the mission facilities. In 1975 their combined population was 99; before the epidemic in 1977 the population was 101; the epidemic brought a decline to 51. By 1980 they were down to 43 people, in 1985 they were 38, and in 1995 they were 37. They had become small villages with the necessity of out-migration for marriage. In twenty years their population had decreased at an annual rate of –4.8 percent.

The third village, the Maxikopiutheri, out-migrated from the Catrimani drainage, and in December of 1981 was located next to the highway at kilometer 211 in the Demini valley, where the construction of the deadly highway had been terminated. Their population was down to fifteen people and dependent on the nearby FUNAI post. After 1981 the village recovered and in 1995 it was a thriving community. This is a reduced population which has recovered.

As in the case of the southern Ninam, construction of the road again brought disease and death to the Yanomami communities of the Catrimani area. But there was a distinct contrast among the Catrimani communities. Those distant from the mission medical program suffered extremely high mortality. The Wakathautheri near the mission experienced high morbidity, but because of the medical program, the mortality did not reach epidemic levels.

In the 1980s and 1990s the Catrimani area suffered high morbidity from malaria and tuberculosis contracted from miners passing through the area on the rivers. But the extensive immunization and treatment program of the Catrimani mission has continued to keep the morbidity from turning into epidemic mortality. From 1984 to 1989, a period that includes the invasion by the miners, the Wakathautheri crude death rate was a 23.8. Although this was a high rate, it was far from the epidemic proportions seen in communities in other areas. From 1990 to 1995 after expulsion of the miners, the rate fell to 14.2, but the morbidity from malaria and tuberculosis remained high. The total middle Catrimani Yanomami population increased from 290 in 1980 to approximately 515 at the end of 1998, an annual growth rate of 3.2 percent in eighteen years.

## V. Experience of the Northern Ninam, the Xiliana

(Migliazza 1972:19, 1978:19, 1980:103, 1998, and pers. comm.; Colchester 1985:59–72; Gomez 1990:1–11; Ramos, Lazarin, and Gomez 1985; Ramos 1995:275; CCPY 1989c)

In 1960 diamond and gold miners—garimpeiros—who had previously worked in the savanna flew into the mission airfield at Boas Novas (17 on map 7) and then hiked for three days over the mountains to reach the upper Paragua rivershed (Paramichi) in Venezuela. As a result of infectious disease from these contacts, Colchester estimates the Venezuelan Xiliana declined by more than 25 percent between 1966 and 1970. Migliazza estimates that the Brazilian Xiliana in 1964 lost about 25 percent of their population. In 1970 ten to twenty Brazilian miners were expelled from Venezuela and began working in an area close to the four Xiliana villages in Brazil. They used the airfield at Ericó (18 on map 7) for supplies. Epidemics and venereal disease accompanied their arrival. Mortality from these sources was mitigated to some extent because of some immunity from prior contacts with Brazilians on cattle ranches in the savanna and by the initial efforts of the missionares' vaccination program.

## VI. Subculture of the Brazilian Miner

As we have seen, Brazilian diamond miners were in the savanna as early as 1912, and gold miners were on the upper Uraricaá in 1960. These small efforts were the precursors of the 1980s Roraima gold rush of an estimated

forty thousand miners into the western forest area, the home of the Yanomami. The invasion would decisively alter the isolation of the Yanomami
from the national society and the world system. Understanding this contact
requires some knowledge of the subculture of Brazilian miners before we
continue the survey of Yanomami communities in Roraima and their contact with the national society.

The Brazilian mining sector is composed of two distinct and frequently
antagonistic groups. The formal sector consists of large national corporations, both public and private, as well as multinational companies. Such
entities use large and high-tech machinery requiring large amounts of capital. As corporations, these miners have a legal definition and government
regulation of their mining activities. Completely different from this is the
informal sector of garimpeiros, a subculture of individuals based on small-
scale technology and a distinctive infrastructure of their own. The relationship of this subculture to the law has evolved over time, from what might
somewhat simplistically be characterized as outlaw status to being ignored
by the law and only in more recent years to legal recognition. This informal
sector of garimpeiros has dominated mining efforts in Roraima. (Garimpeiros means those who work around the sites as well as miners proper, the
sector is known as garimpagem, and the mining pit itself as garimpo.)

This subculture has a tradition dating back to the seventeenth and eighteenth centuries (Schmink 1985:185–99; Cleary 1990:27–50). It was originally marked by a simple technology of hand tools, but beginning in the
1940s miners have also employed small-scale mechanization. Anthropologist David Cleary (1990) has written an extensive ethnography of the subculture and Gordon MacMillan (1995) has examined its extension to
Roraima.

When a mineral-yielding area (garimpo) is located, the finder lays claim
to it if the land is considered open or common. If it is on private land, by
Brazilian law the owner cannot forbid mining activity but is entitled to 10
percent of the gold found. Frequently Indian land is in a confused legal
status. If the land has not been formally demarcated as an Indian reserve,
garimpeiros consider it open or common land regardless of the history of
land use or of government declarations of intent to demarcate it. This was
the situation in Roraima in the 1980s.

The prospector recruits garimpeiros under one of several customary arrangements. If he provides them with food and the necessary equipment,
then the garimpeiros pay 50 percent of their production to the founder of
the pit. If each garimpeiro provides his own food and supplies, he pays 40

percent (MacMillan 1995:152–55). In either case, the miner remains free of debt, thereby maintaining his independence and mobility.

The traditional garimpeiro was usually a full-time miner who placed a high value on his personal independence and mobility but at the same time prized a code of sharing with fellow miners. Many of these men were marginal to Brazilian society. Such traditional miners have continued as a minority in the subculture associated with the Amazonian gold rushes but with an important role as custodians of garimpeiro wisdom about mining and philosophy of life. Sometimes they are called professional garimpeiros.

In more recent Amazonian gold rushes, many of the garimpeiros were part-time miners from agricultural or ranching backgrounds or were lower-income urban workers. Some middle-class Brazilians also became involved in managerial and financial functions of mining activity. In Roraima, surveys (MacMillan 1995:32–33) indicate that many of the garimpeiros were from eastern Brazil—especially the northeast, and Maranhão in particular—who were escaping difficult conditions there (see chapter 21). The miners in the Santa Rosa phase of the gold rush (discussed later) were primarily settlers drawn to Roraima by colonization programs. They worked part-time as miners, spending other portions of the year in agriculture or on ranches. In Roraima the farms grew annual crops (rice, manioc, maize, beans), which meant a lighter work load during the drier part of the agricultural cycle, allowing time for other activities. This was a more suitable time to work in the water-soaked gold pits using the hydraulic machinery described in chapter 19 in relation to the spread of malaria. Such supplemental activities assumed greater importance after the failure of the government's plans for agricultural development.

In the major phase of the Roraima gold rush, garimpeiros poured into the state. Most were also originally from eastern Brazil. In the early 1980s many had worked as miners in southern Pará, including Serra Pelada, Cuca, and Tucuma (see Schmink and Wood 1992). When these mines declined in the mid-1980s, they worked in northern Mato Grosso, Tapajós, and Rondônia. In the latter part of the 1980s they flooded into Roraima.

Having their origin in eastern Brazil, many of the garimpeiros knew the Yanomami only through Brazilian stereotypes of the Indian. Many were afraid of the Yanomami. But they perceived the Yanomami territory as open land available to anyone who worked it, although they did not intend to take permanent possession of the land they mined.

To understand garimpeiro mining in Roraima, the role of the airfields needs explanation. When a site yielding sufficient gold is located in the forest area, the only feasible way to bring in supplies is by air. Therefore all the main mining areas are marked by airfields, as shown on map 7. The map shows where within the Yanomami territory mining was concentrated. In this discussion, mining locations are identified by the number of the airfield on that map.

The original airfields in the Yanomami area (numbers 1, 2, 16, 17, 34, 35, 42, 50) were constructed by missionaries, but they remained the property of and under the jurisdiction of the Brazilian military. All were used by miners. (During the 1980s, missions were no longer in existence at airfields 17, 34, 35, and 50.)

The airfield with its accompanying store, bar, and brothel became the focal point for garimpeiros working the nearby pits. The store sold food and mining supplies. The owner of the airfield received ten grams of gold for each landing. Owners of the planes, sometimes the same as the owners of the site, charged fifteen grams of gold per round-trip to bring miners and other personnel into the area.

As the garimpeiros pushed on to new areas, they used the airfields as bases of operations. They hiked from an airfield into a new area to locate a mining site in the forest. Air drops supplied them while they worked the exploratory pits. Then they would return to the airstrip to sell their gold until they could afford to build an airstrip at the new site. This hopscotch effect using the airfields continued as the mining area expanded.

## VII. Preliminary Phase of the 1980s Gold Rush

In 1980 the small group of miners who had worked in the area near the Xiliana villages since the 1970s was expelled by the federal police at the insistence of FUNAI. During these years in the upper Uraricaá area, the miners had frequent contact with the Xiliana. One miner married a Xiliana and remained as a son-in-law in the faction headed by his father-in-law. Some Xiliana learned Portuguese and how to mine gold themselves. A Xiliana who in-migrated for marriage to village E passed this knowledge on to his new affines. In 1985 the same Xiliana visited the Malaxi theli and taught some of them how to mine gold (Ramos, Lazarin, and Gomez 1985:46).

In the 1970s a diamond mine was opened in the Furo de Santa Rosa region (airfield 22) of the Uraricoera River, just outside the Yanomami area. At the beginning of the 1980s the garimpo was converted to gold production. This initiated a gold rush. About two thousand garimpeiros came into the area and some advanced northwest up the Uraricaá into the southern part of northern Ninam territory (19 and 20).

The garimpeiros brought with them malaria, which was transmitted to the Ninam. A medical report in 1983 states: "Serious problems of chronic visceral malaria. 27% . . . were children between four and twelve years of age. 36% had clinical anemia probably related to the high rates of malaria and to intestinal parasites." Because of the invasion of Yanomami land and the threat to their health, the miners were removed by the federal police in 1986. The garimpeiros returned to their farms or ranches but had now gained the experience to work a garimpo.

## VIII. Major Phase of the Roraima Gold Rush

MacMillan (1995, especially 24–54), who spent sixteen months among the garimpeiros of Roraima, has chronicled some of the developments in the major phase of the gold rush.

### A. Apiaú Velho

In the early 1980s local garimpeiros who had worked at Santa Rosa began seasonal prospecting in the area between the middle Apiaú and Catrimani rivers (CCPY 1989d:37–40). They initiated a garimpo called Apiaú Velho (79) within traditional Yanomami territory and the home area of about three hundred semi- or completely isolated villagers. Requests by the Catrimani missionaries and FUNAI to the government to expel the miners at first went unheeded, and later when an effort was made, it was unsuccessful.

By 1983 there were two hundred miners in the region in spite of the fact that all the Yanomami territory had been interdicted by the government in 1982. Conflicts arose between the garimpeiros and Yanomami incensed by the invasion. Armed attacks followed, in which at least one garimpeiro was killed. In 1984 the Yanomami of the area began to suffer from infectious disease. Three members of a village died from malaria, including the wife of the headman. This same village had lost half its population in the measles epidemic in 1977. Later in the year a young Yanomami from the lower Catrimani was murdered by a garimpeiro and the Yanomami vowed revenge.

Word of the finds on the Apiaú spread. In September of 1984, garimpeiros from Rondônia and other regions of the country began to arrive in Roraima over the recently constructed roads. The gold rush that was to eventually draw an estimated forty thousand miners had begun in earnest. The missionaries and CCPY (Commission for the Creation of a Yanomami Park) pleaded with the government to expel the invaders. Some attempts were made by FUNAI personnel, but their efforts were thwarted by other sectors of the state and federal governments, including the military, who wanted mining development in the area. To avoid FUNAI's blockade of the Apiaú River, garimpeiros began to infiltrate the region on foot.

By 1985 there were six hundred garimpeiros working this area, all of which lies within traditional Yanomami territory. Frustrated by the government's ineffective effort to expel the invaders, Davi Kopenawa, a Yanomami educated at the Demini mission in Amazonas, led a group of fifty armed Yanomami from the region in raids on garimpos between the Catrimani and Apiaú rivers. They destroyed whatever supplies and equipment they could find. In the face of this force, the miners temporarily retreated.

## B. Rio Novo

In 1984 an important find was made at Rio Novo (airfield 77), a tributary of the upper Apiaú (CCPY 1988, 1989d:40–44). By July of 1985 eighty men were working in this area and by September the number had doubled. Again the miners' claim was resisted in armed clashes, both with the Yanomami and with police authorities when they attempted to remove the miners.

## C. Cambalacho

In 1986 a sizable amount of gold was found at Cambalacho (73) near the headwaters of the Apiaú. This site was about a two-week hike by trail from the colonization settlement also called Apiaú (see map 6). News of this find unleashed a torrent of miners who poured into Roraima (CCPY 1988; MacMillan 1995:30).

## D. Couto de Magalhães Region

With the garimpos on the headwaters of the Apiaú as a base, the garimpeiros continued their ascent toward to the Parima Highlands. In July 1987 a farmer colonist from Alto Alegre (see maps 6, 7) moved into the drainage of the Couto de Magalhães River, a tributary of the upper Mucajaí River. This was the home of the Malaxi theli, the marriage exchange partners of villages C and E of the Mucajaí group. He found a small gold mining operation belonging to the Malaxi theli with no one present at the time. The Malaxi theli had learned how to mine gold from a Xiliana in-migrant to village E. The garimpeiro claimed the site and called it Novo Cruzado (59). Whether an agreement was worked out with the Malaxi theli is disputed, but the final result was an armed clash leaving four Yanomami and one garimpeiro dead. Reports of other clashes and deaths filtered back to Boa Vista. Federal authorities as well as international attention began to focus on the problems in Roraima (CCPY 1988, 1989d, 1989f; Castro, Albert, and Pfeiffer 1991:369–70; MacMillan 1995:37–45, Ramos 1995:276–80; O'Connor 1997:1–75; Albert and Goodwin Gomez 1997:41–43).

A short distance to the west at Paapiú was an airfield (50) originally built by the Malaxi theli to invite visits by the missionaries. It had been 300 meters (about 320 yards) in length. In 1986 the military widened and extended this airfield to a length of a kilometer (about 1,093 yards) for no apparent reason. It was a secret part of the Calha Norte Project. In 1987 the Brazilian military policeman who was the custodian of the airstrip observed the gold being mined in the area by the Malaxi theli. He made an agreement with a local Yanomami headman, assembled a group of armed garimpeiros, landed them at the airstrip, and established his own garimpo. This large airfield become one the main gateways of the gold rush without any interference from the military.

Epidemics of infectious diseases soon broke out in the Yanomam communities. At Paapiú between August 1987 and January 1990, Albert and a medical team found that 84 percent of the population suffered from malaria, 53 percent from respiratory infections, 22 percent from intestinal infections, and 4 percent from tuberculosis. All these infections were helped by malnutrition. Serious malnutrition was present in 36 percent of the population, including 62 percent of the children two to nine years of age. Intestinal parasites further complicated the infectious disease–malnutrition synergism. *Ascaris lumbricoides* were present in 88 percent of a sample from the village at the Paapiú airstrip, *Entomoeba hysolitica* in 49 percent, *A. duodenale* in 42 percent, trichiura (hookworm) in 37 percent and lamblia in 29 percent.

Malnutrition was brought on by a number of factors. Degradation of the environment due to the miners' activities reduced the resources collected and hunted by the Malaxi theli. The miners' indiscriminate hunting and the noise of their pumps depleted game in the area. Peccaries, an important source of meat, disappeared completely. This was true not only of Paapiú but also of the middle Mucajaí area of the Xilixana, even though there was no extensive mining in that area. Another reason for malnutrition was the inability of some families to take care of their gardens because of malaria and other infectious diseases. The final months of the year are the time for opening a new portion of the garden as an older portion fatigues. Albert has noted that sickness in a family during this period diminishes the yield from the garden for two years. If sickness prevents a family from performing these tasks, the family must wait a year to begin cultivating this ground and another year for the plants to mature and return the garden to its normal level of production.

Pollutants fouled the waterways, the source of the water supply and fish. As earlier noted, a study of mercury concentration in hair from a sample of 107 Malaxi theli in 1990 found that 4 percent of them had levels above the acceptable limit set by the World Health Organization.

All this resulted in a high mortality rate, although no mortality figures are available. At Paapiú 43 percent of recorded individuals lost from one to seven close relatives between 1987 and 1989. Communities were destroyed by the continuous epidemics of malaria, and the few survivors were forced to join relatives in other communities who were also suffering. Journalist George Monbiot (1991:108–17) visited and described one of the communities laid low by sickness and death. The full extent of the mortality in this region probably will never be known.

### E. Headwaters of the Mucajaí River

With the gold finds increasing as the search moved west into higher elevations, the garimpeiros next moved into the drainage of the upper Mucajaí River (Monbiot 1991:67–121; MacMillan 1995:41–44). Beyond its confluence with the Couto de Magalhães, the main part of the Mucajaí makes a sharp bend to the south, paralleling the Couto de Magalhães. Using the airstrip at Novo Cruzado (59) as a base, a group of garimpeiros walked for about eight days searching for a new site. They befriended a Yanomami they met in the forest, who led them to a site rich with gold ore. Being unaware of the Xiliana influence in the area, the garimpeiros thought the missionaries had taught the Yanomami to extract gold for the benefit of the missions. This was a frequent charge made against missionaries when they assisted Yanomami protests against the invasions. The garimpeiros immediately claimed the site and named it Grota de Tarzã (32), a nickname of one of its claimants. This site in turn became the base for the founding other mining sites: Baiano Formiga (33), Jeremias (31)—visited and described by Monbiot (1991:67–74)—Pedro Jacaranda (28), and Popunha (29).

### IX. Contact Experience of the Highland Yanomam

In the Parima Highlands there was a concentration of about forty-five hundred Yanomam speakers (Taylor 1979:43–98; Ramos 1979a:7, 1995:276–80; Brooks et al. 1973:64–65, 119; CCYP 1989a, 1989b, 1989f; Castro et al. 1991:368–70). This is about half the Yanomami in Brazil and their heartland, where they established themselves several centuries ago to escape slavers along the main rivers. In the middle of the highlands is Surucucu, a table mountain rising 1,000 meters (about 3,280 feet) above sea level. The top of the mountain is a grassland and scrub plateau, 20 by 16 km (about 12.5 by 10 mi.). To the west are the headwaters of the Parima and Orinoco rivers; to the south and east lie the headwaters of the Mucajaí River. Compared to other Yanomami areas, the forty-six villages in the rain forest at the base of the Surucucu plateau had a dense population of twenty-eight hundred people in the 1970s.

UFM had established a mission and airfield (34) at Surucucu in 1961. In 1972 the same APS delegation that had previously visited the Catrimani mission also evaluated the mission at Surucucu. They noted (Brooks et al. 1973:65) that "the number of Indians might well soon increase in consequence of the vaccinations completed at the mission. . . . Measles vaccine has been flown in and administered and so too have small pox, diphtheria and whooping cough vaccines. . . . [These indications] hint at a potentially buoyant demographic situation once the killer epidemics are mastered among the Yanomami." The intense conflict between the Yanomam groups in the area—even giving rise to a raid on the mission store for its machetes— hindered mission work. The APS reported that the tension "helped remind us of the courage needed to man these lonely stations" and described and highly praised the mission's nondependency program of introducing people to and educating them about monetary exchange. The mission was closed in the late 1970s.

In 1975–76 the Surucucu area was invaded by five hundred miners seeking cassiterite, a mineral used to produce tin. About two hundred of the miners were controlled by Mineração Além-Equador, a company owned by businessmen in Boa Vista. The remainder were independent garimpeiros entering on clandestine flights. In the latter part of 1976 armed conflict erupted between the Yanomami and the miners, resulting in deaths on both sides. With international pressure playing a role, the Brazilian minister of the interior ordered expulsion of the miners from the area. There were reports of tuberculosis and venereal disease left by the miners.

In 1985 a Boa Vista mining investor, claiming that the government was about to hand Roraima over to foreign mining companies, armed sixty miners and airlifted them into Surucucu. They attacked the FUNAI post tracking their illegal entry. After a pitched battle, federal police removed these miners.

In 1987 garimpeiros infiltrated the Surucucu region from the upper Mucajaí. Soon the old missionary airfield, recently reconstructed and extended by the military, was pressed into use, as was the nearby strip (35) FUNAI had built for its post. Garimpeiros spread out over the area. Again reports of infectious disease laying low the villages of this densely populated Yanomami area reached Boa Vista. Armed clashes with the Yanomami took place as the miners ran roughshod over the highlands. Tuberculosis and venereal disease became health problems. At the Surucucu FUNAI post, over 40 percent of the medical cases were malaria. A study of mercury concentration in hair from a sample of forty people from the Surucucu area found that 18 percent of them had concentrations above the World Health Organization's acceptable limit.

## X. Contact Experience of the Sanumá

To the northwest of the Mucajaí group in the Auaris rivershed there was a group of Sanumá villages (one in-migrant village spoke Yanomam) for whom Ramos (1993:20–29; 1995:32–55, 289–309) has described contact experiences. Ramos enumerated censuses of two villages in 1970 and 1990. The population of the village of Kadimani increased from 52 to 112, or a 3.9 percent per annum rate of total increase. The Sanumá population of the village of Auaris increased from 94 to 237, or a 4.7 percent per annum rate of total increase. Ramos attributes these high rates of increase primarily to the fall of infant mortality, which was significantly helped by the health program of the MEVA missionaries at Auaris.

These conditions were drastically altered due to the appearance of miners using the mission airfields (1, 2) and then hiking to a mining area in nearby Venezuela. The miners were infected with malaria, which was transmitted to the Sanumá. In 1991 a severe malaria epidemic broke out in these communities.

## XI. The Aftermath

By 1989 all of the Brazilian Yanomami area was in the grip of a malaria epidemic spread by the conditions miners created. Because of pressures brought by national and international groups, the government finally expelled the miners, who retreated to Boa Vista to wait until the protests subsided. By 1992 an estimated eleven thousand had resumed mining activities, only to be expelled again. In 1995 half of the Yanomami population in Brazil (499.5 per 1,000 population) suffered from malaria. This far surpasses the 30 per 1,000 norm of the World Health Organization, indicating a grave public health situation (Gomez 1999).

The Surucucu and adjacent regions contain the headwaters of various rivers flowing into the Rio Branco and the Rio Negro. Mining introduced mercury poisoning into the whole region. As earlier noted, the middle Mucajaí villages can no longer draw their water from Mucajaí River itself.

Ramos (1995:271) has summed up the health crisis of the Yanomami:

The largest indigenous people in the Americas to retain their traditional way of life, the Yanomami, have been caught in the trap of fast and mindless development schemes, both governmental and private. The result has been social turmoil and a staggering death rate. . . . Road building, agribusiness, and mining have brought the Yanomami in contact with Western-style expansion. Whereas in previous decades of this century only the outer villages had been affected by the activities of isolated groups of Brazil nut gatherers, jaguar skin hunters, and other small scale ventures, the 1970s and 1980s brought an avalanche of intruders that ultimately spilled over into the entire Yanomami area from its fringes to its innermost, still isolated recesses.

## XII. Summary of the Impact of Yanomami Contact with Brazilians in Roraima

Table 22.1 summarizes the existing, fragmentary quantitative data about the impact on Yanomami villages in Roraima of contact with the national society. Qualitative accounts from all Yanomami areas in western Roraima indicate high morbidity, especially from malaria and tuberculosis. These conditions have resulted in high mortality in areas of close contact with road construction crews and miners. An exact demographic assessment for most areas is impossible owing to a lack of data.

### A. Impact of the Road

The effect of construction of the Northern Perimeter Highway is the best documented example of the effects of contact as well as offering highly contrasting examples of both kinds of intermittent contact outlined in Ribeiro's model in chapter 5. The devastating effect of contact with the construction workers is shown by the middle Ajarani villages, which lost 20 percent to 77 percent of their populations from death or the dispersal of many of the survivors. The Nainashiuteri village on the upper Ajarani (where some mortality was due to a raid by another Yanomami group shortly prior to contact) became extinct.

In diametric contrast to these villages, those of Opikteri and Wakathautheri on the middle Catrimani had close contact with the construction crews but did not suffer any deaths as a result of the measles epidemic the road brought, although they did suffer high morbidity. The difference was the effect of missionary intervention through the medical program and its preventative emphasis. The Opikteri apparently suffered cultural disorganization as a result of the contact, but there is no demographic data on the ultimate effect on this group. The case with the sharpest contrast is the Wakathautheri. Not only were they able to overcome the

**Table 22.1. Known Impact of Entrance of National Society into the Yanomami Area of Roraima**

| Language and Riveshed | Village | Year | Pop. | Deaths* # | Deaths* CDR | Scatter # | % Pop. Decline | Epidemic and Other Reasons |
|---|---|---|---|---|---|---|---|---|
| **Ninam–North** | | | | | | | | |
| 1. U. Paragua | | 1950s | | | | | | wc, mea, mal |
| 2. U. (Venezuela) | | 1960–75 | 150 | | | | −25%+ | mal |
| 3. " | | 1981 | | | | | | mea |
| 4. U. Uraricaá | | 1960–75 | 100 | | | | −25% | mal |
| 5. " | | 1980–86 | | | | | | mal |
| **Ninam–South** | | | | | | | | |
| 6. L. Apiaú | | 1967–75 | | 100 | | | −100% | mea |
| 7. M. Ajarani (Yawarib) | Km 33 | 1973–75 | 20 | 2 | 100 | 2 | −20% | inf. disease |
| 8. " | Arapishi | 1973–75 | 22 | 8 | 364 | 9 | −77% | mal, pn |
| 9. " | Castanheira | 1973–75 | 24 | 5 | 208 | 5 | −42% | pn, dy |
| 10. U. Ajarani | Nainashiuteri | 1973–75 | 30 | 11 | 367 | 19 | −100% | disease, raid |
| **Yanoman–South** | | | | | | | | |
| 11. M. Catrimani | Opikteri | 1974 | | 0 | | | | mea |
| 12. " | Wakathautheri | 1974 | | 0 | | | | mea |
| 13. " | Iropitheri | 1977 | 69 | 35 | 507 | | −51% | mea |
| 14. " | Uxiutheri | 1977 | 32 | 15 | 469 | | −47% | mea |
| 15. " | Maxikopiutheri | 1977 | 33 | 10 | 303 | | −30% | mea |
| **Yanomam–Central** | | | | | | | | |
| 16. Parima | Surucucu sample | 1990 | | | | | | 18% merc. |
| 17. U. Mucajaí | Paapiú sample | 1990 | | | | | | 84% mal+, 36% mnu, 4% merc |

## Sanumá

| | | | | | | | Rate | Reason |
|---|---|---|---|---|---|---|---|---|
| 18. Auaris | Kadimani | 1991 | | 6 | | | 114% | mal+ |
| 19. " | Mission | 1991 | | 1 | | | 32% | mal+ |
| 20. " | Olomai | 1991 | | 5 | | | 25% | mal+ |
| 21. " | " | 1992 | 92 | 12 | | | 60% | mal+ |
| 22. " | Shikoi | 1992 | | 37 | | | 61% | mal+ |
| 23. " | Tucushim | 1992 | | 5 | 130 | | 62% | mal+ |

## Ninam-Xilixana

| | | | | | | | Rate | Reason |
|---|---|---|---|---|---|---|---|---|
| 24. M. Mucajaí | A | 1957 | 17 | 4 | 267 | 13 | -100% | pn |
| 25. " | B | 1960 | 30 | 7 | 233 | 0 | | pn |
| 26. " | C | 1960 | 87 | 7 | 80 | | | pn |
| 27. " | Sample | 1990 | | | | | 7% | merc |

* Many of the death figures are for less than one year; see sources. Denominators of crude death rates are not always the midyear population.

*Abbreviations:*

Rivershed: U = Upper, M = Middle, L = Lower

Reasons: dy = dysentary; mal = malaria (+ = % testing positive); mea = measles; merc = % testing above World Health Organization norm for mercury contamination, mnu = malnutrition, pn = pneumonia, wc = whooping cough.

*Sources:*

1. Colchester 1985:65, 72 note 2
2. Colchester 1985:64; Migliazza, pers. comm.
3. Colchester 1985:65
4. Migliazza 1978:19 and personal communication
5. Ramos 1995:275
6. Taylor 1979:75–76; Ramos 1995:274
7. Ramos 1979a:14–17
8. Ramos 1979a:14–15
9. Ramos 1979a:14–19
10. Ramos 1979a:13
11. Ramos 1979a:20–22
12. Ramos 1979a:24–30
13. Saffirio and Hames 1983:12; Ramos 1995:274
14. Saffirio and Hames 1983:12
15. Saffirio and Hames 1983:12
16. Castro, Albert, and Pfeiffer 1991:369–70
17. Albert and Gomez 1997:43; Castro et al. 1991:369–70
18. Ramos 1993:20–29; 1995:295–96, 300
19. Ramos 1993:20–24; 1995:293
20. Ramos 1995:280, 290–91, 300
21. Ramos 1995:300
22. Ramos 1995:302
23. Ramos 1995:301
24. This study
25. This study
26. This study
27. Castro, Albert, and Pfeiffer 1991:369–70

high morbidity, but they have continued to increase their population at a rate 5.2 percent per year over a thirty-year period.

## B. Impact of the Miners

There are no acceptable mortality or dispersion data to specify the full impact of the miners in areas of concentrated mining as distinguished from areas through which the miners merely passed. The qualitative accounts and conjectural or absolute numbers (without data on population sizes to make them comparable), especially from the Auaris, Surucucu, and Paapiú areas, indicate losses of at least the same magnitudes as those from road construction and perhaps greater losses. CIMI (1993), the Indigenous Missionary Council, estimates that two thousand Yanomami died from disease or violence due to the miners. But whereas this is given on the first page of the report as representing an estimate since the early 1970s, on page two this figure is given for the mortality for the period 1988–89. The full extent of mortality from the garimpeiros' invasion will probably never be known. The absence of reliable estimates is partially due to the lack of missions in many of the mining areas as a source of such information.

There are some data estimating the morbidity resulting from contact with miners. Sanumá data from the Auaris show that in some communities, up to 60 percent or more of the population tested positive for malaria. Confirming this is the high incidence of malaria morbidity reported for the Catrimani and Mucajaí villages. The Yanomami Health Agency (DSY 1999:6, 8) estimates that in 1996, 27.2 percent of the Yanomami population were infected with malaria. This is probably an under-enumeration due to the difficulties of communication in this area. At Casa do Índio, the Indian hospital FUNAI eventually opened in Boa Vista, 32.5 percent of Yanomami deaths were due to malaria (Pithan, Confalonieri, and Morgado 1991:572).

A study of mercury contamination was carried out in 1990, just after the expulsion of the miners. Levels unacceptable by World Health Organization standards were already found in 18 percent of the Yanomami in the Surucucu sample. Since humans take in mercury through the food chain, a protracted period is required for its full impact to be felt. Future testing will probably reveal a higher incidence of unacceptable contamination.

## C. The Xilixana Communities

As map 2 shows, the communities so far examined in this chapter encircle the Xilixana villages on the middle Mucajaí except toward the east, where there is savanna occupied by Brazilian farmers and ranchers. How do the Xilixana communities compare with those around them?

The Xilixana villages did not have contact with road construction crews. Their contact with miners was less intense than that in other communities, as the miners passed through the middle Mucajaí area but did not develop garimpos there. In addition, they had the protection of the missionaries' medical program. As a result, mortality of the villages during the Brazilian phase was elevated but it never reached epidemic proportions. Nevertheless, the Xilixana mortality level was higher in the Brazilian phase than it was in the Precontact phase in spite of the conflict and infanticide levels of the earlier period.

The early contacts of the Xilixana villages illustrate contrasting effects of first contact. The initial contact of village A was with ranchers or agriculturists of the national population during their first downstream trip in 1957. It resulted in the extinction of the village due to a crude death rate reaching 267 and to the dispersion of the remainder of the village, not only because of the high level of mortality but also because of the important position in the social structure of those who died. This village conforms to Ribeiro's model.

In contrast, village B illustrates the result of indirect contact. Most likely the deadly pneumonia epidemic in this village in 1960 resulted from their contact with another Yanomami group, the Malaxi theli, who may have contracted it from the Catrimani Yanomami along the trade route of that river, which connected them with Brazilians. It shows how villages isolated from outside contact may become victims of the contact experience of other indigenous groups. A number of cases of tuberculosis among the Mucajaí groups were due to indirect contact with the national society through the mediation of Aica in-migrants who had contracted it from Brazilian farmers and ranchers. Once tuberculosis had been brought into the communities, Yanomami eating customs helped spread it.

Village C also suffered high mortality in this period, though significantly less than in village B, apparently from infectious disease from the same source. The reason for the lower incidence is unknown.

## XIII. Summary

This examination of the impact of government efforts to colonize and promote economic development in one Amazonian state, Roraima, reveals a net effect of little development. The efforts have, however, directly and indirectly assisted large-scale intrusions into the rain forest of western Roraima, the Yanomami homeland. These intrusions have resulted in high morbidity and mortality as well as depletion of the environment, and government efforts to remedy the situation have been anemic. The impact of the road program is the best documented. It led to the extinction of one Yawarib village and losses of 20 percent, 30 percent, 42 percent, 47 percent, 51 percent, and 77 percent in the Catrimani and other Yawarib villages. It is difficult to quantify the mortality impact of the miners due to a lack of data. But given the anecdotal and qualitative information, the impact of mining has been severe, leading to extinction of a number of Yanomami villages in the highlands and to extremely high morbidity in all of western Roraima. Even in the villages benefiting from missionary medical programs, high morbidity has led to elevated levels of mortality, higher than the mortality level of the Precontact period. Although the Xilixana have serious health problems, the survey in this chapter indicates that they are one of the more fortunate Yanomami groups in western Roraima.

# 23

# A Model of Self-Determination

At the end of the twentieth century, the results of the national society's penetration into the Yanomami area of Roraima raise a critical question for these Yanomami villages: Will they recover from the endemic and in some cases epidemic diseases and be able to manage their own future? Or is the present health crisis the precursor of more invasions and removal from their land by biological, physical, or legal assault, as would be predicted by Ribeiro's historical model?

## I. Shortcomings of Ribeiro's Conflict Model

In Ribeiro's model as outlined in chapter 5, the ultimate outcome of the contact situation is seen as extinction of many indigenous groups and the integration of a surviving remnant into the national population. These outcomes are the results of the conflict arising from invasions of Indian areas by extractors, farmers, or ranchers. In this model, the Yanomami would appear to be passive and unwilling partners to contact with the nation. Saffirio and Hames (1983:5) have pointed out the incompleteness of this conception:

> Some have argued that the Brazilian government, in historical continuity with all other state-level political organizations in the New World, has mounted a deliberate campaign of genocide and ethnocide against the Yanomama. Others have argued that although governmental actions have not been aimed at deliberately destroying the Yanomama as a culture or people, this has been the inevitable effect of development policies. Curiously absent in the analysis of ethnocide and genocide is the role the Yanomama play as the passively affected or the actively behaving. Many studies imply that the Yanomama are simple automatons unable to distinguish, for a variety of reasons, what is and what is not in their best interests as individuals. . . . Some Yanomama eagerly drop old customs and imitate those of Brazilians. Frequently this is the result of relentless persuasion and ridicule by

whites of Yanomama customs, but at other times it is the result of a belief that they can do better by changing.

There is no single attitude toward contact and social change among the Yanomami. It can differ from village to village in Brazil and Venezuela. It can also differ from individual to individual within the same village. As in any human group, there is a continuum of attitudes ranging from the arch conservative defending traditional ways to the raging radical who wants to do away with all aspects of being Yanomami and become Brazilian or Venezuelan. Most Yanomami are somewhere between these two extremes (see the differences among the Kayapó, a Brazilian indigenous group with a longer and more intense experience of contact, in Rabben 1995).

The Yanomami as active agents in the contact situation with their own attitudes and motivation for change have not been fully appreciated, as Saffirio and Hames point out. This characteristic is emphasized by service organizations (protective intervention) working with the Yanomami, especially the various missionary groups. As seen in chapter 22, these programs have had some success. In many respects, the missionaries in their multifunctional capacities are carrying on the spirit of Rondon and the Villas Bôas brothers, an impulse that faltered in the decline and ineptitude of the SPI and FUNAI. The Xilixana and Catrimani data contradict Ribeiro's model for drawn-out intermittent contact. Ribeiro posited decline of the indigenous population during this period in spite of service agency efforts. He was probably thinking of the difficulties and relative ineffectiveness of the SPI and FUNAI medical programs. An examination of the missionaries' approach shows the characteristics of protective intervention required to ensure the human rights of the Yanomami in the face of Brazilian expansion in the Amazon.

## II. A Model of the Active Yanomami

To understand "protective intervention," we have developed an alternative model to Ribeiro's conflict model. Ours emphasizes indigenous groups as active agents of change in a relatively peaceful contact situation where they are not overwhelmed by invaders of the national population. As Saffirio and Hames (1983:5) have noted:

It is our position that the Yanomama ought to be able to make decisions which are in their own self-interests as they believe those interests to be. The major stumbling block they have in making such decisions is their gross ignorance of the long-term consequences of whatever decisions they do make. Crucial to making decisions is having a set of alternatives from which to choose.

Our model focuses on the correlation between the indigenous desire and choice to acquire manufactured goods of increasing complexity, the increasing intensity of contact required by such acquisitions, and the resulting changes in the traditional indigenous culture. The model is based on ideas contained in a number of sources: Hemming (1978, 1987) in his comprehensive histories of Brazilian Indians; Bodley (1999) in his survey of tribal peoples in contact with the capitalist world; Wolf (1982) in his survey of the spread and impact of the capitalist mode of production in societies organized by a differing mode of production; Ferguson (1995) in his synthetic history of the Yanomami; and our own experiences of working with indigenous people (Early 1970a, 1970b, 1973, 1982, 2000; Early and Peters 1990; Early and Headland 1998; Peters 1973, 1998).

In this model, the descriptions of each stage and transitions to the next are "ideal types" with all the methodological precautions that go with such constructions. There is no necessity that all contact situations pass through all these stages or that the process be linear, although Ribeiro implies that the stages of his model are linear and fixed. Skipping of stages and reversals can take place.

## III. Intermittent Stage

The model retains the outline of Ribeiro's model but involves a different development for each of the stages. Most nationals, either as individuals or as corporate groups, usually seek contact to acquire factors of production from indigenous people: their land and/or labor. Frequently initial contacts take place in what Bodley (1999:30–45) has termed "the uncontrolled frontier . . . by the direct action of countless individual traders, settlers, missionaries, and labor recruiters who, in seeking their own self interest, dealt directly with native peoples in frontier areas beyond government control."

Missionaries initiate contact to communicate a form of religious expression according to their interpretation of the human condition, including a psychological attitude and resulting conduct. This motivation is as strong as the nationalist desire for land and/or labor. In most world religions, missionaries with a fundamentalist stance see their worldview and its values as intrinsically linked to the acceptance of a specific cognitive content based on a literal interpretation of a sacred text. Other missionaries, representing the same world religions whose missiology (the intellectual basis of mission policy) has been influenced by symbolic theology, see the same set of values symbolically expressed in the same sacred texts but understand that the values can be expressed in a number of other cultural ways. The primary function of the missionary is to give witness to a set of values not necessarily restricted to the symbols of a particular worldview. Of special importance is assisting indigenous populations with the problem of understanding how their traditional values are to be implemented in a situation of social and cultural change (see Bortoli 1997:70; Mbefo 1987; Salamone 1997:22–23).

The term *missionary* is frequently used with a restricted meaning. For some, the term is associated with a negative stereotype of narrow-minded authoritarianism accompanied by cultural insensitivity. For others, the term frequently refers only to working for the conversion of the indigenous population to a worldview embodying the form of religious expression embraced by the missionaries themselves. Such a concept does not express adequately the religious goal of some missionary programs and completely omits the provision of human services, which can be of immense importance in the contact situation. The values of many missionaries impel them to engage in providing technical services for the betterment of the indigenous communities.

Indigenous groups are driven by a desire for manufactured goods and technological services. The force of this drive can be as strong as the desire by members of the national society (sometimes called "white man") for wealth and the means to obtain it, such as land, cash, or gold. Ribeiro (1967:97) points out the strength of the Indians' desire for these goods, noting that to make contact, they must overcome their strong fear of strangers. A Venezuelan Yanomami (Salamone 1997:80) expressed the initial desire in this way, with perhaps some exaggeration: "I want medicine for all kinds of diseases. Even if I have a lot of things, I can still die. Because of that I am not saying that I want a lot of things. I just want machetes and axes. When we don't have those. we don't have food to eat. Because of that I want those." Hemming (1978:9, 11, 37, 78, 154) has shown that this motivation has been a constant compelling factor in the history of Brazilian-Indian relations.

> Metal axes and tools seemed miraculous to people who spent much of their year in the laborious business of clearing forest with stone axes. Indians had always made skilled artefacts but, as one chronicler explained, "they took a very long time to make anything. This is why they value metal so greatly—because of the ease they experience in making things with it. For this reason they delight in communication with the whites." It was a fatal fascination, the greatest weakness of Brazilian Indians. (Hemming 1978:9)

Hemming calls the desire for metal tools a "fatal fascination" because the final result of these desires is the outcome projected by Ribeiro's conflict model.

The desire for manufactured goods can be an expanding one, as noted in the pattern of the Xilixana desires discussed in chapter 5. It began with the desire for metal cutting tools and grew from there as shown in table 5.1 and in the Catrimani tables (Saffirio and Hames 1983:15, 20–21). Without ceasing to acquire cutting tools, people shifted their emphasis to specialized hand tools and consumer goods. Some examples were guns for hunting, adzes for canoe building, and aluminum pots and pans for cooking. Beads, combs, mirrors, and a few items of clothing were the typical consumer goods of this stage. The continual acquisition of these goods requires at least intermittent contact between the tribal group and the national society. (This does not preclude their acquisition from other indigenous groups.)

### IV. Cultural Impact of Initial and Intermittent Contact

The specialized tools and consumer goods typical of this stage allow the tribal group to perform traditional tasks with greater ease and efficiency. They are integrated into the traditional patterns of the culture without initially changing them.

During this phase, indigenous groups begin to learn about the need for cash to obtain these items when opportunities for barter are not available. A Yanomami schoolteacher (Salamone 1997:82) said: "When I started working as a teacher I wanted to get thread for tying arrows and red cotton thread for making hammocks. Some of us want shorts, shoes, pants, hats, watches, fishhooks, matches, combs. In order to get these things we want to work."

### V. Permanent Contact

The desire of the tribal group grows to include more complex tools and a much wider range of consumer goods, and this draws them into permanent contact with the national society. The more complex tools are small-scale technologies that require a source of power beyond that of the human body. Examples are various types of power grinders, which can prepare the staple crop for consumption much more quickly than can human hands, or outboard motors used by riverine people. Frequently the source of power is a small gasoline motor. The Yanomami quoted in our description of the initial phase added (Salamone 1997:80): "I also want a machine to grind manioc roots." Another Yanomami (Salamone 1997:20), who had been encouraged by the anthropologist Chagnon to retain his traditional ways, said: "I told Shaki [Chagnon] that when he first came here he had an old boat with an old motor. His boats got better as time passed. Then he came in helicopters. I asked him why he could improve and we could not? Why must we paddle in old canoes when we can get motors for our boats?"

With permanent contact, the traditional tribal culture undergoes substantial change as elements of the national culture are adopted. Before this stage, the manufactured goods had been fitted into the traditional village framework of kinship, reciprocity, and so on. Acquisition of more complex tools locks the group into economic and social structures required for the use and maintenance of such tools. For example, tools powered by small gasoline motors require the continual acquisition of gasoline, which in turn requires money and participation in a market economy. The maintenance of a gasoline motor involves some cognitive understanding of electricity and combustion. As the indigenous groups become more involved in acquisition of manufactured goods, they begin to realize that these goods depend on and are necessarily linked to certain kinds of economic, social, and cognitive structures of the national society, some of which are contradictory to their tribal ways. They may go through a period of trying to deny the contradiction, but eventually it must be confronted.

For example, adoption of new skills and social structures implies that reciprocity can no longer be the universal mechanism for the distribution of goods and services, with a consequent lessening of the importance of the basis of reciprocity: tribal kinship. The more complex tools also require the insertion of new cognitive frameworks of explanation and legitimacy in addition to the traditional tribal worldview. A Venezuelan Yanomami (Salamone 1997:76–77) expressed it in this way: "Some of us need to become health workers, so that when the missionaries go, we will be able to get medical help. If we don't think like that, other outsiders will come here and live, and they will decide over us . . . and take our land away from us. Some of us need to become teachers, some need to become medical workers. I want to represent our people to the outside, even though I don't know a lot of Spanish yet."

## VI. Assumptions of the Model

In the model, this desire for increasingly complex manufactured goods brings about greater intensity of contact, with resulting changes in the tribal culture. The model is not specific to indigenous populations but is applicable to any group with a simpler technology in contact with the international system and the results of its more complex technology. Based on historical experience, the model sees these desires and their implementation eventually leading the indigenous group to choose freely to integrate into the national society as long as they can retain their economic viability and cultural distinctiveness as an ethnic group. But this will take place only under peaceful conditions in which indigenous rights are respected. This assumption is the great problematic of the model.

## VII. Historical Experience

Under peaceful conditions, few groups have looked at the products of industrial technology (or its precursors) and rejected them. The exception proving the statement would be some Old Order (Anabaptist) groups dating from the sixteenth century, such as the Hutterites and various Mennonite groups, including the Amish. Understanding their position provides a contrasting case that helps in understanding indigenous motivation. The insight of the Old Order position is simple but profound. Traditional adherents of the Old Order say that in terms of what they would lose of their communal society (expressed by their religious symbols and values) through the adoption of industrial technology, the technology is not worth it. They refuse to see their fellow men and women primarily as customers, clients, or economic competitors, as required by a market economy. The Old Order position does not see evil in technology itself but understands that technology does not exist by itself, that technology is intrinsically linked to certain types of economic and social structures. (Marx later made this one of the cardinal points of his theory.)

Consequently Old Order groups realize they cannot have it both ways— that is, adoption of the goods of industrial technology and rejection of the economic and social structures linked to these goods and their technology. It takes time for individuals and groups including tribal societies to arrive at this realization. In the interim, they usually try to have it both ways. Very few groups in history, including indigenous groups faced with this choice under peaceful conditions, have made the Old Order decision. In the contemporary technological world, the Old Order groups themselves frequently have difficulty passing on their traditional subculture to their younger generation.

## VIII. Integration: The Big Decision

Up to this point, the desire for manufactured goods has been pursued without people being fully conscious of its implications. But at this point, the

23.1. The Xilixana meet to discuss political matters (John Peters, 1995).

Old Order realization that indigenous groups cannot have it both ways becomes explicit and fully conscious. It requires indigenous people to make a decision about social change. Usually the indigenous community divides into opposing political factions (different from but related to the traditional factions) ranging from extreme conservatism to favoring radical change. The question at issue usually is not the dilemma to change or not to change. Rather the dispute is about the rate of change and the way it should be accomplished. It takes time for any group to work through this problem. As long as there is no coercion or discrimination, cultural change will take place and the tribal culture will change. In this model, the decision to cease the ways of tribal culture and to integrate into the national culture is freely made and not a matter forced on a depopulated or a landless remnant group, as in the conflict model.

## IX. Implementation of the Model

Our model is an attempt to lay out the consequences of protective intervention initiated by the SPI and sketched by Ribeiro as an alternative intermittent stage of his model. Implementation of the model requires respect for indigenous rights. A difficulty with the model of self-determination is that historically, the conditions for its full implementation have seldom been found. The development of further stages of the model were frustrated by bloody conflict between nationals and indigenous groups so that programs of protective intervention were unable to attain their potential. In this respect, Ribeiro's thesis of seeing conflictive permanent contact as following upon either conflictive or peaceful intermittent contact is the more frequent pattern. The question for Brazil with regard to the Yanomami is: In this period of intermittent but increasing contact, will the necessary conditions be maintained for the unfolding of the model of self-determination with its basis in human rights, or will the intermittent stage be followed by the conditions of permanent contact as outlined in the conflict model?

# 24

# Contact and Survival in the Amazon

National and international pressures for the development and colonization of the Amazon, how these pressures have brought the Yanomami in the state of Roraima into contact with the national society, and the consequences of this contact are addressed in the preceding three chapters. We turn now to some of the crucial issues facing the Yanomami as they attempt to implement the model of self-determination.

## I. The Growing Population of Roraima

The increasing problems of the Yanomami in the rain forests of western Roraima can be seen in the growth of the state's population shown in figure 24.1. From 1960 to the late 1970s the entire state had only 30,000 to 50,000 thousand people. Beginning with the government's colonization projects in the late 1970s, the population increased to around 160,000 by 1985. The first part of gold rush in the early 1980s drew from farmers and ranchers of the colonization projects who had previously migrated to the state. But with the finds on the middle Apiaú in 1986, the population soared between 1987 and 1989 as miners and merchants poured into the state and the population reached over 285,000, living mostly in the savanna and the eastern part of the state but closely linked to the mining in the Yanomami area. Roraima has become one of the fastest growing states in Amazônia, with a very high 7.0 percent rate of annual population increase from 1962 to 1981 and an explosive 9.3 percent from that date to 1991. There has been a slight decline of population due to the expulsion of miners, but many remain and work clandestinely in the Yanomami area.

The population figures we use here and in figure 24.1 are taken from the reports of the malaria control commission in Roraima (SUCAM) up to 1991. These figures are probably more realistic than census data because of better communication with local communities, including the mining population, who are not permanent residents. In 1991, SUCAM estimated the state population as 286,729 while the census enumeration for the same year was 217,583; in 1998 the census estimate of the Roraima population was 260,705.

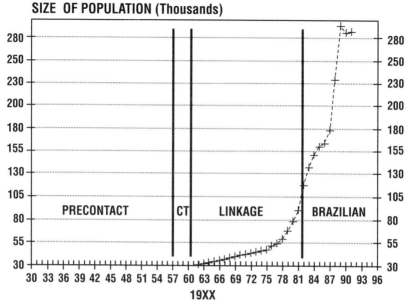

24.1. Population of Roraima.

The Yanomami in western Roraima now face in eastern Roraima a national population almost forty times larger than their own. The Roraima population will probably continue to grow. The question for the future is: In the face of the explosive population growth in eastern Roraima with its potential for increased contact with the Yanomami, will the Yanomami be able to survive and have the right of self-determination in how they survive?

The answer to this depends to a large extent on the Yanomami retention of their land as a basis of economic self-sufficiency. This allows them time to understand their options and to choose their future course as well as providing a place where they may have some provision for their health needs and for acquiring some immunity to infectious diseases. Our focus in this chapter is on the key problems of health and land.

## II. Health Programs

The experiences of contact between the Yanomami and Brazilians in Roraima indicate the importance of health programs, both to sustaining the initial shock of contact and to providing treatment in the face of the continuing danger of infectious disease.

The Wakathautheri and Opikteri cases show that the initial disease shock, frequently from measles or pneumonia, can be avoided. Both these groups had been immunized by the missionary medical program at Catrimani, and they escaped the fate of the Yawarib in the Ajarani area. The shock in other areas also appears to have been mitigated by missionary medical programs—for the Xiliana on the upper Uraricaá in the 1960s and at Surucucu in 1975 by the immunization efforts of UFM missionaries and the Yanoama Project formulated by anthropologist Kenneth Taylor. This project was initially adopted by one of the companies working in Surucucu before operations were suspended. Among the health provisions were vaccination of all mining personnel and a quarantine period upon arrival. The latter provision proved not feasible, but it indicates the type of program needed. The lack of such programs can be seen in the high mortality in the Apiaú, Ajarani, and upriver Catrimani groups.

After the initial shock of contact, health problems continued as the Yanomami were just beginning to acquire some immunity. Some may have survived the initial shock but remain in a weakened condition that leads to high morbidity from other diseases. This is especially true if the Indian group is overwhelmed socially and psychologically by the contact experience, as appears to have happened to the Opikteri and other Yawarib groups. The Wakathautheri case illustrates the importance of missionary health programs both for controlling the biological onslaught of the initial contact and for maintaining health during the gradual process of Indians learning to interact with the national life.

Missionary resources have always been insufficient to reach the majority of the Yanomami in Roraima. Health care was to be a primary concern of the government through FUNAI. Observations in the literature present a dismal picture of inefficiency, incompetence, and woefully inadequate financing. At the main hospital in Boa Vista there was a FUNAI Indian ward. In 1979 Ramos found it to be a small room with three bare mattresses on the floor, where people with infectious diseases were deposited with little care. During the malaria epidemic in the Auaris area in 1991, "ten patients were sent to the Boa Vista public hospital, three of whom died there for lack of proper attention" (Ramos 1995:295). As seen in the last chapter, the high mortality of the upriver Catrimani villages began with measles contracted in this ward.

In the 1970s FUNAI opened the Casa do Índio in Boa Vista and in the 1980s moved it to the outskirts. In FUNAI's structure, it was the place to which the FUNAI posts sent their sick for treatment, making it the nerve center of the FUNAI and later the Yanomami Health District system. In

1989 an independent Brazilian national commission, Ação Pela Cidadania, evaluated the contact problems in Roraima. The medical doctor in charge of the Casa do Índio lamented the conditions under which he worked, as the commission reported (translated from Ação Pela Cidadania 1989:19):

> The Casa do Índio was not architecturally designed or adequately equipped for the proper treatment of Indians. It does not have the facilities to isolate patients with infectious diseases so that Indian patients are always subject to infection during their stay here. The consulting rooms and recuperation wards do not meet acceptable aseptic standards. In the rainy season, water comes into the wards. There is no dietary regime adjusted to indigenous habits. The hospital food is strange to the Indians, so that many times patients suffer from diarrhea or gastric upset soon after their arrival. There are occasions when the hospital cannot furnish food for the patients. . . . In addition to these deficiencies, he pointed out that all the medical efforts of FUNAI on behalf of the Indigenous population of the region were exclusively curative and not preventative. There is no systematic collection of information about the health of the Indian. The personnel at the FUNAI posts do not understand basic health concepts. In emergency cases they administer excessive amounts or unnecessary medicines which hinder normal treatment. Finally, FUNAI has only two medical doctors to take care of the needs of the Indians of Roraima—about 35 thousand.

Thus, ironically, an important source of infectious disease in the Yanomami area was the Casa do Índio, the government health center. Ramos (1979a:9) has described a FUNAI medical post for the Yawarib that verifies this picture.

The situation became so bad in the early 1990s that medical care for Indians was removed from FUNAI's administration and given to the National Health Foundation, which created the Yanomami Health Agency (DSY). The administrators of this program have organized all the FUNAI posts and mission and other private medical programs into a network and have attempted to expand medical services. They have conducted immunization programs for tuberculosis, diphtheria-whooping cough-tetanus, polio, measles, and hepatitis B. Their equipment has included an airplane to transport patients from FUNAI posts to the Casa do Índio for treatment. Ramos (1995:291) cites the example of a dedicated doctor from this organization during the malaria epidemic in the area of the Auaris River. But in spite of these efforts, the health needs of the Yanomami and the difficulties of access in the area require far more resources and personnel than the Health District can supply at its present level of government support (DSY 1999:5, 6, 14).

Another health facility in Boa Vista is the Casa de Hekura founded by the Consolata missionaries, a fifty-bed (-hammock) facility for long-term care of Indian patients. It has received assistance from the National Health Foundation and international sources.

The government-sponsored Yanoama Project in the mid-1970s among the Surucucu and Ajarani groups directed by the anthropologists Taylor and Ramos had some initial success. But it was undermined by elements in the government hostile to indigenous rights, in spite of the fact that it was a government program (Ramos 1979a:31–33). The Yanoama Project shows a basic dilemma still confronting the situation. Only the government has the required financial resources to undertake a program to deal effectively with the large number of Yanomami. Only the government has the legal authority and police powers to enforce restricted access to Indian areas and to require immunization and medical examinations of those entering. These restrictions provide the necessary conditions for the buildup of immunity, and for the gradual learning process. Yet at the same time, Brazilian history has shown that national governments have invariably ignored the human rights of indigenous groups and have failed to implement such programs—circumstances not unique to Brazil.

In spite of the weak government efforts on behalf of the Yanomami, what have been some significant factors for the ability of some Yanomami to survive these contact experiences? The Catrimani case shows that the biological impact of contact can be controlled by a competent medical program. The Mucajaí and Catrimani cases demonstrate the necessity of the continuation of a competent medical program during the postcontact period to control infectious disease and to provide public health instruction. In both cases missionaries were the key providers of outside assistance. In their roles of medical personnel, traders, and teachers, the missionaries became cultural brokers who have been effective because of their continuous on-the-scene presence, knowledge of the language, and the trust engendered by their dedication to their work. These were the key qualities for effective communication.

Although these qualities are not necessarily restricted to missionaries, in Roraima few besides the missionaries have displayed them. This statement may be interpreted as interest pleading in that we have used demographic data provided by the missionaries. But it is affirmed by the conclusions of the APS report in 1972 (Brooks et al. 1973:149):

We were struck by the role being played by religious missions. These deal with far more Indians than is realized outside Brazil. Moreover, the medical and educational assistance they provide is markedly superior to that coming from FUNAI. We are glad to see that many of the missions, both Catholic and Protestant, are re-thinking their attitude to tribal religions and are improving the anthropological side of their work. Nevertheless, it is imperative to stop the rivalries between Christian missions that are dividing so many tribes—Xavante, Kayapó, Tirio, Yanomami and many more; and in the long run we would like to see an improved and properly administered FUNAI shoulder full responsibility for all the Indians of Brazil.

In addition to the missions, another significant private undertaking on behalf of the Yanomami in Roraima has been the work of Claudia Andujar and her associates as the CCPY (Comissão Pró-Yanomami, formerly known as Comissão pela Criação do Parque Yanomami). It has been highly effective in bringing notice of the Yanomami situation to the attention of legislators, media, and the general public as well as helping to mobilize private medical assistance to Yanomami areas. In recent years the French organization Médecins du Monde (Doctors of the World) has been providing assistance.

In 1999 the National Health Agency, seeing the success of the NGOs' medical programs and the failure of its own agencies due to bureaucratic confusion, corruption, and funding delays, requested the CCPY to assume the administration and staffing of twelve health posts responsible for 6,000 Yanomami located in areas of difficult access (CCPY 1999). The CCPY has been assured of financial assistance from the government for this work and is adding 70 people to a separate division for health matters within its organization URIHI–SAUDE YANOMAMI. Since the NGOs do not have the financial resources to maintain an extensive program on their own, it remains to be seen if government assistance will be maintained. As the APS report pointed out, health care is ultimately a governmental responsibility.

### III. The Basic Necessity: Land

All the characteristics of the model of self-determination—protection from concentrated exposure to infectious disease, time to build up immunity, time to learn about national life so that there is some understanding of future options, the ability to carry on traditional subsistence so that decisions can be freely made without coercion by severe economic constraints—

all these depend on the ability of the Yanomami to retain their land. Saffirio and Hames (1983:5) have clearly stated this necessity: "As long as the Yanomama do not have full control over their aboriginal territory, from which their life derives, then they will not have the choice of staying as they are or becoming Brazilians."

Brazilian constitutions and Indian statutes have consistently stated the right of indigenous peoples to their lands. Until recently, however, there had never been a clear definition of what was considered Indian land. In the confusion, many indigenous groups lost their land. The Indian Statute of 1973 decreed that all Indian lands were to be demarcated by 1978, but by 1981 only 15 percent of identified Indian lands had been legally ratified. A clear statement was embedded in the 1988 Brazilian Constitution, chapter VIII, article 231, paragraph 2: "The lands traditionally occupied by the Indians are those inhabited by them permanently; those used for their productive services, those indispensable for the preservation of the environmental resources necessary for their well being; and those lands necessary for their physical and cultural reproduction, according to their uses and customs and traditions" (Santilli 1989:15).

## IV. The Political-Legal War over Land Boundaries

The phrasing of the 1988 Constitution represented a single battle in the long war between those wishing to expropriate Indian land and those defending indigenous rights. Ramos (1998) has described the history of this struggle. In chapter 21 we looked at a recent phase of this war, starting with the decision to occupy and develop the Amazon as the means to accomplish the industrialization of Brazil, to solve its internal problems of inequity, and to provide for its national security. Figure 24.2 sketches the progression of the political and legal war over Yanomami land in Roraima. The figure is divided into three columns. The first column, titled "Constitution," involves the foregoing statement from the 1988 Constitution regarding Indian land rights. The enclosed area under it represents all the land of western Roraima that the Yanomami have traditionally occupied and that is therefore included under the constitutional statement. The second column, "Forced Development," lists the various programs and legal instruments implementing the policy of forced development of the Amazon. In Roraima and Amazonas, one of the goals of these policies and legal documents was the expropriation of Yanomami land in spite of the constitution. The third column lists cases of Yanomami contact described in the previous chapter that have influenced the political and legal battle over land described in the first two

| Year | Constitution | | Forced Development | Contacts | Year |
|------|-------------|---|--------------------|----------|------|
| 1963 | Traditional Land | | - | Miners 1 | 1963 |
| 1960s | - | | Operação Amazônia | Miners 2 | 1960s |
| 1968 | Park Proposal | | - | - | 1968 |
| 1970 | - | | PIN | - | 1970 |
| 1974 | - | | Poloamazônia | Road 3,4 | 1973-75 |
| 1977 | - | | FUNAI Proposal | Miners 6 | 1975 |
| 1982 | Interdiction | | - | Miners 1 | 1982 |
| 1986 | - | | Calha Norte | - | 1986 |
| 1987 | - | | - | Miners, All | 1987 |
| 1988 | | | Decrees 160, 250 | - | 1988 |
| 1990 | 25% | 75% | Miner Reserve | - | 1990 |
| 1991 | | | Demarcation | Miners 6 | 1991 |
| 1996 | ? | | Decree 1775 | - | 1996 |

24.2. Expropriation of Yanomami land.

columns. (The numbers in the third column next to the source of contact refer to the code numbers for the Yanomami groups listed on map 2).

For years there was little dispute about what was Yanomami land in western Roraima. The northern and western boundaries were fixed by the dividing line between the watersheds of the Orinoco and Rio Branco, which had been accepted as the international boundary between Brazil and Venezuela. The southern and eastern boundaries were the forested areas historically used and occupied by Yanomami groups.

Realizing the dangers to the integrity of Yanomami land as a result the early contact experiences listed in the "Contacts" column in figure 24.2, in 1968 anthropologist Kenneth Taylor sketched the boundaries of Yanomami land based on the known Yanomami distribution at that time. He proposed that the government formally demarcate this area and designate it as a reserve (park) for the protection of the Yanomami. This was the first of fifteen such proposals (CCPY 1978). All but the two government proposals defined Yanomami territory as a continuous area that the Yanomami had traditionally occupied.

## A. Interdiction

World public opinion had been aroused by news of the epidemics among the Yanomami as a result of contact with construction workers on the government's Northern Perimeter Highway in 1973–75 and the miners in 1975 at Surucucu. Bowing to international pressure, including that of the

Organization of American States, in 1982 the minister of the interior interdicted Yanomami territory and ordered FUNAI to establish vigilance posts to enforce the designation. Interdiction recognizes an area as occupied by Indians, forbids entrance into the area by unauthorized outsiders, and makes known the intention to legalize (demarcate) the Indian claim.

Map 8 shows the boundaries of the interdicted area (the series of dashes). To carry out the interdiction seriously and avoid being subject to international scorn, the government had to face the reality of the situation and recognize what was de facto Yanomami territory. Therefore the boundary of interdiction outlined an area that was a good approximation of the area of traditional Yanomami land. In figure 24.2 this territory is symbolized by the boxed area in the first column. The area of the zone of interdiction was 9,419,108 hectares (5,956 sq. mi.). It represented the land on which the Yanomami had their gardens, hunted and collected, and over which they traveled to form marriage ties and to trade with other villages. It was the area used to relocate their villages when game became scarce or the land fatigued. The continuous area was needed for the cultural continuity included in the constitutional definition of indigenous land. These boundaries were in close agreement with the area proposed for demarcation of the Yanomami Park (reservation) in the various nongovernmental proposals. The boundaries were the basis for the temporary expulsion of the miners in 1986 from the Xiliana area and in 1989 from all the Yanomami area.

The expropriation of Yanomami land was sought by military and mining interests, including garimpeiros, businessmen in Boa Vista, and national corporations, some with ties to multinational corporations. The government projects and administrative decrees used to implement the whittling away of Yanomami land rights are listed in the second column of figure 24.2 under the heading "Forced Development," the root of the projects and policies of the military-mining interests. Some of these projects are discussed in chapter 21.

The area interdicted in 1982 was not the area the government had in mind for demarcation but a bow to international pressure at that time. The government's intention about demarcation (legal recognition of land claims) had been revealed in a 1977 FUNAI proposal for the Yanomami Park. It created a Yanomami reserve of twenty-two enclaves for specific Yanomami population blocs, but these were separated from each other by territory to which the Yanomami would not have exclusive rights. This was a rejection of all nongovernmental proposals that the reserve be a continuous area of land.

An interministerial work group (GTI) replaced FUNAI as the government's agent to deal with demarcation of indigenous lands. In 1988 they issued two decrees (160 and 250) dripping with terms such as *national parks, national forests,* and other phrases of environmental concern and protection. But inserted within this rhetoric were administrative provisions that had the effect of opening up these areas to mining interests as determined by government agencies independent of the Brazilian Congress. This was contrary to the Brazilian Constitution.

The final version of the decrees (250) declared parts of the Yanomami area to be national forests or national parks. As can be seen on map 9, the outer boundaries of the national forests in Roraima encompass a substantially smaller area than the boundaries of demarcation in 1982. This was a loss of 13 percent of traditional Yanomami land to Brazilian settlers or the government.

Within the national forests and parks, the decree created nineteen separated indigenous enclaves for the exclusive use of the indigenous population. In Roraima as shown on map 9, there were ten indigenous enclaves. Land within the national forest but not contained within the indigenous reserves (in map 9 the hatched area between the indigenous enclaves) fell under the jurisdiction of a government agency, which could allow the land to be used for non-Indian economic activities. In other words, the land could be expropriated for the use of mining and timber interests. This method of expropriation involved 62 percent of traditional Yanomami land as defined by the area of interdiction in 1982. Albert (1992:43) notes that by 1987, 37 percent of the Yanomami territory had been open to intrusion: 27 permits and 363 applications for authorization to prospect for minerals had been registered by Brazilian and multinational companies.

In Roraima, the only land left for the exclusive use of indigenous groups was the ten indigenous enclaves. This was about 25 percent of the traditional land marked at the time of interdiction. (In Amazonas, the situation was more complicated because of establishment of a national park as well as a national forest, although the result was much the same.) In spite of the rhetoric, decree 250 was a decree of expropriation of 75 percent of traditional Yanomami land. Albert (1992:40–45) has dissected the environmental rhetoric by which the expropriation was accomplished.

## V. Mobilizing for Defense of Yanomami Land

The decrees were declarations of intent and a preliminary step to demarcation. This set the stage for the war: the Yanomami constitutional rights to their traditional land on the one hand versus the continual effort to whittle down the area and to undermine the constitutional basis of the rights. The Yanomami knew little about the designs on their land except that they had seen the road workers, the miners, and the epidemics. The political and legal battles were taking place in other parts of the world system. A coalition came to the defense of Yanomami rights, including Brazilians defending the democratic process resurrected in 1985, Brazilian national and international nongovernmental organizations (NGOs) concerned with environment and/or indigenous rights, and the international media, with its concern for the fate of the Amazon Basin. The fight radiated around the world system.

Opposition to the military worldview regarding the Amazon centered on these points:

1. Undermining of the constitution, especially that of 1988, where Indian land rights were clearly delineated.
2. Undermining of the democratic process whereby instead of the constitutional authority of the president, Congress, and the Indians themselves, an autocracy of unaccountable government agencies would make decisions about the exploitation of mineral resources on Indian lands.
3. The end of Indian communities as distinct ethnic groups.
4. Lack of social or environmental controls.
5. Problems created with neighboring countries.

The military reacted negatively to these criticisms, regarding efforts to preserve the Amazon forest and to protect Indian land rights as subversive activities by foreign interests. They saw the criticisms as preludes to encouraging the formation of independent Indian nations in the border areas.

## A. Demarcation

On November 15, 1991, the official demarcation reflecting decree 250 was signed, partially due to the pressure exerted by the United Nations and the organizers of the Rio-92 Earth Summit. But it was a hollow victory. The national forests, land lost to the Yanomami, could be opened to mining interests. As Albert (1992:42) states, "The strategy was to force the Yanomami into a sedentary life and by so doing, provoke such a change in their economic activities as to preclude their traditional spatial mobility over a large territory for hunting-gathering and shifting cultivation." The ultimate goal was the forced integration of the Yanomami into the national culture as part of the agricultural proletariat. Given the condition of this underclass within the Brazilian nation, this was not a future to which either Brazilians or Indians would aspire.

The demarcation provided the legal basis for the future use of Yanomami land, but there was no immediate occupation of the land. The Mucajaí people know little about demarcation and the involvement of the world in these matters taking place in Boa Vista and Brasília. The western boundary of the Mucajaí reserve would be an immense surprise to the Mucajaí people. Villages C and E consider the land between themselves and the Malaxi theli as their hunting areas shared with the Malaxi theli, among whom they have affinal relatives.

## B. Decree 1775

But the decree of demarcation leaving the Yanomami with 25 percent of their land was not the final battle. The war continued as the partisans of forced development chipped away at indigenous land interests. On January 8, 1996, President Fernando Henrique Cardoso issued decree 1775, which gave squatters, miners, ranchers, and state and local governments the right to challenge the boundaries of any indigenous land demarcated since February 4, 1991. Yanomami demarcation had taken place on November 15, 1991. Turner (1996) has described the legal arguments and the political reality behind this decree.

Brazilian groups defending the rights of indigenous people (Turner 1996:12, note 1) have sprung into action petitioning various international bodies to withhold loans and grants to Brazil until the decree is withdrawn. These include the ambassadors of the G-7 countries, the World Bank, the German government, and the European Parliament. Other national and international organizations of the world system (Turner 1996:14–15) have become part of the opposition as the war over Yanomami land in the Amazon continues in this new phase. The 25 percent of the traditional Yanomami holding could be reduced even further.

## VI. An Ancient Process—The Confirmation of a Thesis

The health and land problems facing the Yanomami at the beginning of the twenty-first century are not new. Indigenous groups in the Americas have faced them since the first European contacts at the end of the fifteenth century. It appears that the historical process is as old as civilization itself. The eminent world historian William H. McNeill has read, researched, and written about the history of many civilizations, including some of the first ones known. In his work, he kept noticing a demographic pattern in the history. Although there were insufficient data, he thought there were enough clues in the historical record to propose it as a hypothesis that merited further research. He set forth the thesis in a book entitled *Plagues and People* (McNeill 1976:69–71):

> When civilized societies learned to live with the "childhood diseases" that can only persist among large human populations, they acquired a very potent biological weapon. It came into play whenever new contacts with previously isolated, smaller human groups occurred. Civilized diseases when let loose among a population that lacked any prior exposure to the germ in question quickly assumed drastic proportions, killing off old and young alike instead of remaining a perhaps serious, but still tolerable, disease affecting small children.
>
> The disruptive effect of such an epidemic is likely to be greater than the mere loss of life, severe as that may be. Often survivors are demoralized, and lose all faith in inherited custom and belief which had not prepared them for such a disaster.
>
> . . . Warfare characteristically mingled with and masked this epidemiological process. Trade, which was imperfectly distinct from warlike raiding, was another normal way for civilized folk to probe new lands. And since war and trade relations have often entered civilized records, whereas epidemics among illiterate and helpless border folk have not, historians have hitherto failed to take anything like adequate notice of the biological weapon urban conditions of life implanted in the bloodstreams of civilized peoples.
>
> In fact, it is fundamentally because of this phenomenon that civilized societies throughout history have so persistently tended to expand their geographical size.

The Yanomami of Roraima at the end of the twentieth century provide a case that confirms the thesis. Ramos (1995:308) states it succinctly: "Malaria it would seem has the potential to produce the much heralded demographic voids of Amazônia, an important ideological piece in the politics of conquest. Apiaú and Ajarani are examples of how epidemics . . . can wipe out indigenous populations and leave the terrain free for colonization."

An understanding of this may be of little consolation to the Yanomami, but at least ignorance can no longer be used as a justification for social injustice raising the specter of genocide by "civilized" nations and the international system of the contemporary world.

## VII. Biological Warfare?

Monbiot (1991:100) and Ramos (1993:2–3; 1998:237) report that the pattern described by McNeill may not be an unconscious result of biological ignorance but rather a deliberate strategy being used to acquire Yanomami land. The question is whether the large national and multinational corporations have assisted or will assist in a conscious effort to gain access to Yanomami land by removing the people from it. Removal could be by death or dispersion. Corporations realize that if they tried to do this directly, national and international protest would force the government to halt their efforts. But if they encouraged and financed garimpeiros and small local companies in their invasion of Yanomami land, they would be placing the biological weapons carried within the bodies of the garimpeiros into the Yanomami area. In the circumstances of contact, the biological weapons would automatically fulfill their function by transmitting measles, malaria, pneumonia, and other infectious diseases. Many Yanomami would die and the remnant would disperse. In Roraima this would result in the much talked about demographic emptiness of the Amazon. At this point, large corporations could apply to the government to use the land for mining. By now, the land would be depopulated and environmentally degraded due to the rivers dead from mercury poisoning. The land would have lost its value for any other use than mining. Monbiot notes that twenty-one big mining companies had applied for exploration rights in the Yanomami area. While to date there is no proof of a deliberate attempt to implement such a scenario, the lessons of history show it is a possibility to be guarded against.

Even if the complete chain of causality described in the this scenario is not deliberately intended by any individual or corporate groups, the scenario describes an unplanned outcome that may take place if the full dimensions of the problems of the Yanomami in Roraima and elsewhere are not confronted. Perhaps this research may help focus attention on the larger picture and the need for social justice based on human rights.

## VIII. Land: The Crucial Issue

The Yanomami are going through a period of cultural change. They are desirous of the technology and consumer goods of international society. The non-Yanomami world wants Yanomami land. The interaction between the two worlds has resulted in a serious health problem that has threatened Yanomami villages. The demographic history of the eight Xilixana villages provides some insight into Yanomami population structure and the qualities needed for assistance to the Yanomami in meeting their health and other transition needs. If their health needs are met, the further question becomes health for what kind of life? Present Brazilian policy is to expropriate Yanomami land and to force the Yanomami to integrate as rural laborers. Such a prospect may not answer any need, judging from the situation of the Brazilian underclass, especially in northeastern Brazil (see Scheper-Hughes 1992). The Kayapó Indians in southern Pará (summaries in Schmink and Wood 1992:253–75; Rabben 1995) have already faced a number of these issues and their reactions and problems may foreshadow the future of the Yanomami.

## IX. Appendix—Corporate Interest in Yanomami Land

Here are some of the mining companies that have shown interest in the Yanomami Reserve. These are Brazilian or multinational corporations, all with close ties to the world system.

The first list (Taylor 1979:56, 62, 66) were companies that sought information or prospecting rights around 1975 when there was some mining of cassiterite at Surucucu: Companhia Estanífera do Brazil, which is partly owned by Compagnie Française d'Entreprises Minières Métallurgiques et d'Investissements, an affiliate of the Patiño Tin Syndicate; Companhia Industrial Amazonense; Companhia Indústria e Comércio de Minérios, a joint company formed by Bethlehem Steel and Companhia Auxiliar de Empresas de Mineração, a large Brazilian holding company; and Companhia Vale do Rio Doce, which had previously undertaken joint ventures with U.S. Steel and Alcan Aluminum.

There is no published account of the financial structure behind the 1987 gold rush. Many participants were small investors in the garimpos. Some financing came from politicians and businessmen in Boa Vista (see MacMillan 1995:138–40). The following companies (CCPY 1989e:48) were in possession of prospecting rights for the region, although this does not necessarily mean they were actively involved in the 1987–89 invasions: Best, Pompeia, Crasa, Aracati, Cia Mineração e Participações, Meqimbras, Vila do Principe, J. R. Scalabrin, Peguina, Vale do São Joao, Montes de Roraima, Tratex, Codesaima, Brumadinho, Mineral, Parima, Curd, Mearim, Itacua, Paranapanema, Rio Vivenda, Brascan, CPRM, Mutum, and Bozzano Simonsen.

The government had hoped that private companies would undertake and finance geological research following government efforts in the various development programs for the Amazon. MacMillan (1955:26–27) points out that this has not happened in Indian areas:

By law, claims for mining concessions on indigenous reserves may be registered by the DNPM (Departmento Nacional de Pesquisa Mineral), but companies can only work in these areas with the permission of FUNAI and the consent of the relevant Indian group. Notwithstanding the legal complexities of mining on Indian lands, geological surveying in the remote parts of Amazônia is sufficiently expensive, and risky, to dissuade investment. Thus companies that hold registered claims, both in and beyond Indian reserves, often do not research their geological potential. Frequently the mineral rights for these speculative claims are upheld only after garimpeiros have discovered economically significant deposits on them.

This shows that there is an important link between the garimpeiros and the mining companies but without any expense for the companies—allowing them, in a legalistic sense, to disclaim any responsibility for uncontrolled garimpagem. Social justice and human rights are frequently the victims of the legal and psychological disconnection of connected realities.

# 25

# The Future as Seen from the Past and Present

In attempting to understand the Xilixana and other Yanomami in Roraima, we have followed Eric Wolf's (1982:385) lead in his study of the spread of industrial capitalism:

> This book has asked what difference it would make to our understanding if we looked at the world as a whole, a totality, a system instead of as a sum of self-contained societies and cultures; if we understood better how this totality developed over time; if we took seriously the admonition to think of human aggregates as "inextricably involved with other aggregates, near and far, in web-like, netlike connections." . . . As we unraveled the chains of causes and effects at work in the lives of particular populations, we saw them extend beyond any one population to embrace the trajectories of others—all others.

We have attempted to provide a window on a group of tribal peoples both before and after their encounter with the international world. The sections concerning this encounter are a case history of the continual need for social justice founded on human rights. Such concerns are the basis of world peace in the single global society. Frequently the escape from the imperatives of social justice lies in seeing social structures in solitary fragmentation. Such narrow vision absolves participants in the world system from responsibility for the social implications of their own actions and those of their communities.

The future of the Yanomami in Roraima depends on which of the two models will prevail—the conflict model or the model of self-determination, which is based on social justice and human rights. For the model of self-determination to be successful, the problems of Yanomami health programs and land rights must be addressed. The health problem must be confronted by the implementation of effective programs. This requires adequate financing and sufficient personnel with the required qualities.

The land problem must be confronted either by undoing the current legal basis for future external occupation or by simply preventing such occupation. Where does the danger of future occupation of land come from? As land becomes a scarcer resource, agriculture, ranching, and possibly logging always pose a threat. But an even greater threat may be mining by large national and multinational corporations in this area known to be rich in minerals. Garimpeiro miners have traditionally been mobile and may withdraw from the forests of western Roraima as the yield of gold diminishes, given the low level of their technology. But this raises the specter of the national and international mining companies moving into the Yanomami area with their permanent mining sites, large-scale technology, and wage-earning labor force. This will lead to more disease, forced eviction of the Yanomami from their land, and forced integration into the underclass. The surviving remnant will become part of the Brazilian peasantry, trying to eke out a minimal subsistence on land no longer their own. This is the land that once provided a satisfactory subsistence and the basis for the Yanomami determining their own cultural future.

Due to the desire of many factions of the world system for mineral wealth from Yanomami land, and the consistent trend of the long-range policy of the Brazilian government to expropriate this land, it appears doubtful that the Yanomami will be able to retain enough land for their independent subsistence. Funding for an effective health program also appears unlikely. As these lines are being written, Brazil is in economic crisis. A casualty of this crisis has been a key project for the protection of the Amazon. On the first day of 1999, the *New York Times* (Schemo 1999:A9) reported:

> Under intense pressure to reduce its spending, the Brazilian Government has slashed funds intended for a $250 million pilot project backed by seven leading industrial nations that has been the centerpiece of Brazil's efforts to save the Amazon rain forest. . . . Brazil was to provide just 10% of the $250 million. . . . The pilot program, which pays for surveying the vast rain forest, has been the principal vehicle for marking off 40,000 square miles for Indian reservations. Surveying is seen as the first step toward protecting the Amazon from destruction by ranchers, loggers, farmers and miners.

We believe the future outlook for most Yanomami is bleak because the forces of conflict appear to be stronger than those of human rights and social justice. The twenty-five thousand Yanomami will find it difficult to assert their human rights in a world of six billion people. Historically the forces of economic gain, laissez-faire capitalism, and racism and elitism have not had room for the basic human rights of the disenfranchised and those who live in "simpler" cultures. In this book we have examined these forces and furnished the background to understand the 1997 words of a Yanomami spokesman, Davi Kopenawa Yanomami (1999).

## TO ALL WHO WISH TO HEAR ME

The biggest problem for the Yanomami now is the *garimpeiro* (gold miners) who are in our land, and the illnesses they bring with them.

The government's National Health Foundation say that 1300 Yanomami had got malaria up until May this year [1997]. They have counted 24 airstrips opened by *garimpeiros* in the forest and they said that over 2500 men have illegally entered our reserve to pan for gold. This information was published in the newspaper Folha de Boa Vista in May, you can see for yourselves. Among them [the miners] some have illnesses like flu, TB and venereal diseases, and contaminate my people. Now we are afraid they will bring measles and also AIDS, this illness which is so dangerous that we do not want it among us. But the worst illness for us is malaria, which comes in with the gold miners. It is the Indians who keep the forest alive, because the Indians do not destroy nature looking for gold. The Indians do not spoil nature because they know it is important for the salvation of planet Earth. This is why we want the help of all those who understand that we only want to live in peace. If they do not help us, the *garimpeiros* will spoil all the rivers and leave us without fish or drinking water or game, destroying the health of the Indians, the whites and the planet.

When I go to the big city I see people who are hungry, without anywhere to plant, without drinking water, without anywhere to live. I do not want this to happen to my people too, I do not want the forest to be destroyed, which leads to misery. I am not saying that I am against progress. I think it is very good when whites come to work amongst the Yanomami to teach reading and writing, how to breed bees, how to use medicinal plants, the right ways of protecting nature. These white people are very welcome in our land. This for us is progress.

What we do not want are the mining companies, which destroy the forest, and the *garimpeiros,* who bring so many diseases. These whites must respect our Yanomami land. The *garimpeiros* bring guns, alcohol, prostitution and destroy nature wherever they go. The machines spill oil into the rivers and kill the life existing in them and the people and animals who depend on them. For us, this is not progress. We want progress without destruction. We want to study, to learn new ways of cultivating the land, living from its fruits. The Yanomami do not want to live from dealing with money, with gold, we are not prepared for this. We need time to learn.

This is what I wanted to say to the whites who will listen to me, so that they can understand what the Yanomami want. We do not want to live without trees, hunting, fish and clean water. If this happens misery will come to our people. That is why I am here, defending my land and my people. I hope you will help me in this fight.

# APPENDIX

## Correction of Table 9.3 in Early and Peters 1990:109

In the previous volume of this research (Early and Peters 1990), there were several calculating and typographical errors. The more serious appeared in table 9.3, page 109 of that volume due to a computer error in generating the table. Below is a corrected version of the table. It does not change the analytical significance of the table. There were a number of other typographical errors in that volume. Most of them are in the textual numbers; the table numbers are usually correct.

**Years Difference in Age between Males and Females in Various Types of Marital Unions**

| # Years | 1950 | 1960 | 1970 | 1980 | Total |
|---------|------|------|------|------|-------|
| M>F 40+ | 1 | - | 3 | 6 | 10 |
| 30 | - | 3 | 5 | 13 | 21 |
| 20 | 3 | 12 | 17 | 18 | 50 |
| 10 | 6 | 8 | 19 | 18 | 51 |
| 0 | 12 | 12 | 6 | 11 | 41 |
| F>M 0 | - | 2 | 6 | 2 | 14 |
| 10 | - | 2 | 6 | 2 | 10 |
| 20+ | - | - | - | - | - |
| Total | 22 | 39 | 62 | 74 | 197 |
| | | Percentages | | | |
| M>F 40+ | 4.5 | - | 4.8 | 8.1 | 5.1 |
| 30 | - | 7.7 | 8.1 | 17.6 | 10.7 |
| 20 | 13.6 | 30.8 | 27.4 | 24.3 | 25.4 |
| 10 | 27.3 | 20.5 | 30.6 | 24.3 | 25.9 |
| 0 | 54.5 | 30.8 | 9.7 | 14.9 | 20.8 |
| F>M 0 | - | 5.1 | 9.7 | 8.1 | 7.1 |
| 10 | - | 5.1 | 9.7 | 2.7 | 5.1 |
| 20+ | - | - | - | - | - |
| Total | 100 | 100 | 100 | 100 | 100 |
| M>F 20+ | 54.5 | 41.0 | 29.1 | 25.7 | 33.0 |

# REFERENCES CITED

Ação Pela Cidadania
1989    *Roraima: O aviso da morte.* São Paulo: CCPY/CEDI/CIMI/NDI.
1990    *Yanomami: A todos os povos da terra.* São Paulo: CCPY/CEDI/CIMI/NDI.
Albert, Bruce
1985    *Temps de sang, temps des cendres: Représentation de la Maladie, système ritual et espace politique chez les Yanomami du sud-est (Amazonia brésilienne).* Ph.D. dissertation. Paris: University of Paris X.
1988    La fumée de métal: Histoire et représentations du contact chez les Yano-amai (Brésil). *L'Homme* 28 (2–3):87–119.
1992    Indians Lands, Environmental Policy, and Military Geopolitics in the Development of the Brazilian Amazon: The Case of the Yanomami. *Development and Change* 23:34–70.
1994    Gold Miners and Yanomami Indians in the Brazilian Amazon: The Hashimu Massacre. In *Who Pays the Price? The Sociocultural Context of Environmental Crisis,* ed. Barbara Rose Johnston, 47–55. Washington, D.C.: Island Press.
Albert, Bruce, and Gale Goodwin Gomez
1997    *Saúde Yanomami: Um manual ethnolinguístico.* Belém: Museu Paraense Emílio Goeldi.
Allen, Elizabeth
1992    Calha Norte: Military Development in Brazilian Amazonia. *Development and Change* 23:71–99.
Baer, Werner
1995    *The Brazilian Economy: Growth and Development.* Westport, Conn.: Praeger Publishers.
Bodley, John H.
1999    *Victims of Progress,* 4th ed. Mountain View, Calif.: Mayfield Publishing Co.
Bortoli, Jose
1997    The Missionary Effort to Help the Yanomami Speak for Themselves. In *The Yanoamami and Their Interpreters: Fierce People or Fierce Interpreters?* ed. Frank Salamone, 67–74. Lanham, Md.: University Press of America.
Brooks, Edwin, Rene Fuerst, John Hemming, and Francis Huxley
1973    *Tribes of the Amazon Basin 1972.* London: Charles Knight and Co.

Bugos, Paul E., Jr., and Lorraine M. McCarthy

1984    Ayoreo Infanticide: A Case Study. In *Infanticide: Comparative and Evolutionary Perspectives*, ed. Glenn Hausfater and Sarah Blaffer Hrdy, 503–20. New York: Aldine Publishing Co.

Castro, M. B., B. Albert, and W. C. Pfeiffer

1991    Mercury Levels in Yanomami Indians' Hair from Roraima, Brazil. *Proceedings of the 8th International Conference on Heavy Metals in the Environment*, ed. J. G. Farmer, 367–70. Edinburgh: CEP Consultants.

CCPY (Committee for the Creation of the Yanomami Park)

1978    Yanomami Indian Park: Proposal and Justification. In *Yanoama in Brazil 1979*, ed. A. Ramos and K. Taylor, 99–163. Document 37. Copenhagen: International Work Group for Indigenous Affairs (IWGIA).

1988    The Gold Fever in Roraima: Synopsis of News Items Carried in the Press, Sept. '87–Feb. '88. *Urihi* no. 6 (Aug.): 8–34.

1989a   Serra de Surucus: River Parima Basin. *Urihi* no. 11 (Dec.): 7–16.

1989b   The Taking of Sururucus. *Urihi* no. 11 (Dec.): 17–23.

1989c   The Santa Rosa "Hole" Rio Ericó Region. *Urihi* no. 11 (Dec.): 24–36.

1989d   Garimpo at Apiaú. *Urihi* no.11 (Dec.): 37–45.

1989e   Serra Couto de Magalhães, Paapiú. *Urihi* no. 11 (Dec.): 45–59

1989f   Death and Gold in the New Eldorado. *Urihi* no.11 (Dec.): 60–72.

1999    CCPY Update 102. Electronic Mail.

Chagnon, Napoleon A.

1968    *Yanomamo: The Fierce People*. 1st ed. New York: Holt, Rinehart and Winston.

1972    Tribal Social Organization and Genetic Microdifferentiation. In *The Structure of Human Populations*, ed. G. A. Harrison and A. J. Boyce, 252–82. Oxford: Clarendon Press.

1977    *Yanomamo: The Fierce People*. 2nd ed. New York: Holt, Rinehart and Winston.

1983    *Yanamamo: The Fierce People*. 3rd ed. New York: Holt, Rinehart and Winston.

1992    *Yanamamo*. 4th ed. Fort Worth: Harcourt Brace Jovanovich College Publishers.

1997    *Yanomamo*. 5th ed. Fort Worth: Harcourt Brace Jovanovich College Publishers.

Chagnon, Napoleon A., Mark V. Flynn, and Thomas F. Melancon

1979    Sex-Ratio Variation Among the Yanomami Indians. In *Evolutionary Biology and Human Social Behavior: An Anthropological Perspective,* ed. Napoleon A. Chagnon and William Irons, North Scituate, Mass.: Duxbury Press.

Chagnon, Napoleon A., James Neel, Lowel Weitkamp, Henry Gershowitz, and Manual Ayres

1970    The Influence of Cultural Factors on the Demography and Pattern of Gene

Flow from the Makiritare to the Yanomama Indians. *American Journal of Physical Anthropology* 32:339–49.

Chahnazarian, Anouch
1988   Determinants of the Sex Ratio at Birth: Review of the Recent Literature. *Social Biology* 35:214–35.

CIMI (Indigenous Missionary Council)
1993   *Chronology of the Yanomami Genocide.* Brasilia: CIMI.

Cleary, David
1990   *Anatomy of the Amazon Gold Rush.* Iowa City: University of Iowa Press.

Cocco, P. Luis
1987 (1973)   *Iyëwei-teri: Quince años entre los yanomamos.* Caracas: Liberia Editorial Salesiana.

Colchester, Marcus
1985   The Venezuelan Ninam (North Eastern Yanoama). In *Health and Survival of the Venezuelan Yanoama,* ed. M. Colchester, 59–72. Document 53. Copenhagan: International Work Group for Indigenous Affairs (IWGIA).

Commission on Development and Environment for Amazônia
1992   *Amazonia without Myths.* Washington, D.C.: Inter-American Development Bank, United Nations Development Programme, Amazon Cooperation Treaty.

Conniff, Michael L., and Frank D. McCann
1989   *Modern Brazil: Elites and Masses in Historical Perspective.* Lincoln: University of Nebraska Press.

Cultural Survival
1979   *Special Report: Brazil.* Cambridge: Cultural Survival.

Davis, Shelton
1977   *Victims of the Miracle: Development and the Indians of Brazil.* Cambridge: Cambridge University Press.
1988   *Land Rights and Indigenous People: The Role of the Inter-American Commission on Human Rights.* Report 29. Cambridge: Cultural Survival.

Davis, Shelton H., and Robert O. Mathews
1976   *The Geological Imperative.* Cambridge: Anthropology Resource Center.

Dias de Aguiar, Brás
1944   Geografia Amazônica: Nas Fronteiras do Norte. *Revista Brasileira de Geografia* 6:19–40.

Dickemann, Mildred
1984   Concepts and Clarification in the Study of Human Infanticide: Sectional Introduction and Some Cautionary Notes. In *Infanticide: Comparative and Evolutionary Perspectives,* ed. Glenn Hausfater and Sarah Blaffer Hrdy, 427–37. New York: Aldine Publishing Co.

Divale, William, and Marvin Harris
1976   Population, Warfare and the Male Supremacist Complex. *American Anthropologist* 78:521–38.

1978a    Reply to Lancaster and Lancaster. *American Anthropologist* 80:117–18.
1978b    The Male Supremacist Complex: Discovery of a Cultural Invention. *American Anthropologist* 80:668–71.
Divale, William, Marvin Harris, and Donald T. Williams
1978    On the Misuse of Statistics: A Reply to Hirschfeld et al. *American Anthropologist* 80:379–86.
DSY (Distrito Sanitario Yanoamami, Yanomami Health Agency)
1999    *Roraima, E Os Distritos Sanitarios Indigenas.* http://www.fns.gov.br/acoes/saude/rrlink.htm
Early, John D.
1970a    A Demographic Profile of a Maya Community: The Atitecos of Santiago Atitlan. *Milbank Memorial Fund Quarterly* 48:167–78.
1970b    The Structure and Change of Mortality in a Maya Community. *Milbank Memorial Fund Quarterly* 48:179–201.
1973    Education via Radio among Guatemalan Highland Maya. *Human Organization* 32:221–29.
1982    *The Demographic Structure and Evolution of a Peasant System: The Guatemalan Population.* Gainesville: University Press of Florida.
2000    *La Estructura y Evolución Demográfica de un Sisrema Campesino: La Población de Guatemala con un Prólogo por Ricardo Falla.* South Woodstock, Vt.: Plumsock Mesoamerican Studies/CIRMA, Serie Monográfica No. 11.
Early, John D., and Thomas N. Headland
1998    *Population Dynamics of a Philippine Rain Forest People.* Gainesville: University Press of Florida.
Early, John D., and John F. Peters
1990    *The Population Dynamics of the Mucajai Yanomama.* San Diego: Academic Press.
Eguillor, Maria Isabel
1984    *Yopo, shamanes y hekura: Aspectos fenomenologicos del mundo sagrado Yanomami.* Caracas: Liberia Editorial Salesiana.
Ferguson, R. Brian
1995    *Yanomami Warfare: A Political History.* Santa Fe, N.M.: School of American Research Press.
Ferreira Reis, Arthur Cezar
1943    En las Selvas del Demini. *Revista Geográfica Americana* 20:271–76.
1944    Cabceiras do Orinoco e a Fronteira Brasileira-Venezuelana. *Revista Brasileira de Geografia* 4:93–105.
Flavio Pinto, Lucio
1989    Calha Norte: The Special Project for the Occupation of the Frontiers. *Cultural Survival Quarterly* 13:40–41.
Gomez, Gale Goodwin
1990    *The Shiriana Dialect of Yanam (Northern Brazil).* Ann Arbor, Mich.: University Microfilms International #9127863.

1999    *Genocide by Neglect: The Impact of Gold Mining and Government Response on Yanomami Health and Survival.* In *El Dorado Revisited. Gold, Oil, Environment, People and Rights in the Amazon,* ed. Leslie Sponsel. In press.

Good, Kenneth Robert

1989    *Yanomami Hunting Patterns: Trekking and Garden Relocation as an Adaptation to Game Availability in Amazônia, Venezuela.* Ann Arbor, Mich.: UMI Dissertation Services #9021853.

Goodman, David, and Anthony Hall, eds.

1990    *The Future of Amazonia: Destruction or Sustainable Development?* New York: St. Martin's Press.

Hames, Raymond B.

1983    The Settlement Pattern of a Yanomamö Population Bloc: A Behavorial Ecological Explanation. In *Adaptive Responses of Native Amazonians,* ed. Raymond B. Hames and William T. Vickers, 393–427. New York: Academic Press.

Harris, Marvin

1984    A Cultural Materialist Theory of Band and Village Warfare: The Yanomamo Test. In *Warfare, Culture and Environment,* ed. R. Brian Ferguson, 111–40. Orlando: Academic Press.

Haub, Carl, and Diana Cornelius

1997    *1997 World Population Data Sheet.* Washington: Population Reference Bureau.

Hauser, Philip M., and Otis D. Duncan

1959    Overview and Conclusions. In *The Study of Population: An Inventory and Appraisal,* ed. P. Hauser and O. Duncan, 29–44. Chicago: University of Chicago Press.

Haviland, William A.

1997    *Anthropology.* 8th ed. Fort Worth: Harcourt Brace College Publishers.

Heinen, H. Dieter, and B. Illius

1996    The Last Days of Eden: A Review Essay on Yanomami Warfare. *Anthropos* 91:552–60.

Hemming, John

1978    *Red Gold: The Conquest of the Brazilian Indians.* London: Macmillan.

1987    *Amazon Frontier: The Defeat of the Brazilian Indians.* Cambridge, Mass.: Harvard University Press.

Hirschfeld, Lawrence A., James Howe, and Bruce Levin

1978    Warfare, Infanticide and Statistical Inference: A Comment on Divale and Harris. *American Anthropologist* 80:110–15.

Holdridge, Desmond

1933    Exploration between the Rio Branco and the Sierra Parima. *Geographical Review* 23:372–84.

Howe, James
1978    Ninety-Two Mythical Populations: A Reply to Divale et al. *American Anthropologist* 80:671–73.
James, Preston E., and C. W. Minkel
1986    *Latin America.* 5th ed. New York: John Wiley and Sons.
James, William H.
1987a   The Human Sex Ratio. Part 1: A Review of the Literature. *Human Biology* 59:721–52.
1987b   The Human Sex Ratio. Part 2: A Hypothesis and a Program of Research. *Human Biology* 59:873–900.
Keesing, Roger M.
1981    *Cultural Anthropology.* New York: Holt, Rinehart and Winston.
Knauft, B. M.
1987    Reconsidering Violence in Simple Societies. *Current Anthropology* 28:457–500.
Koch-Grunberg, Theodor
1979    *Del Roraima al Orinoco.* 3 vols. Ed. E. Armitano. Caracas: El Banco Central de Venezuela.
Kopenawa Yanomami, Davi
1999    Statement by Davi Kopenawa Yanomami, São Paulo, August 25, 1997. http://kafka.uvic.ca/~vipirg/SISIS/sov/aug25yan.html
Kottak, Conrad Philip
1991    *Anthropology: The Exploration of Human Diversity.* New York: McGraw-Hill.
Lancaster, Chet, and Jane B. Lancaster
1978    On the Male Supremacist Complex: A Reply to Divale and Harris. *American Anthropologist* 80:115–17.
Lizot, Jacques
1976    *The Yanomami in the Face of Ethnocide.* Document 22. Copenhagen: International Work Group for Indigenous Affairs (IWGIA).
1977    Population, Resources and Warfare Among the Yanomami. *Man* 12:497–517.
1988    Los Yanomami. In *Los Aborigenes de Venezuela* (ed. Walter Coppens), vol. 3, *Etnologia Contemporanea,* ed. Jacques Lizot, 2:479–584. Caracas: Fundación La Salle de Ciencias Naturales.
1994    Words in the Night: The Ceremonial Dialogue—One Expression of Peaceful Relationships among the Yanomami. In *The Anthropology of Peace and Nonviolence,* ed. L. Sponsel and Thomas Gregor, 213–39. Boulder: Lynne Rienner Publishers.
MacMillan, Gordon
1995    *At the End of the Rainbow? Gold, Land and People in the Brazilian Amazon.* New York: Columbia University Press.
Marcano, Teodoro
1997    Yanomami Health Problems. In *The Yanomami and Their Interpreters:*

*Fierce People or Fierce Interpreters?* ed. Frank Salamone, 53–55. Lanham, Md.: University Press of America.

Mbefo, Luke
1987    Theology and Inculturation: The Nigerian Experience. *Cross Currents* 37:393–403.

McNeill, William H.
1976    *Plagues and Peoples.* New York: Anchor Press–Doubleday.

Meggers, Betty
1975    Application of Biological Model of Diversification to Cultural Distribution in Tropical Lowland South America. *Biotropica* 7(3):141–61.
1976    Vegetational Flucuation and Prehistoric Cultural Adaptation in Amazonia: Some Tentative Correlations. Unpublished manuscript, Smithsonian Institution.

Melancon, Thomas
1982    *Marriage and Reproduction Among the Yanomami Indians of Venezuela.* Ann Arbor, Mich.: UMI Dissertation Services #8213331.

Merrick, Thomas W., and Douglas H. Graham
1979    *Population and Economic Development in Brazil.* Baltimore: Johns Hopkins University Press.

Migliazza, Ernest
1972    *Yanomama Grammar and Intelligibility.* Ann Arbor, Mich.: University Microfilms International Dissertation Services 72–30432.
1978    *The Integration of the Indigenous People of the Territory of Roraima.* Document 31. Copenhagen: International Working Group for Indigeneous Affairs (IWGIA).
1980    Languages of the Orinoco-Amazon: Current Status. *Antropológica* 53:95–102.
1982    Linguistic Prehistory and the Refuge Model in Amazônia. In *Biological Diversification in the Tropics,* ed. G. Prance, 479–519. New York: Columbia University Press.
1998    Brief History of the Uraricaá River Ninam. Unpublished manuscript.

Migliazza, Ernest, and Lyle Campbell
1988    *Panorama General de las Lenguas Indigenas en America.* Vol. 10, *Historia General de América, Periodo Indígena,* ed. Guillermo Moron. Caracas: Academia Nacional de la Historia de Venezuela.

Missão Catrimani
1995    *Relatório Anual 1995.* Boa Vista: Missão Catrimani.

Monbiot, George
1991    *Amazon Watershed.* London: Michael Joseph.

Neel, James, and Kenneth Weiss
1975    The Genetic Structure of a Tribal Population, the Yanomami Indians. *American Journal of Physical Anthropology* 42:25–52.

Norton, Helen H.
1978   The Male Supremacist Complex: Discovery or Invention? *American Anthropologist* 80:665–67.

O'Connor, Geoffrey
1997   *Amazon Journal: Dispatches from a Vanishing Frontier.* New York: Dutton, Penguin Putnam.

Oficina Central de Estadística e Informática
1985   *Censo Indígena de Venezuela.* Caracas: Oficina Central de Estadística e Informática.

Pacheco de Olivera Filho, Joao
1990   Frontier Security and the New Indigenism: Nature and Origins of the Calha Norte Project. In *The Future of Amazonia: Destruction or Sustainable Development?* ed. David Goodman and Anthony Hall, 155–76. New York: St. Martin's Press.

Peters, John
1973   *The Effect of Western Material Goods upon the Social Structure of the Family among the Shirishana.* Ph. D. dissertation, Western Michigan University.
1998   *Life among the Yanomami.* Peterborough, Canada: Broadview Press.

Pithan, Oneron A., Ulisses E. C. Confalonieri, Brenda Anastacio F. Morgado
1991   A Situação de Saúde dos Indios Yanomami Diagnóstico a Partir da Casa do Indio de Boa Vista, Roraima, 1987–89. *Cadernos de Saúde Publica,* 7(4):563–80.

Poppino, Rollie E.
1973   *Brazil: The Land and People.* 2nd ed. New York: Oxford University Press.

Rabben, Linda
1995   Kayapo Choices: Short-term Gain vs. Long-term Damage. *Cultural Survival Quarterly* 19(2):11–13.

Ramos, Alcida
1979a  Yanoama Indians in Northern Brazil Threatened by Highway. In *The Yanoama Indians in Brazil,* ed. A. Ramos and K. Taylor, 1–41. Document 37. Copenhagen: International Work Group for Indigenous Affairs (IWGIA).
1979b  On Women's Status in Yanoama Societies. *Current Anthropology* 20:185–87.
1979c  Personal Names and Social Classification in Sanuma (Yanoama) Society. In *Peasants, Primitives, and Proletariats,* ed. David Browman and Ronald A. Schwarz, 191–205. The Hague: Mouton Publishers.
1993   *O Papel Político das Epidemias o Caso Yanomami.* Série Antropologia 153. Brasília: Universidade de Brasília, Departamento de Antropologia.
1995   *Sanumá Memories: Yanomami Ethnography in Times of Crisis.* Madison: University of Wisconsin Press.
1998   *Indigenism: Ethnic Politics in Brazil.* Madison: University of Wisconsin Press.

Ramos, Alcida Rita, and Bruce Albert

1977 Yanoama Descent and Affinity: The Sanumá/Yanomam Contrast. *Actes du XLIIe Congrès International des Américanistes* 2:71–90. Paris: Société des Américanistes.

Ramos, Alcida Rita, Marco Antonio Lazarin, and Gale Goodwin Gomez.

1985 *Yanomami em tempo de ouro, relatório de pasquisa.* Série Antropologia 51. Brasília: Departamento de Antropologia, Universidade de Brasília.

Ribeiro, Darcy

1967 Indigenous Cultures and Languages of Brazil. In *Indians of Brazil in the Twentieth Century,* ed. and trans. Janice Hopper, 77–165. Publication no. 2. Washington, D.C.: Institute for Cultural Research Studies.

Rice, A. Hamilton

1928 The Rio Branco, Uraricuera and Parima. *Geographical Journal* 71:113–43, 209–23, 345–56.

Roosevelt, Ana, ed.

1994 *Amazonian Indians from Prehistory to the Present: Anthropological Perspectives.* Tucson: University of Arizona Press.

Saffirio, Giovanni (John)

1985 *Ideal and Actual Kinship Terminology among the Yanomama Indians of the Catrimani River Basin (Brasil).* Ann Arbor, Mich.: University Microfilms International #8521530.

1986 Cultural Orientation of Population Control. Unpublished manuscript.

1996 Adattamento as mutamenti ambientali. In *Yanomami: Indios sel Amazzonia.* ed. Guguelmo Damioli and Giovanni Saffirio, 116–27. Turin, Italy: Il Capitello.

Saffirio, John, and Raymond Hames

1983 The Forest and the Highway. In *The Impact of Contact: Two Yanomamo Case Studies,* ed. J. Saffirio, R. Hames, N. Chagnon, and T. Melancon, 1–52. Occasional Paper 11. Cambridge: Cultural Survival.

Salamone, Frank, ed.

1997 *The Yanomami and Their Interpreters: Fierce People or Fierce Interpreters?* Lanham, Md.: University Press of America.

Sanford, Greg

1997 Who Speaks for the Yanomami? A New Tribes Perspective. In *The Yanomami and Their Interpreters: Fierce People or Fierce Interpreters?* ed. Frank Salamone, 57–64. Lanham, Md.: University Press of America.

Santilli, Marcio

1989 Notes on the Constitutional Rights of the Brazilian Indians. *Cultural Survival Quarterly* 13(1):13–15.

Schemo, Diana Jean

1999 Brazil Slashes Money for Project Aimed at Protecting the Amazon. *New York Times,* January 1, 1999, p. A9.

Scheper-Hughes, Nancy
1992    *Death without Weeping: The Violence of Everyday Life in Brazil.* Berkeley: University of California Press.

Schkolnik, S.
1983    Aspectos Demograficos de la Poblacion Yanomami de Sierra Parima Territorio Federal Amazonas, Venezuela. In *Filariasis Humanas en el Territorio Federal Amazonas, Venezuela,* 111–26. Publ. Cient. No. 2. Caracas: Proicet Amazonas.

Schmink, Marianne
1985    Social Change in the *Garimpo.* In *Change in the Amazon Basin,* vol. 2, *The Frontier after a Decade of Colonization,* ed. John Hemming, 185–99. Manchester: Manchester University Press.

Schmink, Marianne, and Charles H. Wood
1992    *Contested Frontiers in Amazonia.* New York: Columbia University Press.

Shryock, Henry, and Jacob Siegel and Associates
1973    *The Methods and Materials of Demography.* 2 vols. Washington, D.C.: U.S. Bureau of the Census, U.S. Government Printing Office.

Skidmore, Thomas E.
1988    *The Politics of Military Rule in Brazil, 1964–85.* New York: Oxford University Press.

Smole, William J.
1976    *The Yanoama Indians.* Austin: University of Texas Press.

Sponsel, Leslie
1981    *The Hunter and the Hunted in the Amazon: An Integrated Biological and Cultural Approach to the Behavorial Ecology of Human Predation.* Ann Arbor, Mich.: UMI Dissertation Services #8129634.
1997    The Master Thief: Gold Mining and Mercury Contamination in the Amazon. In *Life and Death Matters: Human Rights and the Environment at the End of the Millennium,* ed. Barbara Rose Johnston, 99–127. Walnut Creek, Calif.: AltaMira–Sage.
1998    Yanomami: An Arena of Conflict and Aggression in the Amazon. *Aggressive Behavior* 24:97–122.

Taylor, Kenneth I.
1977    Raiding, Dueling and Descent Group Membership among the Sanumá. *Actes du XLIIe Congrès International des Américanistes* 2:91–104. Paris: Société des Américanistes.
1979    Development against the Yanoama. In *The Yanoama in Brazil, 1979,* ed. A. Ramos and K. Taylor, 43–98. Document 37. Copenhagen: International Work Group for Indigenous Affairs (IWGUA).

Treece, David
1990    Indigeneous People in the Brazilian Amazon and the Expansion of the Economic Frontier. In *The Future of Amazonia: Destruction or Sustainable Development?* ed. David Goodman and Anthony Hall, 264–87. New York: St. Martin's Press.

Turner, Terence
1996    *Brazil's Giant Step Backward on Indigenous Rights*. Report to the Commission for Human Rights. Washington, D.C.: American Anthropological Association.
United States Bureau of the Census
1975    *Historical Statistics of the United States. Colonial Times to 1970, Part I*. Washington, D.C.: Government Printing Office.
1996    *Statistical Abstract of the United States, 1996*. Washington, D.C.: Government Printing Office.
Valero, Helena
1984    *Yo Soy Napëyoma*. Monografia no. 35. Caracas: Fundación La Salle de Ciencias Naturales.
Wagley, Charles
1971    *An Introduction to Brazil*. Rev. ed. New York: Columbia University Press.
*Webster's New Geographical Dictionary*.
1988    Springfield: Merriam Webster.
Weyland, Kurt
1996    *Democracy without Equity: Failure of Reform in Brazil*. Pittsburgh: University of Pittsburgh Press.
Whitehead, Neil Lancelot
1988    *Lords of the Tiger Spirit: A History of the Caribs in Colonial Venezuela and Guyana, 1498–1820*. Providence, R.I.: Foris Publications.
Wolf, Eric R.
1982    *Europe and the People without History*. Berkeley: University of California Press.
Wood, Charles H., and Jose Alberto Magno de Carvalho
1988    *The Demography of Inequality in Brazil*. Cambridge: Cambridge University Press.

# INDEX OF PERSONS

# INDEX OF TOPICS

John D. Early, retired professor of anthropology at Florida Atlantic University, Boca Raton, is the author of several books about population anthropology, most recently (with Thomas Headland) *Population Dynamics of a Philippine Rain Forest People* (UPF, 1998).

John F. Peters is professor of sociology at Wilfrid Laurier University in Waterloo, Ontario, Canada, and the author of *Life among the Yanomami* (1998).